THE VETERANS

OF

HISTORY

A Young Person's History
of the Jews

Mitchel

D1495481

BOSTON WORKMEN'S CIRCLE
CENTER FOR
JEWISH CULTURE
& SOCIAL JUSTICE
www.circleboston.org

For Raful and Kalman

מיינע יידישע ברידער

Table of Contents

Acknowledgements

For seventeen years as Educational Director of the Y.L. Peretz School of Boston Workmen's Circle, and eighteen years as Cultural Director of Camp Kinderland, I was fortunate to work with people who shared my interest in immersing young people in a secular interpretation of Jewish history shaped by progressive values.

At the Boston Workmen Circle Chris Colbath-Hess, Deborah Good, Martha Katz, Karen Klein, Wayne Lencer, Steve Ostrow, Laura Punnett, and Kay Seligson read sections of the original manuscript and made helpful suggestions. Lisa Gallatin created a framework for this work to get done, and her daughter, Phoebe Rosen, was an early young reader whose reaction was enlightening. Daniel and Sarah Albert-Rozenberg made helpful suggestions about the discussion questions at the end of the book.

At Camp Kinderland Maddy Simon and Judee Rosenbaum read and discussed large sections of the book with me, and I benefited greatly from those discussions.

Other readers whose comments made this a better book than it would otherwise have been: Kolya Borodulin, Adam Chalom, Henry Feingold, Ora Gladstone, Cheryl Klausner, Hadass Silver, Isaac Silver, and Ronald Silver.

I learned from talks with Joel Marks, who challenged the very idea of a book such as this.

I benefited from Michael Albert's expert advice regarding copyrights, and Dovid Goldberg's last-minute Yiddish grammar guidance.

Milt Kotelchuk and Solon Beinfeld read the entire manuscript with care and intelligence; their many suggestions were always thoughtful and well informed.

In his commentary on the manuscript, Barney Zumoff, generously gave of his enormous general erudition, his especially deep and broad Jewish learning, and his scrupulous concern for good English.

Dorothée Rozenberg has provided great encouragement, and spurred me to make public a neglected manuscript; her energetic help in project management and outreach was invaluable in bringing this project to fruition. Her enthusiasm, and that of others who have provided help and support on this project, triumphed over my indolence—no small feat.

I am grateful to all of the above, but I did not follow every suggestion, so it is likely that the remaining errors or infelicities are my fault.

A Note to Parents and Teachers

As the new principal of the I.L. Peretz School of the Workmen's Circle of Brookline, it fell to me to recommend a Jewish history text for our sixth graders. Although there are many Jewish histories for children, some quite good, none were quite right for the needs of a Jewish Sunday school that defined itself as secular, progressive, and non-Zionist (*but not anti-Zionist*). Our school needed a text that spoke of religion's importance in Jewish history without presuming the "truth," or even high value of any particular religious doctrine. We needed a book that described the Zionist movement knowledgeably without abandoning a critical or diasporist perspective. We needed a book that explored the progressive themes and values in Jewish history and traditions, without chauvinistically pretending that everything in the Jewish past is liberal, egalitarian and humane.

In addition to the lack of a good ideological fit, there were other deficiencies I found in previous Jewish histories for youth. One was grossly distorting simplification. Jerome Bruner has said that "any subject can be taught effectively in some intellectually honest form to any child at any stage of development." As a literal statement this is clearly false, a bit of hyperbole. But it is in the spirit of Bruner's statement that I have attempted to write this book. Most books aimed at young people simplify the social, economic and philosophical issues at work in Jewish history, that is if they pay any attention to them at all. *The Veterans of History* tries to give substantial attention to the complexity of complex issues by analyzing social, economic, and ideological forces into their simpler components and by conveying the issues through a sixth grade vocabulary.

Another inadequacy I saw in most Jewish histories for young people was their relative inattention to the broader historical context in which the story of the Jews unfolded. These books seem to assume either that Jewish history was self-contained or that young people were already familiar with the broader historical contexts. I think both these assumptions are false. Today's students don't usually bring broad, basic, historical knowledge to their study of Jewish history and therefore need it provided to them. *The Veterans of History* attempts to give world historical context to Jewish history. It emphasizes that the Jewish story can only be understood as part of the story of all humanity. So, for example, an explanation of feudalism is given in the chapter on medieval European Jewry.

Finally, I was dissatisfied with the form of many Jewish histories for young people. Many older texts are little more than a string of biographies of heroes. Other, more recent ones, are either primarily episodic, "scenes from Jewish life in the past," or a compilation of units on different aspects of Jewish history. What is needed, I felt, is a strong, continuous narrative that, as good stories do, holds the readers' interest and simultaneously incorporates as part of the story all of the disconnected theme units found in the other children's histories. *The Veterans of History* attempts to do that.

Introduction

A Note to Young Readers

In this book I tell the story of the Jewish people. The story begins thousands of years ago, and although I am old, I'm not *that* old. I was not around for most of the story I will tell. So, how do I know it? Well, I have read many other books that tell the story of the Jews, or parts of the story. In the back of this book I list some of those other books. But most of the authors of *those* books didn't see the things they were writing about either. They were not eyewitness reporters. Instead, like detectives investigating a crime, they tried to figure out what really happened from the evidence they gathered. These authors are historians, and historians try to describe what happened to people in the past and why it happened. They do their detective work by reading things that people in the past wrote—letters, diaries, old newspapers, birth records, business papers, maps—whatever they can find that will help him or her understand what happened. That is historical evidence. Archeologists, who are a kind of historians, try to understand the past by studying the things left from the past— buildings, tools, weapons, pots, statues, paintings, furniture— anything made by people. That is archeological evidence. The story I am going to tell you is a story I have learned from reading historians and archeologists. It is a version of the story they have put together from studying documents and objects from the past.

I hope it is a true story. I have certainly tried to make sure that nothing in this book is false. But, even though I tried, this book is probably not completely true. Historians and archeologists seldom have enough evidence to be sure about everything that happened. So they have to fill in some parts of the story with good guesses. A good guess is one that makes sense out of the facts that are known by fitting them together in a sensible way. A true story is more than just a list of facts. It is more than simply saying, "this happened, and this happened, and this happened," and so on. You have to connect the things that happened in the right way, and highlight the most important events. Good guesses fill in the missing pieces, especially the missing connections. Maybe most of these good guesses I have used are right, but some are bound to be wrong. Also, some historians guess one way and some another way, and I have had to choose which seemed to be the better guess. I hope I have chosen wisely, but in some cases I may have believed a mistaken historian's guess.

In addition to making smart guesses to fill in the missing facts in order to create a sensible, true story, a historian has to decide *which* true story is most interesting. There may be a number of different ways to connect the facts in a way that is true and makes sense. The whole truth would describe all those ways, but no historian can tell the whole truth. The whole historical truth would be a collection of all of the true stories. To tell the whole truth a historian would have to write a book that was as long and detailed as the history itself. The historian has to select the interesting and important parts of the truth to tell. In other words, the problem of telling the true story of what happened in the past is not just a problem of guessing correctly about the things we don't know, it is also a problem of deciding what are the important parts of the story we do know, what are the parts worth telling, what are the parts that should most interest *us*.

What people find interesting and important depends on who they are and what they care about. Before you read my version of the story of the Jews, which I tried to make certain is *one* of the true versions, that is, one sensible way to connect the facts, I am going to tell you who I am and what I care about.

I am an American Jewish man. My grandparents and great grandparents came to America from Eastern Europe. The family I grew up in was only a little religious and I am not religious at all. I try to tell the story of the entire Jewish people, but I certainly concentrate on those parts of the story that will be of most interest to American Jews, especially American Jews whose ancestors, like mine, came from Eastern Europe. So, for instance,

I spend more time telling about what happened to Jews who came to America than about Jews who went to Argentina. I also spend more time discussing Yiddish, the language of Eastern European Jews, than Ladino, the language of Mediterranean Jews. Yiddish and America are not more important than Ladino and Argentina, but I think they may be more important to many of my readers.

I also write a lot about non-religious Jews. There is plenty in this story about religious Jews and the Jewish religion. It is impossible to tell *any* sensible, true history of the Jews without the Jewish religion being at the center of the story. But I also write a lot about non-religious Jews because their story is a part of the Jewish story that I care especially about.

I believe that all people should have a chance to live a free and a good life, and that we all have some responsibility to try to make that happen. I think it is a great evil to treat people unequally because of their race, or sex, or culture. The progress people have made to end all sorts of discrimination, and to give people more control over their own lives, are the parts of history I most want to emphasize.

Everyone writes history with some biases, that is, some attitudes they start out with. Now you know mine. I hope that in spite of these biases I have not changed any facts to make them be the way I would have liked them to be instead of the way they actually were, and I hope I don't ignore any really important parts of the story because I am too biased to see that they are important. But it is good for readers of history to always be at least a little suspicious that the author may be shaping the facts to fit his or her own opinions.

Perhaps every group of people believes that its own story is very interesting. I certainly think the Jews have an interesting story. Jews are an ancient people and their story goes back very far. Jews have lived in many parts of the world with many people. As a result, the Jewish story contains parts of the whole world's story. If you are Jewish, it is your story, the story of how you and your people fit into the human story.

NOTE: *Jewish languages, such as Hebrew and Yiddish, use the Hebrew alphabet. When those words are written in another alphabet it is called "transliteration." In this book I use a few different ways of transliterating depending on which seemed best for the part of the story I was telling.*

Prologue

The Veterans of History

The historian Simon Dubnow called Jews "the veterans of history." What could he have meant? He might have just meant that Jews have ancestors that go way back. But so does everybody else. Everyone has gotten here through ancestors who stretch through all of human history. So in that sense all people are veterans of history.

But we might also call someone a veteran who has long experience in doing something. A veteran doctor is someone who has lots of experience being a doctor. But that doctor doesn't have meaningful experience if he or she forgets everything she or he has done as a doctor in the past. Genuine *long* experience means you remember what you did and what happened to you. Veterans of history have long experience of history. For that you must record history and remember it. Unrecorded and unremembered, the past doesn't even become history.

From nearly the beginning of recorded history Jews have remembered and carried their story from generation to generation. Their story includes great sadness and great happiness, great accomplishments and great failures. There were times that Jews treated other peoples badly, and many times when Jews were treated horribly by other peoples. There are ways in which Jews cared for each other and ways in which they were unfair to each other. It is a story that was centered in Europe and the Middle East but had important scenes throughout the world. Today the United States is one of its main settings.

The Jewish story is also one that has affected the whole human story. Only one out of five hundred human beings today is Jewish, but more than half of humanity are Christian and Muslim, and both those religions evolved from the religion of the Jews. And something about Jewish history seems to have led to new ideas that have helped shape the world and how we think of the world. St. Paul, Karl Marx, Sigmund Freud and Albert Einstein were Jews or the descendants of Jews. Jewish history is dramatic and Jews have added drama to world history.

Jews are veterans of history because they carry all this with them. In fact, Dubnow thought that that is what makes Jews Jews. If you think the Jewish story is your story, if you want it to be your story, if you want to help continue that story, then you are a member of the Jewish people. Assimilation, blending in with the non-Jewish population, just requires forgetting. Being Jewish requires remembering. You must tell the story of the Jews to your children and you must say "this is what happened to us."

THE VETERANS OF HISTORY

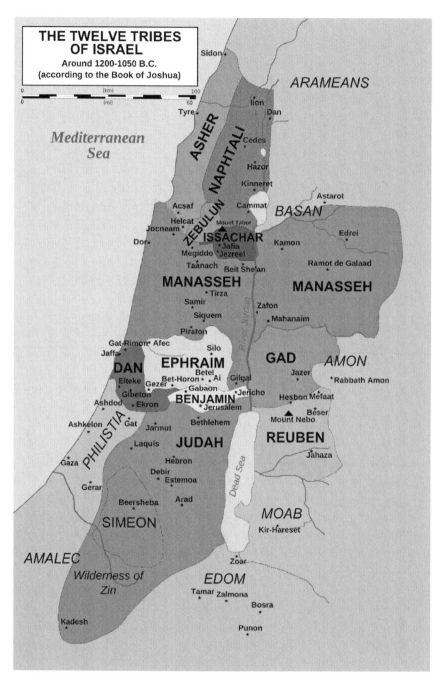

FIGURE 1 – The territories of the 12 Tribes of Israel according to the Bible.

Chapter 1

Hebrew Tribes

In the Beginning

We do not know exactly where or when the Jewish people started, but we do know that they began somewhere in the Middle East between three and four thousand years ago. Today the Middle East has countries in it such as Egypt, Jordan, Israel, Palestine, Syria, Saudi Arabia, and Iraq. Four thousand years ago things were different. Then the Middle East had one great kingdom along the Nile River and others in the valley between the Tigris and Euphrates Rivers. These kingdoms along the rivers of the Middle East are where the earliest human civilizations began. There people first learned to farm and build towns. There they first built roads and great buildings. There they first organized into countries, with government workers and large armies. It is also where writing began and where we find the first historical records.

At that time there were many groups of peoples living in the Middle East. Some of these groups were Semitic peoples. These were peoples who all spoke a language from the family of languages called Semitic. In the family are languages that are very similar to each other, but are still different languages. The Jews started as one of these Semitic peoples and the language they spoke was, or became, Hebrew. In fact, at that point in their history, we should call them Hebrews.

Not all of the peoples of the ancient Middle East were settled members of the great kingdoms. Like many of the Semitic peoples, the Hebrews were nomadic. They didn't build permanent houses and live in one place all the time. They lived in tents and moved around a great deal. They earned their living as shepherds. When their flocks of sheep and herds of goats could no longer graze in an area, they moved on. The Hebrews lived in family groupings, and related families lived and traveled together. There were other Semitic peoples who were also nomadic and lived as the Hebrews did. But there were also settled peoples in the area, who lived in one place as farmers. Eventually the Hebrews settled down. But that did not happen for some time and it did not happen all at once.

It was the kind of life that we can still find among a few nomadic desert people today. They lived in big family groupings and earned their living raising animals—sheep, goats, camels and cattle. Most of the things they used—the tents they lived in, the food they ate, the tools they worked with and clothing they wore—came from these animals. The animals and control of water-wells were their most important wealth. When a family had to move to new grazing lands, they would have to find a spot near a water-well. Water in a desert is hard to find and precious. The right to use a well was a very important family possession.

Everything belonged to the entire family, but the family itself belonged to the head father, the patriarch. The patriarch was the ruler of his wives (a man could have more than one wife) his children, grandchildren and servants. He made all the important decisions for the family. When a family became too big to stay as one group, one of its men went off with his wives and children and started his own family group. The two families stayed connected. They considered themselves related, children and grandchildren of the same patriarch.

Life was always difficult for desert nomads. Not only was it difficult to earn a living from nature, other groups of people were also a danger. In those harsh living conditions there was a lot of competition to get the things your family needed to stay alive—water and grazing land especially. Often there was fighting or stealing between nomadic groups.

With so many things that could go wrong and turn their lives into disasters—no water, no grazing land, disease to their herds and flocks, defeat in fighting—nomadic people had to be very concerned about things *they* couldn't control, but that they thought the gods—powerful, mythical, person-like immortal beings—could control. Naturally they were very interested in learning about the gods and keeping the gods happy.

The harsh living conditions also required the desert nomads to develop strict rules and strong customs that would help them survive. There was little room to experiment with new ways of doing things. If the experiment didn't work the family could die. It was very important that everyone do what the family tradition said they were supposed to do. These customs were treated as rules from the gods.

The Hebrew Bible

The Hebrews told many stories about their earliest days. Later on they wrote these stories down and they became part of the Bible. Certainly, many of the stories are completely made up. For instance, we know that the Bible stories about how the world was created by God in six days is a myth, similar to the myths that other peoples made up long ago to try to explain to themselves where the world came from. But there is probably some truth to many of the Bible stories that describe the earliest times of the Hebrew people. Even if they didn't happen just as the Bible says they did, these stories describe the kind of people and the kind of life in those days.

The Hebrews believed that their founder, the first patriarch, was a man named Abraham. Abraham was supposed to have come from Ur, a city in the land of Babylonia. A Jewish legend tells how Abraham fled north from his father's house in Ur after he smashed all of his father's idols—statues of gods. The legend says Abraham did this because he heard the voice of the one true God. Jewish tradition made Abraham the discoverer of the idea that there is only one God. Abraham and his family are supposed to have gone from Ur, north to Mesopotamia, where Iraq is today, and then with his family on to Canaan, a land Jewish legend says was promised to Abraham and his descendants by God.

It is quite possible that some nomadic ancestors of the Hebrew people did come from around Mesopotamia. The Bible begins the story of the Jewish people, the ancient Hebrews, with the adventures of Abraham and his wife Sarah and their children, especially Isaac and his wife Rebecca. We are told that Isaac and Rebecca had a son named Jacob, and that Jacob had two wives, Leah and Rachel. Jacob and his wives had thirteen children, twelve sons and a daughter. According to Jewish tradition the Jewish people are descended from the twelve sons of Jacob. In the Bible, Jacob is given another name, Israel, and so Jews are sometimes called the children of Israel, and the ancient Hebrew people were called Israelites.

According to Jewish legend, the Israelites lived in groups of related families called tribes, their territory divided between 12 tribes said to be descended from sons and grandsons of Jacob: Asher, Benjamin, Dan, Ephraim, Gad, Issachar, Judah, Manasseh, Naphtali, Reuben, Simeon, and Zevulun.

Even though these Bible stories certainly aren't precisely true and may even be very far from the truth, they are important to know when studying the history of the Jewish people. That is because, not only are the stories good clues to what life was like and to what may actually have happened, but also because for so long almost all Jews thought the stories were true. When they had decisions to make or tried to understand what was happening to them, Jews would be influenced by what they read in the Bible. They thought it was the true story of who they were and what they had done. That was where they could read about past mistakes, and past successes. It was also the place they believed they could find out about promises they had made and promises made to them.

Exodus

Probably the Bible stories that made the biggest impression on the Jewish people, and the ones that some historians think has at least some truth, and maybe a lot of truth, are the stories about Moses and the liberation of the Hebrews from slavery in Egypt.

Egypt had one of the first great civilizations and for thousands of years in ancient times it was a very powerful nation. In Egypt today you can still see many of the great buildings, temples, palaces and tombs (pyramids) that the ancient Egyptians built.

The Hebrews may have first come to Egypt to escape famine. They settled there and according to the Bible legend lived well in Egypt for a time. But their situation got worse. The Jews became laborers forced to work on the great building projects of the Pharaohs, the Egyptian Kings. The Bible says that they had bad working conditions and even that there were government attempts to wipe out the Hebrews by killing all of their baby boys.

According to the Hebrew myth, Moses was the leader who arose among the Hebrews and led them to freedom out of the land of Egypt. But not only was Moses portrayed as a political leader, he also was considered a great religious thinker. The Jews have always called Moses "Moshe Rabeynu," that is "Our Teacher Moses." When, a thousand years after Moses was supposed to have lived, the Israelites gathered their histories, legends, folktales, myths, customs and laws together into the Bible, they said that it had all come from Moses, who had gotten it directly from God.

Jewish legend says that under the leadership of Moses, the Israelites wandered in the Sinai desert for forty years. The long journey was remembered not only as a journey out of the slavery of Egypt, but also as one to a land the Israelites believed God had promised to them. This was Canaan, the land that Abraham had brought his family to, the "promised land" that has played such an important part in Jewish history and Jewish beliefs. The goal of their travels in the desert was to return to Canaan, the land that the twelve sons of Jacob, the Children of Israel, had left generations before.

Although the story of the trip in the Sinai desert was important to Jews because it represented leaving slavery and heading towards the Promised Land, these were not the most important memories of their time in the desert. It was during that time in the desert that Moses was said to have received the Torah from God. The Torah consists of the first five books of the Hebrew Bible, and is the holiest part of the Bible to Jews. The belief that Moses was given God's laws at Mount Sinai, and that there all the Israelites accepted God's law, has had a greater effect on Jewish history than any other belief, and some think that belief actually helped form these Hebrew speaking tribes into one people and held them together through three thousand years. There is even a Jewish tradition that not only the Jews who were alive during the journey through the desert, but all the souls of any Jew who would ever live was present at Sinai when the Children of Israel accepted God's law, the Torah.

Conquest of Canaan

We cannot know how much truth there is in the Bible tales about Abraham and Moses, but we do know that about 1300 B.C. Hebrew speaking tribes began to invade Canaan from the East. The Bible gives us the names of some of the military chieftains who led this conquest. First amongst them was Joshua, the leader who in legend followed Moses. Later came Gideon, Deborah, Barak and Jeptha, who, along with other heroes, were called Judges. They were called Judges because not only did they lead the people in battle, but they also enforced the law.

The conquest of Canaan by the Hebrew tribes took a long time, probably many generations. Eventually they conquered much of Canaan, but not all of it. Different groups of Canaanite peoples continued to live in the land and the Hebrews lived next to them, with each Hebrew tribe settling in a particular area. In time the Hebrew tribes gave up their wandering, nomadic way of life. They settled down and mostly became farmers like their Canaanite neighbors. Often they lived in peace with these neighbors, but there were also times when they fought. Living so close together it was natural that the Canaanites and Hebrews would learn from each other and influence each other. In fact, Hebrews and Canaanites often married each other and had children, so after a while the Israelites were really a people made out of a merger, a mixture, of these two groups. Still for a long time some people in Canaan were thought of, and probably thought of themselves as Canaanites, and others as Israelites.

One great difference between the Canaanites and the Israelite Hebrews was in their religions. The Canaanites believed in local gods and nature gods. For instance, Astarte was an earth goddess who was worshipped for making the land fertile—she made the crops grow. The Hebrews' god, who was called Yahweh, started off as a local god, much like the other gods of Canaan. Maybe he (the Hebrews thought of Yahweh as being male) started as a God of the Sky. It is very interesting to see how the Hebrews' idea of their god Yahweh changed and grew over time. He started as the personal God of Abraham and his descendants. But in time the idea of Yahweh grew. At first he became the strongest of gods, then the most important of gods and finally the only God. His characteristics also changed. Early on Yahweh is described as an angry and jealous God. But as he developed in the legends of the ancient Hebrews recorded in the Bible, Yahweh becomes more and more interested in justice. We will see how in a few hundred years, in the times of the Prophets, the Hebrews' come to believe their god had become the God of all the world, a God who demands that people be honest, pursue peace, and take care of the poor. But that is jumping ahead. For now we must see how the early Yahweh was worshipped by the Israelites.

Early Israelite Religion

When the Israelites were nomadic people they believed their God traveled around with them and lived in a mobile sanctuary they had built to carry him around. This was the Holy Ark. (Later the Holy Ark was believed to hold Moses' tablets and God's "presence" instead of God himself). The Bible has some detailed descriptions of what the Holy Ark was like. When the Israelites settled in Canaan, the Holy Ark was placed in the city of Shiloh. The Canaanites, like many farming peoples, had holidays to celebrate the important times of year in farming life. So there was a holiday when they planted in early spring, a holiday when they gathered their first fruits in late spring and a holiday when they took in most of the crops in the fall. As the Israelites settled among the Canaanites and became farmers, they celebrated these holidays too. But instead of just treating them as holidays about planting and harvesting, the Israelites made them holidays to celebrate and remember important events in their history. The early spring holiday to celebrate the planting became Passover, a holiday to celebrate the liberation from Egyptian slavery. The late spring holiday of first fruits became Shavuot, the day God was supposed to have given the Torah to the Israelites. And the fall harvest holiday became Succot, the week to remember their wanderings in the Sinai desert. Each of these holidays became a pilgrimage. On these festival days, Israelites would travel to Shiloh to make sacrifices and offerings to Yahweh. Back then, people seemed to have believed that you had to give gifts to the gods so that the gods would help you in growing food, having children, winning battles, and avoiding diseases. One way of giving gifts was sacrificing people—killing them as an offering to the gods. One big step forward in the Israelites' religion was that the Israelites decided that their god, Yahweh, didn't approve of sacrificing people. Probably the Bible story in which God first asks Abraham to sacrifice his son Isaac, and then stops him, was the Israelites way of remembering that they once sacrificed people but came to understand that they shouldn't do that.

FIGURE 2 – Engraving by Rembrandt showing the Bible story of Joseph telling his dreams, one of the many works of art inspired by the Bible.

FIGURE 3 – Map of the Kingdoms of Israel and Judah.

Chapter 2

Ancient Kingdoms

The Israelites Unite

The Bible stories should never be taken as fully accurate history. The stories of the previous chapter are largely mythical. However, the stories of this chapter are a mix of Bible legends and history based on real evidence. We cannot know how close to the truth they are, but they may be quite close. In any event, they are important because almost all Jews until about 1800 thought they were completely true. Many still do.

Although in time the wars with the Canaanites mostly stopped, there were other groups that the Hebrew tribes fought with in the days of the Judges. First, from across the Jordan River came peoples, such as the Moabites, who just as the Israelites had done, tried to conquer Canaan from the east. Another group, the Philistines, had sailed from the west and established themselves along the Mediterranean coast of Canaan.

At this point, the Hebrew tribes had not yet formed one united country. Each tribe ruled itself. Sometimes when they fought other groups, such as the Moabites or the Philistines, only one or a few tribes fought against them. Sometimes, when there was a common threat, many tribes joined together. But when they did cooperate, they were still not one country. They were a coalition, a group of separate groups that worked together to get a job done. But finally the Philistines, the people on the coast, became so strong that the Israelites believed that all the tribes had to unite permanently into one country, under one leader, to be able to fight the Philistines.

One of the respected Judges of that time, Samuel, arranged to have someone from one of the small, weak tribes become king of all the Israelites. Samuel probably did this so that the big tribes, especially Ephraim and Judah, wouldn't be jealous that the king came from another big tribe. And so, in order to lead them into battle against the Philistines, Saul, of the tribe of Benjamin, became the first king of the Israelites,

The Israelite Kingdoms

Saul's first battles were not against the Philistines, but against the Ammonites, an enemy of some Israelite tribes settled east of the Jordan River. Saul also led battles against the Amalekites, the Israelites arch-enemy to the South. But it was the Philistines that were the greatest threat to all the tribes, and it was to fight them that the tribes united under the leadership of Saul.

The Philistines, who had started on the coast, had been steadily moving inland, into the heart of Israelite territory. Military leaders, such as the legendary Samson, had been fighting them for decades. But by Saul's time it had become clear to the Israelites that they all would be completely conquered by the Philistines unless they fought together as a united people.

Probably, the Hebrew tribes had already gone a long way to becoming one nation even before Samuel helped make Saul king of all the Israelites. Besides the religious traditions and language that they shared, people from one tribe must have gotten mixed up with people from other tribes, and perhaps some smaller tribes had already been swallowed up by bigger tribes. A judge like Samuel must have been respected by all the tribes. Samuel may even have acted like a leader of all the Israelites. The difference now was that Saul was going to be the official leader of all the tribes, and not just a leader, but a king. That meant his sons would become rulers after him. Judges were picked as leaders because they had some special quality—they were good fighters, smart politicians or inspiring religious leaders. But a king becomes king because his father was king. At least that was the way it was supposed to have worked. And that was going to be a new thing for the Israelite tribes.

Saul had good success in his war against the Philistines. His uncle Abner and his son Jonathan were excellent generals. With their help, King Saul's armies drove the Philistines out of Israelite territory and back to the coastal areas. Saul seems to have been mostly a war king and not to have done much to change the way the Israelites lived. In fact, other than being a good general, Saul probably wasn't a very good king at all.

A young man from the big and powerful tribe of Judah became important in the court of King Saul. His name was David. Legend has it that David first came to Saul's attention by killing a mighty Philistine warrior in single combat (this is the famous story of David and Goliath). David became very popular in King Saul's court. He was a poet, a singer and a soldier. Some of our most beautiful poems in the Bible, the Psalms, are said to have been written by David. In addition he came from the important tribe of Judah. Although David had become a close friend of Saul's son Jonathan, Saul started to distrust David and fear him. Saul feared that maybe David was trying to take his place as king.

David ran away from Saul's court before Saul could hurt him. In the south, where David had fled, he formed a group of warriors that were loyal to him. To be safe from Saul, David agreed to cooperate with the Philistines. The Philistines had their own purposes for making this deal with David. They thought this quarrel among the Israelites would give them an opportunity to reconquer them. So after they had made the deal with David, the Philistines marched against Saul's forces. A battle was fought in the north, on Mount Gilboa. Many Israelites were killed there, including the king's son Jonathan. Saul was so unhappy after the great defeat that he killed himself. It looked as if the Philistines would now be able to fully conquer the Israelites.

The Rise of David

David had set himself and his followers up in Ziklag, under Philistine protection. But now that Saul was gone, David didn't need the Philistines and wanted to be free of them. He moved out of Philistine territory to the town of Hebron, a city holy to the Israelites because it was believed to be where Abraham was buried. Hebron was located in the middle of the tribe of Judah's territory. David was declared King of Judah. But that did not make him king of all the Israelites. The northern tribes, under the leadership of the tribe of Ephraim, had accepted another of Saul's sons, Ishbaal, as their king.

And so right after Saul's death there were two kingdoms among the Israelites. For a while, not only did each kingdom fight the Philistines, they also fought each other. But Ishbaal and his great uncle Abner, who was the real power behind the throne in the north, realized that David was too strong for them. After a few years the kingdoms agreed to unite under the leadership of David. After the agreement, Abner and Ishbaal were assassinated, which made the northerners very unhappy. But they remained in the united kingdom. David was now the second king of all Israel.

The Reign of David

Hebron was in the far south of Israelite lands, in the heart of Judean territory. Now that he was king of both the north and south, David wanted to establish his capital city in a more central place. The city of Jerusalem was between the north and the south and David thought that that would be a good place to establish his capital. But Jerusalem had never been conquered by the Israelites. Located on hills, where it was easy to defend, Jerusalem had remained a Canaanite city. It was only now, a little before 1000 BCE (**B**efore the **C**ommon **E**ra—sometimes called "BC", that is, about 3000 years ago) with David as king, that the Israelites first conquered Jerusalem. David established Jerusalem as the capital of his kingdom. This city, which had probably had a Canaanite shrine, a holy place, in it, would become holy to the Israelites and the central place of their religion. The Holy Ark, which had been in Shiloh, was now brought to Jerusalem, and Jerusalem would be the place to which Israelites traveled three times a year to make their festival offerings to their God.

David had even greater success against the Philistines than Saul did. He ended their threat to the Israelite tribes for good. David also fought against other peoples that the Israelites had conflicts with: the Moabites, the Ammonites, the Jebusites, the

Edomites—David did battle and defeated all of them. As a result, the borders of his kingdom expanded greatly. In part David was lucky. The big power to the south, Egypt, and the big power to the north, Assyria, were weak at that time, so they didn't interfere as David's kingdom got bigger and stronger. But it was not all luck. Besides being a great military leader, David was a good diplomat, that is, he was good at knowing when and how to make deals with other countries. He didn't try to fight everyone. For instance, David made a deal with the Phoenicians (another coastal people living north of the Philistines) and even paid some of their soldiers to be in his army.

David was not just a warrior-king like Saul. He built walls and palaces in Jerusalem. He wrote religious poetry. He gave more people jobs in the government and the government in Jerusalem took more interest and control over the lives of all the Israelites. In general, he did much to unify the kingdom and make it strong.

But David, unlike the kings of Assyria or the Pharaohs of Egypt, never became an absolutely powerful king. There are a number of reasons for this. First, the Israelites believed that their God was their real ruler. It was God, they believed, who made the laws. In Egypt, and many places in those times, the king became a god or the relative of a god. But the Israelites never thought of David as God, so no matter how loyal they became to him, they always thought they were supposed to be more loyal to God.

A second reason that David's power was limited was that the Israelite tribes still kept some of the independent traditions of a nomadic people. People that move around are independent and don't like to be ruled by others. Even after they had been long settled, the Israelites kept an independent streak from their nomadic days.

Finally, the Israelite religion gave them the idea of a covenant. A covenant is like a contract, an agreement, in which each side to the agreement promises to do something. The Israelite religion was based on the idea that the people had a series of covenants with God. God would watch over them, provide them land and make them a great people and in turn they were to follow the Torah, God's laws. The Israelites used this idea of covenant when they thought about their loyalty to their kings. They would be loyal subjects, but the king had to be a good king. He couldn't just do anything he felt like. Each side, king and people, had something they were supposed to do.

David is remembered by Jews as the greatest king they ever had. Although the Bible reports that he had lots of problems in his family with his wives (the Israelites allowed a man to have more than one wife) and his children, and although he was judged to have committed some very serious sins, such as killing innocent people, he is still remembered by some Jews as a model of what a leader should be. In fact, an important part of the Jewish religion became the belief that a future leader would arise who would re-establish the Kingdom of David and would eventually rule the whole world. This leader, who they called the Anointed One, or *Mashiach* in Hebrew (Messiah in Greek) would rule according to God's law in perfect justice. This Messiah was supposed to be a descendant of King David, and tradition had it that like David, he would come from the Judean town of Bethlehem. That belief in the coming of a Messiah ended up playing an important role not only in Jewish history, but in the history of the world. We will return to it later in our story.

David's family problems became political when his son Absalom rebelled against him. Absalom thought he should become king after David, but David had decided to make his youngest son, Solomon, the next king. Absalom's rebellion met with temporary success. David had to run away from Jerusalem. But Absalom's rebellion ended up failing, and Absalom was killed. Solomon, the son of David's favorite wife Bathsheba, did become the King of the Israelites after David's death.

The Reign of Solomon

The kingdom was at peace during Solomon's reign. Solomon was good at making treaties and arrangements with the kingdom's neighbors. Although he lost some territories that had been conquered under David, Solomon managed to keep his kingdom strong and united. He encouraged trade and started building projects all over the country. He built soldier-towns with great stables for the horses of his charioteers. In Israel today, in the

Negev desert, you can still see the ruins of the copper mines he built there.

Solomon's greatest building projects took place in the city of Jerusalem. During his time of peace, Solomon's court became much fancier, with many more luxuries, than it had in the warrior times of David. Palaces were built for his many wives, homes for his friends, and most important of all, Solomon built a temple to house the Holy Ark, the chest that legend said God commanded the Israelites build to hold the tablets of law God gave Moses.

David had already brought the Ark to Jerusalem, but now that Solomon had built a temple for it, more and more Israelites would make the pilgrimage to Jerusalem to make offerings to God. After the Temple was built the Jerusalem priests gained even tighter control over the religious life of the Israelites because there was much less sacrificing to Yahweh at other places around the country. Although the Israelite religion didn't have human sacrifices, it still had animal sacrifices. Animals would be killed on the altar as a gift to God. The only people allowed to perform these religious rituals were priests. All of the priests were supposed to be descendants of Moses' brother, Aaron. They were called Kohens, and to this day, among some religious Jews, only people considered Kohens are allowed to perform certain parts of a service in synagogue. But in the time of the Israelites, when animal sacrifice was very important and when only priests could do it, being a priest was especially important. And they did their important religious work at the Temple. Solomon's Temple was to be the center of the Israelite religion for the next four hundred years.

Tradition has given Solomon a reputation for great wisdom. He kept his country at peace and that is certainly a wise thing to do. He is also said to have written parts of the Bible, which should also give us reason to admire Solomon's wisdom. But he does not seem to have been very wise about spending money. David had left Solomon a rich government. All the conquered peoples paid tribute into David's treasury, a sort of tax, so that the Israelites would leave them alone. But Solomon's great building projects, along with his taste for luxuries, left the kingdom bankrupt, that is, with an empty treasury, at the end of his reign. Solomon also did not wisely arrange for someone to become accepted as the king after his own death. So history gives us some reason to question Solomon's reputation for wisdom.

The Kingdoms of Israel and Judah

The story of the Hebrew tribes for the next three hundred and fifty years is the story of two kingdoms, Israel (sometimes called Samaria) in the north and Judah in the South. There were lots of connections between the two kingdoms. The people in both kingdoms considered themselves as part of the same nation. Both kingdoms were Hebrew-speaking and both followed the same religious traditions and shared the same legends. Although the northern kingdom was destroyed by Assyria after two hundred years and never came back (that is where the legend of the ten lost tribes of Israel comes from) its story is told in detail in the Bible. So even though the rest of Jewish history is really a continuation of the story of the southern Kingdom of Judah, the northern Kingdom's tale has played an important part in Jewish memory.

The Kingdom of Israel

When Solomon died about 933 BCE his son Rehoboam became king, but the ten northern tribes of the kingdom, under the leadership of Jeroboam, revolted. They rebelled because they felt that the Government taxed them too much, mostly to build up Jerusalem. Perhaps they also felt the Government favored the tribe of Judah and was not fair to the northern tribes.

Jeroboam became the first king of the northern Kingdom. At first he made his capital in Schechem, where Nablus is today. He built shrines to make sacrifices to God at Beth-El and Dan in the north, so that his subjects didn't feel they had to go to Jerusalem to do their religious duties. Jerusalem was still the capital of the southern kingdom, and Jeroboam didn't want them going to another country to perform their religious duties. He wanted to keep the pilgrimage business at home.

At first the two kingdoms fought each other frequently. But neither country was able to conquer the other. Israel had more people and was richer. But Judah usually had better governments and its people were more united than the people of Israel. After about fifty years the countries mostly stopped fighting each other.

The northern Kingdom of Israel was always having problems settling on who should be king. The usual custom in a kingdom is that when a king dies his son is supposed to succeed him, that is, his son is supposed to become the next king. But in the Kingdom of Israel the "succession" was seldom smooth. Many times when a king died there would be fighting to see who would become the next king. Often there would be rebellions against a king while he was still alive or he would be murdered. A dynasty is a family of kings, and a long dynasty is one in which the crown is passed from father to son (or daughter, if the country is one that allows women to reign) for many generations. The Kingdom of Israel had short dynasties. And they usually ended in violence, with someone being stabbed or poisoned. Lots of the violence took place within the royal families. There was plenty of jealousy, anger, and greed.

The northern kingdom also had religious troubles. There were still a lot of Canaanite people in the north who had not completely mixed with the Israelites. They had their own religious customs. The northern kings also often married foreign wives and these queens brought their foreign religions with them. This created problems, because, unlike other ancient peoples, the Israelites believed in a God who was jealous. Of course the other ancient gods wanted to be worshipped, but so long as they were worshipped, they didn't mind if the people who worshipped them also worshipped other gods. But the Israelite God was different. In many Israelites' minds, he had become a God who became very angry if the Israelites worshipped other gods. In fact he said there were no other gods. The gods that other people worshipped were fakes, idols. Worshipping them was the worst possible sin, idolatry. To this day, in the Jewish religion worshipping something other than God—idolatry—is the worst of sins.

The second dynasty to rule the Kingdom of Israel, the dynasty of Omri, moved the capital to Samaria and that is why the Kingdom of Israel is sometimes called the Kingdom of Samaria. One of the Omri kings, Ahab, married a Phoenician woman named Jezebel. The Phoenicians worshipped a god called Baal.

Jezebel continued to worship Baal after she became Ahab's queen and she also wanted Baal worshipped throughout the kingdom. This was the sort of thing that was constantly dividing the people, causing quarrels and fights. It also contributed to the succession problem because traditional Yahweh worshippers didn't like having kings who allowed Baal to be worshipped in their kingdom. If they thought there was too much Baal worshipping going on they would rebel and try and put a new king on the throne.

The Kingdom of Israel also had problems because it was near Assyria, a big country that was becoming strong once again. For a while the Kingdom of Israel fought off the Assyrians, with the help of other nearby, small countries. But it couldn't hold the Assyrians off long. First it lost the northern part of the Kingdom, the land of Gilead. Then, some years later, in 722 BCE, the entire country was conquered. The Assyrians killed many of the important people. Others they took away and settled in small groups in different lands ruled by Assyria. They also brought a great many foreign settlers to live in the lands of the fallen Kingdom of Israel. These foreign settlers mixed with the remaining Israelites and Canaanites to form a new people, the Samaritans. The Samaritans considered themselves Israelites and developed a religion based on some of the same writings that are holy in the Jewish religion. Like the Jews, the Samaritans have had a long history, one that included many persecutions, that is, many times when they were killed or badly treated. Small communities of Samaritans still exist, and live in Israel and the West Bank in Palestine. They are the closest thing there is to the "lost" tribes of Israel, but the Jews have not considered them Jews.

The Kingdom of Judah

The Kingdom of Judah did not have as bloody a history as the Kingdom of Israel. Its early kings, Asa and Jehosophat, got the kingdom off to a good start with long reigns and wise rule. The population of Judah was mostly Israelite and there was general respect for the dynasty of David, so there weren't as many fights over religion or succession. But there still were some succession fights and religious quarrels. In fact, one king of Judah, Josiah, is famous for fighting idolatry and trying to get all his subjects to follow the Israelite religion strictly, so we know that Judah had religious quarrels too.

Although it lasted almost 400 years, about 150 years longer than the Kingdom of Israel, Judah too eventually came under pressure from the big countries that surrounded it, pressure that it couldn't withstand. By the time the Kingdom of Israel fell, Judah had become a country paying tribute to Assyria. It would occasionally try to rebel against Assyria or use the help of one of its powerful neighbors, Babylonia and Egypt, to free itself from Assyria. That was what King Hezekiah tried to do. His son, King Manasseh, thought it better to try and get along with the Assyrians and even went along with some Assyrian religious practices to please them. A hundred or so years later, under King Zedekiah, when Babylonia had become the strongest power in the area, Judah tried to get the help of Egypt to free itself from Babylonia.

The Babylonian king, Nebuchadnezzar, invaded Judah. In 586 BCE his forces captured Jerusalem and, on the 9th day of Av destroyed the Temple that Solomon had built over three centuries earlier. Most of the royal family, military leaders, government officials, rich families, religious leaders, and city dwellers were forced to move to Babylonia. The Babylonians allowed one Jewish leader, Gedaliah, and a few followers to set up a government in the town of Mizpeh, north of Jerusalem, but a few years later Gedaliah was assassinated by a member of the old royal family. That was the final end of the Israelite kingdoms of Israel and Judah. Only scattered Judean peasants remained in the land, poor farmers under Babylonian rule.

But although the Judean people had no land or government, they did not disappear. They took their religious traditions and memories of Jerusalem with them and they continued as a people together in Babylonia. Their time in Babylonia is known as the First Exile. Before we turn to that exile, there is one more thing to discuss about the kingdoms of Israel and Judah, and it is the most important thing those kingdoms left us: the writings of the Prophets.

The Prophets

The prophets of Judah and Israel did not come from a special city or a special family. There was no school that taught them how to be prophets and they had no official position in the Israelite religion. They were individual people who believed that they understood what God wanted and that felt they had to tell it to the rest of the Israelites. They viewed themselves as messengers from God, and it seems that that is the way the Israelites looked at them.

The great age of prophecy was the three centuries when both Israelite kingdoms were around. It is difficult to say why there stopped being prophets later in Jewish history. It may be a coincidence, but it is an interesting fact that during the same centuries that the Hebrew prophets were active, there were great religious and moral teachers alive in distant civilizations. In Persia, Zoroaster was teaching (although some scholars think he lived earlier), in India, the Buddha, and Confucius in China. Although local conditions probably best explain the rise of all these religious teachers, maybe there were some worldwide social developments that also contributed to this outburst of religious activities.

The words of the prophets were collected in the Bible. Not everyone who made prophecies has had his or her words recorded in the Bible. Some prophetic words may have never been written down. Some that were written down may have been lost before the Bible writings were collected. Other writings may not have been included in the Bible because the Bible's editors, the people who put together the Bible from these collected writings, felt they were not the writings of true prophets. Even during the days of the prophets, Israelites disagreed about who was a true prophet and who was a false prophet. Some of the people called false prophets may really have been insincere or phony, but others may have been rejected because no one wanted to hear what they were saying or because people were prejudiced against them. For instance we don't have the words of any women prophets. So what we have today probably is only a small part of what was said in the name of God in the Israelite kingdoms. But it was enough to have a very great influence on the thoughts and feelings of humankind for thousands of years.

Each prophet had his own style of speaking and certain things that he was especially concerned with. Elijah, an early prophet in the Kingdom of Israel, preached against the luxury of Ahab's court and against the worship of Baal. Fancy living, greed and idolatry were things that many prophets spoke against. The image of Elijah, in his rough peasant clothing, scolding the greedy rich and fighting idolatry, made such a strong impression on the Israelites, that he became a legendary figure in Jewish folklore who was believed to appear in time of special need.

Amos, Micah, and Hosea were northern prophets who wanted people to really feel their religion and not just do things on the outside. It was more important to love God and be a good person than to make sacrifices. In general, we can say that the prophets hated the violence, the phoniness, the greed, and impiety of royalty. They demanded what they called "righteousness"— following God's will. For them, God's will required living simply, being concerned for the poor and pursuing peace. It meant a real devotion to God, not just going through the motions.

The prophets were also very nationalistic. They loved the Israelite people and were very concerned about their wellbeing. But their love of their people often led the prophets to cry out against what the people were doing. The prophets said they saw that the people's sinful ways, as well as the King's, would lead to disaster and great suffering for the Israelites. The idea that a prophet sees into the future comes from the Israelite prophets, who foretold the troubles that awaited the Israelites. The prophets said the troubles were punishments from God for the wickedness of the people. Jeremiah, one of the last great prophets from the Kingdom of Judah, gave powerful descriptions of the hardships that were coming because of the King's folly and people's wickedness. The prophets pleaded with the people to repent, that is, to change their wicked ways and become righteous.

Not only did the prophets preach righteousness and warn about the punishments of sin, they also tried to console the Israelites, make them feel better, when they were suffering. One way they consoled their people was by describing a wonderful future, when God would make the Israelites triumph and bring peace and justice to the whole world. The words of the prophet Isaiah speak of a time when swords will be changed into ploughshares, and spears into pruning hooks, and nation will not make war against nation. The prophets dreamt of a peaceful world, with food for all and justice for all, and they described those dreams in some of history's most beautiful and powerful poetry.

The prophets' religion had developed an idea of a god who was clearly the lord and ruler of the whole world. They thought of great nations, such as Egypt, Assyria and Babylonia as tools that God used to punish Israelite wickedness. Yahweh, now usually called "the Lord" or "Elohim," had grown from the God of Abraham's family to become master of the universe. And he had become a master who above all demanded justice, justice even more than animal sacrifices or other gifts. It was this idea of God that the exiles from Judah took into exile in Babylonia, and it was with this idea of God that they built the Jewish religion.

Exile and Return

As I described earlier, most of the leaders of the people of Judah were exiled to Babylonia after the Babylonian Empire conquered the Kingdom of Judah. In fact, there were very few people left living in the old Judean lands. There was no Temple left and no place to do animal sacrifices. The people in exile had to find a new way to practice their traditional religion and a new way to feel that they belonged to a separate people. Prophets, like Ezekiel, came forth in exile, urging the Jews to keep to their religion and have faith that they would be able to return to the land of Judah and Jerusalem someday. While they did return after not too long, the exile in Babylonia was the first experience of the Judeans—who we may now call Jews—as a people outside their own territory and without the Temple to make sacrifices in. They had to start to learn to develop substitutes for having a government and for some of their older religious practices. One important substitute was studying their religious laws closely in order to remember them, even those they couldn't follow in exile. From that first exile in

586 BCE, until today, there always have been Jews living in countries outside the land of Israel. For many of these years in many of those countries, Jews really felt and believed that they were not at home. And when they had that feeling of being in exile, they would remember the words of the Bible that told how the Jews felt during that first exile, "By the rivers of Babylon, where we lay down and wept as we remembered Zion." Throughout history, when people have been taken from their homeland, they would often remember the story of the exile of the Israelites to Babylonia.

Under Persian Rule

In 538 BCE the Persian King Cyrus conquered the Babylonian Empire. It was the Persian policy to allow exiled peoples to return to their homelands and rule themselves, as long as they remained loyal to the Persian Empire and paid tribute to the Persian kings. So about fifty years after the destruction of the Temple and the exile into Babylonia, Jews began to return to Judea. Not all the Jews returned. Many remained in Babylonia. The Diaspora had become a permanent feature of Jewish history. The ones that did return settled in the territory around and south of Jerusalem, mostly the old territory of the tribe of Judah. That is why it came to be called Judea, and all remaining Israelites, not just the tribe of Judah, came to be called Judeans, or Jews.

The returning people were under the leadership of Zerubabel, a member of the royal family. In 515 BCE the Temple was rebuilt. It was not as big or fancy as Solomon's Temple. But still this second Temple made it possible to go back to some of the old religious practices. Priests became powerful again and for about 70 years Judea was ruled by priests. It stayed a poor part of the Persian Empire. We don't know much of what happened during this time. We do know that the Judeans had conflicts with the Samaritans. By this time the Samaritans had developed their own religious traditions that were different from those of the Judeans. The Samaritans may have been afraid that the new Temple would help the Judean priests in their attempts to bring the Samaritans back under Judean control. The Persians, however, ruled all of them and had the final say in any dispute. The Persians let the Judeans rebuild the Temple, but the Persians demanded that it be kept small so as not to anger the Samaritans. The Judeans also didn't have enough money to build anything big or fancy.

After 70 years as a poor land ruled by priests, in about 440 BCE, a Jew from Babylonia named Nehemiah arrived in Judea. Nehemiah was a trusted official in the Persian government. After he learned of the poor condition of his homeland, he had the Persians appoint him governor of Judea. Nehemiah did much to improve the Judean government in the twelve years that he ruled. He made it work better and more honestly. He started policies to help the poor and he is also remembered for rebuilding the walls around Jerusalem.

About the same time that Nehemiah returned to Jerusalem from Babylonia, another important exile returned. This was Ezra, the Scribe. A scribe was someone who wrote down the religious laws and stories of the people. Ezra was accompanied by many other religious Jews from Babylonia, and when he arrived with them in Jerusalem he began to reform the religious life of Judea. One of his most important changes was to start to have the Jewish religious laws read out loud in public. If you have ever been to a synagogue service, you may have noticed that the most important part of the service is when the Torah is taken out of the Ark and a part of it is read out loud. This practice began with Ezra. Although in Ezra's day there were still animal sacrifices, eventually the Jewish religion completely replaced the sacrifices with public Torah readings as its most important ritual.

Some people think Ezra was the main editor of the Torah, that is, they believe he was the one to collect the Jewish laws and stories that were around in his day and decide which ones should go in the holy book. Whether he was its main editor or not, it seems clear that he did much to make the Jewish people aware of the Torah and convince them to consider it holy and the proper guide to living a good and religious life.

Even though we know very little about Jewish life the two hundred years that Judea was part of the Persian Empire, there must have been a lot of literary and religious activity going on. First, as we have said, the Torah, the basic part of the Jewish

Bible, which Jews came to believe Moses got from God on Mount Sinai, was compiled and made familiar to all the people. Many other parts of the Jewish Bible were probably written at this time, such as the Book of Job, the Book of Joel, the Book of Ruth and the Song of Songs. This was also the time that the old Hebrew script, which is hard for us to read, was changed over to a Hebrew script which can easily be read today.

Another very important development during the time of the Persian Empire was the beginning of the Oral Law. "Oral" means spoken. The Jewish Torah laws were written and collected at this time, but Jewish scholars also began to discuss what the written laws meant and how they should be applied to people's daily life. Their ideas and discussions were memorized and passed down from generation to generation and it was called the Oral Law. The Oral Law was created over many hundreds of years, but its earliest parts were formed during the Persian Empire. Eventually it was written down in books called the Mishna. One interesting thing about the Mishna is that the Hebrew it is written in is different from the Hebrew of the Bible. It is still Hebrew, but it is more like Aramaic than the Biblical Hebrew. Aramaic was the most widely used language in the Middle East in those days, and probably more and more Jews started speaking Aramaic at that time.

The stories in this chapter have come mostly from the Bible, and as we have said, the Bible is not reliable as history. But unlike the earlier parts of the Bible, the parts about Abraham, Isaac, and Jacob, which are fairly clearly mythical, historians think the Biblical accounts of the Babylonian exile, Ezra, and Nehemiah, probably describe, if only approximately, what actually happened. In the next chapter there is still some reliance on traditional legends for our story, but we begin to enter the time when there is good historical evidence for what happened.

FIGURE 4 – Print of Mattathias, leader of Macabbean rebellion against the Greeks.

Chapter 3

Greeks and Hasmoneans

The Greek Conquest

In 334 BCE a Greek leader, Alexander the Great, went to war against the Persian Empire. Greece is a land on the Mediterranean Sea, a few hundred miles west of Israel. Many of the customs and ideas of today's Europe and America began in ancient Greece. The Greeks developed science, art, history, philosophy, poetry and drama that have had a great influence on world civilization. This Greek cultural influence was first felt in the eastern Mediterranean area and Middle East, then in Rome, then in the rest of Europe, and eventually, when Europe conquered most of the world thousands of years later, Greek culture became part of the entire world's culture. But it first began to spread with the conquests of Alexander the Great.

It did not take long for Alexander to defeat the Persian Empire. He and his troops arrived in Judea in 333 BCE. Even though the Jews had been content under Persian rule, they accepted Alexander as a friendly conqueror. He let the High Priest in Jerusalem and the local Jewish authorities continue to rule. He did not make the Jews change their religion or way of life.

Alexander died young, and after his death his generals fought over who would control the large empire he had conquered. One general, Ptolemy, got control of the Egyptian part of Alexander's empire. Another General, Seleucus, got control of the Syrian part. Judea is right between these two parts, so the Seleucids fought the Ptolemies to see who would control Judea.

At first the Ptolemies won. They brought Greek settlers to live in Judea and introduced Greek customs, but they mostly seemed to leave the Jews alone to lead their own lives. There were some

Judeans that would have preferred to live under Seleucid rule. Maybe that was because so many Jews still lived in Babylonia. Babylonia was in the Seleucid Empire and it would be easier for the Judean Jews to have contact with them if they were part of the same empire. But life under the Ptolemies was fairly good and we don't know of any serious Judean resistance to Ptolemaic rule.

During this time many Jews moved to other parts of the Ptolemaic Empire, especially a new city that the Greek conquerors had built in Egypt, Alexandria. Alexandria became an important center of the Jewish Diaspora. Jews mixed with Greeks in the city and learned about Greek culture and came to admire it. It was there that tradition says the Hebrew Bible was first translated into Greek by seventy scholars. This translation is called the Septuagint, from the word seventy, and it allowed the people who were not Jews to learn about the Jewish religion and read the Jewish holy books.

Ptolemaic rule of Judea lasted one hundred years, but in 199 BCE the Greek Seleucids from Syria finally did take Judea away from the Greek Ptolemies. The Seleucids were more interested than the Ptolemies in having all of the peoples in their empire act and live like Greeks. This created a lot of tension among the Jews of Judea. There were already lots of Jews in Judea who tried to live in a Greek way. In part this is probably because they wanted to imitate the way of life of the powerful rulers, in part because it was the way of life of more and more people in that area of the world, and in part because the ancient Greek culture, with its beautiful buildings, poetry, and ideas was very attractive. But, of course, many Judeans, probably most, wanted to remain traditional Jews. So when the new Seleucid rulers began to heavily favor the Jews who wanted to live a Greek way of life, there was anger and resentment throughout Judea.

The Hasmonean Revolt

The situation became worse when Antiochus IV became king of the Seleucid Empire in 176 BCE. He wanted all the people he ruled to be as Greek as possible. At first he only heavily favored the Greek-style Jews of Judea by doing such things as having a gymnasium for Greek athletics built in Jerusalem. The traditional Jews hated these changes. They believed that things like the gymnasium, where young men competed naked, were insulting to the Jewish way of life and against their religion. They believed that it defiled, that is, made unholy, their holy city. So fights began to break out between the pro-Greek and the anti-Greek Jews. That is when Antiochus' soldiers interfered. In 170 BCE, Seleucid troops entered Jerusalem. They massacred many people. The Temple treasures were taken and the Temple itself was changed into a place of worship for the Greek God Zeus. Antiochus declared laws that made certain Jewish customs against the law. In some places Judaism was completely outlawed.

FIGURE 5 – Bust of Antiochus IV.

The Jews started fighting back. The first resisters were called the First Pious Men. They were good fighters, but they lost when the Greeks found out that they wouldn't fight on the Sabbath. The Greeks attacked them on the Sabbath, slaughtered them, and ended their rebellion.

But in 167 BCE, when the Greeks entered the town of Modi'in to enforce their anti-Jewish laws, the rebellion started again. A priestly family from Modi'in, led by Mattathias the Hasmonean, killed the Greek soldiers. The war Mattathias and his sons fought against the Greeks was a guerilla war. In a guerilla war a group of fighters from the people in the area fight small battles against a bigger regular army. After the battles, the guerilla fighters go back into hiding. The Hasmonean guerilla fighters knew the Judean hills well. Perhaps the Greeks did not take the rebellion seriously at first, but after two years, in 165 BCE, the Hasmoneans were strong enough to conquer Jerusalem. They cleaned up the Temple and re-dedicated it to Elohim, the Jewish God. The rededication ceremony took place on the 25th of Kislev, and to this day Jews remember the event by celebrating the holiday of Hanukah.

By the time the Hasmoneans conquered Jerusalem, Mattathias had died and his son Judah had taken over the leadership of the rebellion. Judah was known as "the Maccabee," which probably meant the Hammer. Judah was an excellent military leader. He also was smart enough to begin a friendship with Rome. Rome was far away, but it was becoming stronger all the time and it was a good friend to have.

Meanwhile, Antiochus had died and the anti-Jewish laws he had made were withdrawn. While that decreased the fighting, it did not stop it. Now the Hasmoneans were fighting to be free from Greek rule altogether. But the rebellion had a setback. In 160 BCE, Judah died. He was replaced by his brother Jonathan. Jonathan was unable to prevent the Seleucid Greeks from reconquering Jerusalem and he fled with some soldiers and followers across the Jordan into the hills and desert. From there the guerilla war against the Greeks continued. In 153 BCE, the Seleucid Greeks started fighting among themselves. They couldn't agree on who was to become their next king. Jonathan used this fight among the Greeks to make a deal. He used his army to help one side and then had himself appointed the ruler of Judea. So the Hasmoneans were ruling in Judea again, but were not completely free of Greek rule. In 143 BCE, Jonathan was killed by one of his enemies among the Seleucids. Immediately his brother Simon took over as High Priest and ruler of Judea. Simon was a ruler who was able to defend Hasmonean rule in Judea and even to expand its boundaries. The Hasmoneans had kept up their friendship with the Romans ever since Judah was the leader. Simon now used that friendship to win complete independence from the Seleucid Greeks. He also gathered a meeting of important Jews, called the Sanhedrin (Great Assembly), to get their agreement that he would be High Priest and ruler of the country. Simon lived till 136 BCE, when he was assassinated. He is remembered in Jewish tradition as a just leader who cared about his people. He was followed to power by his son, Johanan Hyrcanus.

The Hasmonean Monarchy

Johanan Hyrcanus, like his father Simon, made himself High Priest of the Jews and also their ruler. He and his descendants ruled an independent Kingdom of Judea for the next 75 years. Although these Hasmoneans fought among themselves at times, they managed to conquer new territories too, and so made their kingdom bigger. Johanan Hyrcanus himself conquered the Idumaneans in the south and forced them to convert to Judaism. His son Aristobolus conquered territories in the north and also made many people convert. At times the Hasmonean kingdom may have included lands that even King David had never conquered.

But although they had success in foreign conquests, the rule of the Hasmonean kings at home was often troubled. There were a number of different causes for these troubles. Sometimes it was a simple fight between two Hasmoneans to see who would become king. The last Hasmonean rulers for instance, the brothers Hyrcanus II and Aristobulus II, fought each other to see who would be king.

But there were also problems with Jews who didn't like how Greek the Hasmonean kings were acting. Even though the Hasmoneans first came to power in the time of the Maccabees by leading a successful rebellion against Greek culture, their descendants had become very Greek in their ways, and this angered many Judeans. Between 90 and 85 BCE the Hasmonean King Jannaeus cruelly massacred many thousands of Jews who didn't like the way he was ruling.

Part of the problem throughout Hasmonean times was that many Jews thought it was wrong for one person to be both the king and the High Priest, and this is something the Hasmonean kings usually did, that is, they made themselves the High Priest. Another problem was that the Hasmoneans weren't from the right families to hold either position. The king was supposed to be a descendant of David and the High Priest was supposed to be a descendent of Zadok, who was the first High Priest in Solomon's Temple. When the Great Assembly first agreed to allow Simon to become High Priest and ruler, they made it temporary until "a true prophet shall arise." Many Judeans were never happy with having Hasmoneans, who were not from David's or Zadok's family, being king and High Priest.

There were also important religious differences among the Jews during the Hasmonean rule. One group of Jews, who were called Sadducees, thought that the Temple service, with its animal sacrifices and rituals that only the priests could perform, was the most important part of the Jewish religion. The Sadducees believed in following the first Five Books of the Bible, the Torah, very closely. But they thought other parts of the Bible, and other Jewish customs, traditions and the Oral Laws were not important. Since the Hasmonean kings themselves were either the High Priest or close to him, they naturally favored these Sadducees. After all, the Sadducees said the priests were the most important people in the Jewish religion. In general the Sadducees got along well with the government.

Sadducees were very nationalistic and they liked that the Hasmonean kings kept fighting to make their kingdom bigger and kept forcing other people to become Jews. Rich people, government officials, military people, and merchants were usually Sadducees.

Another group of Jews, called the Pharisees, appeared during Hasmonean times. The Pharisees were more connected to the Jewish tradition of the prophets than the Sadducees were. The Pharisees didn't stop believing in the Temple service, but they thought that the most important part of the religion was following a good and pious life. This included a concern for the poor and righteous living. In addition to the Torah, the Pharisees had great respect for the other parts of the Bible. They also followed the Oral Law. Most of the Pharisees' religious activities took place in the houses of worship all across Judea, where the Torah was read out loud, not the Temple where the priests performed the sacrificial service. These houses of worship were also places of study and the Pharisees made studying the Jewish law a very important part of Judaism. That's why most of the scholars were Pharisees. Maybe because of Pharisee concern for the poor, most of the poor Judean farmers, which meant most of the people of Judea, also favored the Pharisees.

The Pharisees emphasized some of the prophets' ideas and introduced some new ones of their own. As the prophets did, the Pharisees thought of God not as a God of the Jews but as everyone's God. The Pharisees also agreed with the prophets that it was more important to be a good person than to just go through all the rituals in the right way without caring about justice. Some ideas new to Judaism introduced by the Pharisees were that a person's soul kept living after he or she died and that when the Messiah comes, pious Jews will be resurrected, that is, they will rise from their graves and live again. These ideas appeal to poor people who don't have good lives and to people who believe that God is just, but who don't see much justice in the world around them. They think, or hope, that something will happen after death or in the future that will make up for all the unfairness. These ideas also help explain why God is letting bad things happen now.

The Hasmonean kings quarreled and sometimes fought with the Pharisees, but they eventually usually made up because they knew that the Pharisees represented the feelings of most of the people. Take the Sanhedrin, for example. The Sanhedrin started during Hasmonean times. It had 71 people in it and was a legislature, that is, it made laws for Judea, and it was also a high court, that is, it made the final decisions about who had broken the laws and what the punishment should be. Most of the time, the Sanhedrin had Sadducees and Pharisees. But the kings would sometimes kick the Pharisees out. In the end they always had to bring them back because a Sanhedrin without any Pharisees was not respected or obeyed by the people.

Hasmonean times were probably mixed for the people of Judea. The farmers were very heavily taxed and many were very poor. But Jewish law made some arrangements for the whole society to distribute food to the poor on a regular basis. Trade flourished in Judea. Merchants went north and south between Arabia and Syria and east and west between Egypt and Babylonia. But the wars to expand the kingdom and the civil wars in the kingdom caused the people hardships.

The final books of the Hebrew Bible were written during the Hasmonean era. Some of the Psalms, the Book of Daniel, and Ecclesiastes are probably from that time. It was also during this period that some of the final choices were made about which writings would be considered holy. All of the holy books were collected into one "Book of Books." The Hebrew word for "books" is "sefarim." When that word is translated into Greek, it becomes "ta biblia" (the books), which is where the English word Bible comes from. So, although it was in the making for over a thousand years, and its oldest part, the Torah, had been written down and agreed upon for hundreds of years, the entire Hebrew Bible was not fixed in its final form till the end of Hasmonean times.

The Oral Law, the commentaries on the Torah, continued to be developed by the Pharisees during this period, and Judaism continued to spread outside of Judea. By the end of the Hasmoneans' rule there were Jewish communities throughout the Greek-speaking world.

In 63 BCE, in the middle of a Hasmonean civil war between Hyrcanus II and Aristobulus II to see who would become king, Pompey, a Roman general, came with his soldiers to Jerusalem to side with Hyrcanus. Pompey conquered Jerusalem but he didn't make Hyrcanus king. He just made him a local ruler who worked for the Romans. The real local power was Antipater, a rich Judean who was friendly with the Romans. So after 75 years of independence, Judea was once again under foreign, this time Roman, rule. The later Hasmonean kings were such bad kings that the people probably didn't mind being ruled by the Romans at first. As we will see, that changed.

FIGURE 6 – Detail of the stone carving on the Roman Arch of Titus
commemorating the conquest of Jerusalem in the year 70.

FIGURE 7 – The fortress of Masada.

Chapter 4

Roman Rule

Herod

Julius Caesar was the leader of the Roman Empire when Judea fell under Roman rule. In 43 BCE, Caesar made Antipater a Roman citizen and appointed him the Procurator of Judea. A procurator was the Roman governor of one of its provinces. When Antipater was killed by a Hasmonean family member who wanted to be the local ruler, a struggle took place between the Hasmonean family and the Antipater family. It was finally won by Antipater's son, Herod. He had the Romans on his side, which of course was a big advantage. He also married a woman from the Hasmonean family so he could say that he represented all of the ruling families of Judea.

In 37 BCE, the Romans allowed Herod to take the title King and he ruled until he died in 4 BCE. To the world outside Judea he was known as Herod the Great. Trade flourished and Herod kept the peace. He also was a great builder. He had forts and castles built all over the country. He built whole cities, like Caesarea, whose ruins you can still visit today on the Mediterranean coast of Israel. He also built in Jerusalem. The entire area of the Temple, and the Temple itself, was enlarged. The "Western Wall" that still stands in Jerusalem today, was built by Herod to help hold up the enlarged hill he created to expand the Temple.

But though in some ways he was certainly a great king, Herod is not remembered fondly by the Jewish people. First of all, he was always considered a bit of an outsider. His family came from a people the Hasmoneans had conquered and forced to become

Jews, the Idumaneans, so some Judeans never thought of him as a full Jew. He also could be very cruel, and showed no mercy if he thought anyone or any group was a threat to his power. Many people were killed during Herod's rule, including many members of his own family that he didn't trust. Herod gathered all of the power into his own hands. He didn't let the Sanhedrin make any important decisions. In addition, he taxed the people very heavily. He had to give a lot of tribute money to the Romans, who were allowing him to be king in the first place. Herod also needed money for the cities, roads, forts, and Temple renovations he had built. All this building benefited the city population, but it didn't help the majority peasant farmers, who just kept becoming poorer from all of the taxes.

Instead of appointing a new king when Herod died, the Romans allowed Herod's four sons to rule different parts of Judea. But that only lasted a few years before the sons died or were removed from their position by Rome. Judea then became a province of Rome directly ruled by the Roman procurator.

Resistance to Rome

The Roman procurators of Judea were not good rulers. They knew nothing and cared even less about Judaism, so they were always doing things that insulted the people's religious feelings. They also were mostly dishonest men. In addition to the tribute that was sent to Rome, lots of the people's tax money went to enrich the procurators.

Under these bad conditions many things happened that were very important in Jewish history. There began to be a great desire to be free of foreign rule, especially among the Pharisees. Some groups, such as the Zealots, started to talk about fighting the Romans. One group of Zealots, the Sicarri, even began assassinating Romans on the streets.

Besides these political reactions to the oppression of Roman rule, there were religious reactions. Some groups of Jews, such as the Essenes, went to live simple and religious lives in the desert caves around the Dead Sea. The Dead Sea Scrolls, two thousand year old texts that were probably written by the Essenes or a similar group, were found recently and can be seen in museums today.

The hope that the Messiah would soon come became widespread and more important among the Jews. Many Jews felt that now, surely, was the time for the Messiah to come. The Messiah was supposed to lead the Jews in some terrible battles against foreigners. After the Messiah's victory, Jews believed there would come a time of peace and justice. There were many people in Judea at this time predicting that the Messiah would soon come. The life of one of them would affect the whole world.

The Beginning of Christianity

A Jewish country preacher named John used to take people to the Jordan River, where he immersed them in the river and said prayers. This is called "baptism," and John was known as John the Baptist. John was always preaching about the coming of the Messiah.

One of the people that John baptized was a Jewish Galilean, probably from Nazareth, named Joshua (in Greek, Jesus). When he was about thirty years old, in about 25 CE (meaning, in the Common Era; I am writing the book you are reading now in 2013 CE), Jesus began to preach. He also became a healer, and there are legends of his curing blindness and leprosy. His activities mostly took place around Lake Kinneret, the Sea of Galilee, in the town of Capernaum. Jesus' teaching was very similar to what most of the Pharisees of his time were saying. Like other Pharisees, Jesus put great emphasis on having the right religious feelings and not just going through the motions of religious activities. And like the Pharisees and the old prophets, Jesus spoke up for the poor and the weak people.

Jesus must have been a very impressive person, because in only a few years he gained a very devoted following. It is not clear whether Jesus thought he was the Messiah, but his followers certainly thought he was.

When Jesus and some followers went to preach in Jerusalem, they caught the attention of the authorities. Apparently, Jesus spoke out against the business activity going on around the

Temple, which he thought was a corruption of religion. This angered the High Priest Caiaphas, who was probably making money from the businesses around the Temple. Caiaphas reported Jesus to the Roman Procurator, Pontius Pilate. The Romans of course, did not like anyone who claimed to be the Messiah, someone who would become king of the Jews and lead a war against Rome. So Jesus was charged with being a rebel against Rome, someone who wanted to be king of the Jews. He was crucified in about 32 CE by the Romans in Jerusalem. Crucifixion, nailing someone to a cross, was the regular way the Romans punished people they condemned to death. Many thousands of people in Judea alone were crucified during the years of Roman rule.

After his execution, Jesus was buried in a nearby cave. His followers did not stop believing he was the Messiah. According to Christian tradition, after three days Jesus was resurrected, that is he rose from death and went up to heaven.

For some time after Jesus' death, Christians remained a group of Jews that believed Jesus was the Messiah. They called themselves the Brethren and other Jews called them Nazarenes, since Jesus and so many of his followers came from around Nazareth. They were not a separate religion yet. Except for the fact that they thought Jesus was the Messiah, their religious beliefs were pretty much like those of other Jews. The Greek speakers called them *Christianos*, which is Greek for "follower of Christ." Jesus was referred to in Greek as Christos, meaning "anointed one;" this word had the same meaning as the Hebrew word Mashiach (messiah).

Paul

Christianity started to change with the work of Saul of Tarsus. Saul was one of the most influential Jews who ever lived, and was the true founder of Christianity. At first he hated the followers of Jesus and harassed them, but he had a religious experience when he was travelling to Damascus that changed his life and world history. As a result of this experience, Saul became a Christian. He changed his name to Paul and is remembered by Christians today as St. Paul.

Paul travelled all over the Mediterranean world spreading the word about Jesus. Some Christians, Paul included, now believed that Jesus was not only the Messiah, but that he was also part of God himself, or as they said "the son of God." They thought that if you believed in Jesus your sins would be forgiven. These beliefs were very different from standard Jewish beliefs. They also believed that Jesus would come back again to do what the Messiah was supposed to do. But the big break with Judaism came when Paul said that you don't have to be Jewish or follow Jewish laws to be a Christian. He believed that you could be "saved," that is, forever keep your soul alive in heaven after you died, without being Jewish; all that was needed was to have faith in Jesus.

These ideas of Paul made it much easier to gain followers. Paul was preaching to people who were gentiles, that is, not Jewish. Many of these people seemed to be ready to give up their pagan religion, but the idea of being circumcised, a requirement for men becoming Jews, and following all the laws of the Torah, required for both men and women, were not appealing to gentiles. So when Paul said you could be a Christian without being Jewish, he made it possible for Christianity to grow into a world-wide religion. Many Jewish religious ideas remained in Christianity, and Christians accepted the Hebrew Bible as holy. But starting with Paul, the two religions grew farther and farther apart. Christianity was influenced more and more by the Greek and Roman traditions and religion of its gentile followers. Before long, Christianity no longer saw itself as a branch of the Jewish religion, and Jews didn't see it as a branch of the Jewish religion either. In fact, by then the two religious groups disliked each other. The authors of the Christian holy books, the Gospels, did not have friendly feelings about Jews. The Christians thought the Jews were stubborn. Why didn't Jews accept Jesus as the Messiah? Why did they stick with the old Jewish laws? Why did they deny the truth?

For Jews, Christians were traitors to the true Jewish religion, people who brought a mistaken form of Judaism to the gentiles of the world. Jews and Christians would sometimes fight and each group would try to get the Romans to persecute the other. There were many periods when the Romans did persecute Judaism, or Christianity, or both. By the time Christianity became the official religion of the Roman Empire, three hundred years after Paul first started to get gentile converts to Christianity, Jews and Christians hated each other. Since Christians became the large, powerful group, this became a big problem for Jews for the next two thousand years. But now let us return to first-century Judea.

The First Judean Revolt

Dissatisfaction with Roman rule increased until finally open rebellion broke out in Jerusalem. In 66 CE, the Roman soldiers stationed in Jerusalem were trapped in a fort and then slaughtered when they came out. The Jews in Jerusalem quickly organized a government and successfully fought off the first Roman attempt to recapture Jerusalem. This success got more Jews from all over the country to join the rebellion against Rome. But not all Jews did. Throughout the war with Rome that followed, many Jews quietly led their own lives and didn't join either side. Jews living in the Diaspora, that is, outside Judea, also didn't give much support to the Judean rebellion.

One big problem the rebels had was that they were disunited. They often fought and even massacred each other. The Zealots thought the more moderate Pharisees would betray the rebellion and make some kind of peace with Rome. There were also disagreements about how strictly to enforce Jewish laws. Only when the Roman forces approached Jerusalem did the Jews there stop fighting one another to face the enemy united.

The Roman Emperor Nero had sent one of his best generals, Vespasian, to put down the rebellion in Judea. First Vespasian conquered the Galilee before he finally approached Jerusalem. By the time Vespasian was ready to lay siege to Jerusalem, all of Judea outside of that city, except for a few strongholds, was under Roman control. But then there was a delay in the siege of the city. Nero had died and Vespasian went back to Rome to fight to become Emperor himself. He sent his son, the Roman general

Titus, to continue the war in Judea. But all of this took time and for a few years the Jews stayed in control of Jerusalem. But finally, in 70 CE, Titus laid a forceful siege to Jerusalem. Jerusalem held out for a while and fought the Romans very heroically, but on the 9th day of the Jewish month of Av, which is in August, Roman troops reached the Temple in the center of the city. We do not know whether the Romans did it on purpose, but on that day, during the fighting, the Second Temple was destroyed. It was, according to Jewish tradition, the exact same date over six centuries earlier when the first Temple was destroyed by the Babylonians. Religious Jews still observe the 9th of Av as a day of national mourning.

A few strongholds of Jewish rebellion held out after the fall of Jerusalem. The most famous of these was a fort built on top of a mountain plateau in the desert along the Dead Sea: Masada. Hundreds of Jewish warriors with their families held out against the Romans for three years in their mountain fortress. In the end, when they could resist the Romans no longer, they decided to kill their own families and commit suicide rather than surrender.

We know a lot of details of the first Jewish revolt against the Romans because of the writings of Joseph ben Mattathias, known to history by his Roman name, Josephus. Josephus was a Jew who was appointed commander of the Jewish forces defending the Galilee. When the Romans conquered the Galilee, not only did Josephus surrender to them, he also joined their side. He tried to convince the Jews that were still fighting to give up. Maybe he really was trying to save Jewish lives by having them stop a hopeless fight against the mighty Roman Empire, or maybe he was just trying to save his own skin or win favor with the Romans. He was with the Roman armies when they laid siege to Jerusalem and three years later at Masada. When the war was over he went to Rome and wrote a history of it. Later he wrote other books that tried to explain and defend the Jewish people to the other peoples of the Roman Empire.

Hundreds of thousands of Jews were killed during and immediately after the revolt. Many died in battle, but many also died in punishment massacres and executions. Some were killed in gladiator contests to entertain the Romans. Some were killed to celebrate Roman holidays. Thousands of others were sold into slavery. The Arch of Titus, which still stands in Rome today, has carvings on it that show the Romans bringing treasures and prisoners from Judea in a victory parade.

Even though many thousands of Jews died in the first revolt and the Temple was destroyed, life in Judea went on much as before. Judea remained a Roman province ruled by a procurator and still had many Jews living in it, even if there were fewer there than there were before the revolt. In fact the Sanhedrin, under the leadership of Johanan Ben Zakai, relocated to Yavneh, a town near today's Jaffa. The Romans permitted the Sanhedrin, filled with religious scholar-teachers called rabbis, to make religious laws for the Jews. The head of the Sanhedrin, "Nasi" in Hebrew, was soon recognized by the Romans as the legitimate local leader of the Jews, and soon things returned to normal.

The Hadrianic Persecutions and Bar Kokhba Revolt

In 96 CE, there were anti-Roman riots by Jews in many Diaspora communities in the Roman Empire. There was not much anti-Roman activity in Judea at this time, but the riots elsewhere made the Romans nervous about the Jews in general. When Hadrian became the Roman Emperor in 117 CE, things got worse. Hadrian thought it was important that all the peoples of the Empire follow Roman customs, including religious customs. Naturally the Jews weren't going to go along with that easily. In 120, Hadrian built a Roman city, Aelia Capitolina, over the ruins of Jerusalem. At the site of the Temple he built a Temple to the Roman god Jupiter. Judean resistance increased until in 132 CE the second Jewish revolt against the Romans became a full-fledged war. It was led by Simon ben Kosiba, who was also called "Bar Kokhba," Son of a Star.

Bar Kokhba seems to have been an excellent military leader and administrator. He conquered Jerusalem and for a year controlled much of the country. One of the most important rabbis of the time, Rabbi Akiva, declared that Bar Kokhba was the Messiah come to lead the Jews in a victorious war against the Romans. Unlike the first revolt, most of the Jews of Judea rallied together to fight the Romans. But the success of Bar Kokhba's rebellion was short lived. The Romans counter-attacked in 133 CE. Bar Kokhba's army fought well and the Romans lost many soldiers in the war, but the Roman army was just too strong. In a couple of years the rebellion was completely crushed. In 135 CE, Bar Kokhba's headquarters at Betar fell to the Romans and he was executed by them.

The Romans took a terrible revenge on the Jews of Judea for this second revolt. Leading rabbis, such as Akiva, were tortured to death. Thousands of Jews were slaughtered. Whole Jewish cities and hundreds of Jewish villages were completely destroyed. Many Jews were sold into slavery. In addition, Hadrian made laws against practicing the Jewish religion: it became against the law to circumcise a child. It was against the law to observe the Sabbath, and it was against the law to study or teach Torah. There are many tales of heroic rabbis who risked their lives to keep Jewish knowledge alive during this Hadrianic persecution. The persecution only lasted three years, till Hadrian's death in 138 CE. The new Emperor, Antonius Pius, let the Jews practice Judaism again, but by then most of the Jews of Judea who hadn't been killed or sold into slavery had fled, many to Babylonia, beyond the Roman Empire. Judea, whose name Hadrian had changed to Syria Palaestina, now had very few Jews left in it. For almost the next two thousand years, Jewish history is mostly the story of the Jews in the Diaspora; the Jews became a people who thought of themselves, and were viewed by others, as exiles, as "guests" in other people's countries.

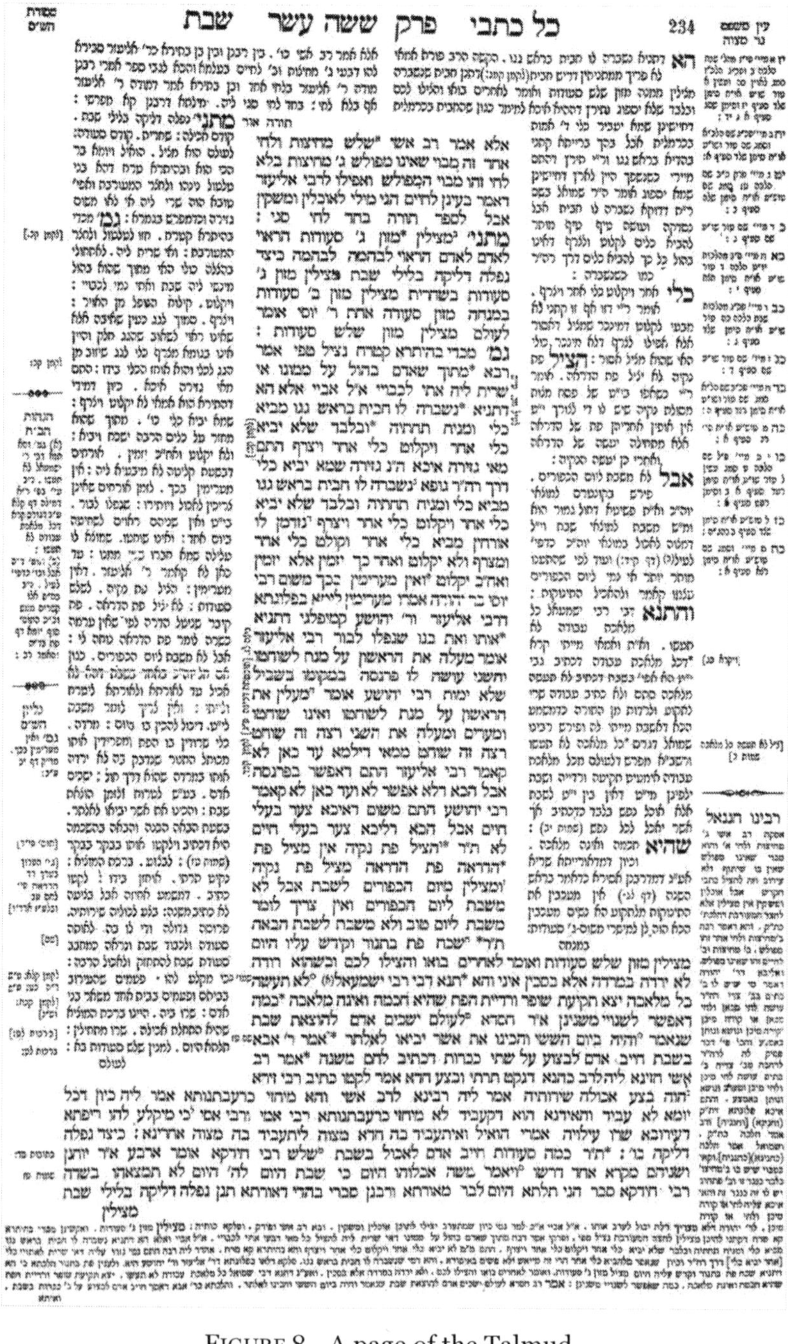

FIGURE 8 - A page of the Talmud.

Chapter 5

Talmudic Times

The Talmud

A few years after the second Judean revolt against Rome there weren't many Jews left in Judea. But by then there were many Jews living in other countries. In Egypt and Babylonia there were very large Jewish communities. In some ways, the Jews in the Diaspora became like the gentiles they were living among. In Alexandria they spoke Greek, like the other people of that city. In Babylonia, they spoke Aramaic, which was not only the local language there, but was also the most common language in the Middle East at that time. (Aramaic was probably the most common language in Judea itself at that time.)

But what is most interesting is not how the Jews in some ways became similar to the people they lived among. That is to be expected, for people living together always learn from each other and influence each other. What is most remarkable is that without a country, that is, without their own government to rule them or a land to live together in, the Jews didn't just melt into other nations. Instead, scattered across many countries, the Jews remained a separate people. How did this happen?

We have already seen some of the reasons the Jews were able to continue being Jewish without a country. First they had developed an idea of one God that wasn't tied to one spot or one land. The Greek gods lived on Mount Olympus, and you might think that if you moved far away from Mount Olympus you moved away from them. The Jewish God you couldn't move away from.

Second, much of Jews' religious activities had come to take place in synagogues, houses of worship and study, which could be built anywhere. Wherever Jews went they could make a place of worship. Third, the basic stories and rules of the Jewish religion were written in a book that all Jews recognized as the official holy book—the Book of Books—the Bible. The Bible could be carried everywhere, and in the centuries leading up to the revolts against Rome the Jews had started schools in their communities so that more and more of them were able to read the Bible. Even after the Temple was destroyed and they had left the Land of Israel, Jews were still able to practice their religion. Their religion could be carried with them.

But it wasn't just their religion that Jews were able to take as they left Judea, it was a whole way of life. This way of life was described in the Oral Law. The Oral Law had been developing for many centuries. These Jewish traditions, rules, and stories had been handed down, told from generation to generation, at least since the days of the Persian Empire, and perhaps from even earlier. Jews believed that some of it, or all of it, was actually told to Moses by God at the same time God gave Moses the written law. However, Oral Law was actually being created throughout all of this time and was always being added to. But the rapid growth of the Oral Law and its collection into a standard form took place mostly from 200 BCE to 550 CE. Finally, when it was all written down, it was called the Talmud, the Teaching, and its study and the guidance it gave to every aspect of daily life was probably the single most important reason that the Jews stayed a separate people while living throughout the Diaspora.

The first part of the Talmud is the Mishna, the Repetition. It was written down by Judah HaNasi, Judah the Prince, or Patriarch, somewhere between 170 and 220 CE. The Patriarchs were the heads of the Sanhedrin, which first moved from Jerusalem to Yahvneh, a town near today's Jaffa, at the time of the first revolt. The Sanhedrin then moved into the towns of Usha and Tiberias in the Galilee. The Patriarchs were descendants of Rabbi Hillel, who had led the Sanhedrin in Jerusalem in the first century BCE. When Judah HaNasi wrote down the Mishna, he was organizing and recording all of the results of those Sanhedrin discussions of the previous few hundred years. The Sanhedrin rabbis, from Hillel through Akiva and his student Rabbi Mier, right up to Judah himself, are called the *Tannaim*, the Repeaters. What they said they were doing was interpreting the first five books of the Bible, the Torah, the written law. The Torah didn't say exactly what to do in every situation, so these rabbis had to decide how to apply it to new situations. Of course, there were always situations coming up that the Torah had nothing to say about at all, and so the rabbis had to make up their own rules about what to do in that situation. But they never would admit, probably not even to themselves, that they really were making up completely new rules. Instead they would always try to find some connection to something that was written in the Torah. So the Mishna is in the form of a commentary on the Torah, that is, it is a book that is discussing another book. But it is also a book about the legal discussions and decisions of rabbis that took place over hundreds of years.

As soon as Judah HaNasi had finished organizing and writing down the Oral Law in the Mishna, other rabbis began to study it and comment on it. And just as the Torah couldn't provide rules about what to do in every possible situation that might come up, so too, the Mishna had nothing directly to say about many of the problems and situations that Jews faced in their lives. So once again rabbis not only interpreted a Jewish holy book, this time the Mishna, but they also made new rules for Jewish life, even though they always tried to connect these new rules to the old ones somehow.

This second part of the Talmud, this commentary on the Mishna, is called the Gemara, the Completion. Sometimes, when people use the word "Talmud" they are only talking about the Gemara and sometimes they mean both the Mishna and the Gemara. Actually Mishna and Gemara are always studied together because the Gemara is a commentary on the Mishna. A page of Talmud has a part of the Mishna and the Gemara that discusses it right on the same page. While the Mishna was written by Jews in Palestine (the Roman name for Judea), there are two different collections of commentaries on the Mishna itself: one collection written in Palestine, known as the Palestinian Talmud, the other written in Babylonia, the Babylonian Talmud.

The Palestinian Talmud is the shorter and less exciting of the two. It was written by the small weak Jewish community that was left in Palestine after the second revolt. That small community hung on for a couple of hundred years, and the Patriarchs of the Sanhedrin, who are responsible for the Palestinian Talmud, remained its recognized leadership. But the Patriarchy itself was abolished in 425 CE and the Jews of Palestine and their Talmud became minor players in Jewish history.

But the Babylonia Talmud was created by a strong Jewish community that had established some great centers of Jewish learning. First the Babylonian Jews had built schools of higher learning to study Torah. They built these academies in the Babylonia cities of Sura and Nehardea. Later on, after the closing of the academy in Nehardea, an Academy was established in Pumbedita. The Babylonia Talmud was created from the discussions of the Mishna that took place at these Academies over hundreds of years. When the Exilarch, that is, the leader of the Jews in the Babylonia Exile, realized that there was a danger of losing or forgetting the Oral Law created in this these discussions, it was decided to write them down. And that is how the Babylonian Talmud came to be written in 477-499 CE. Some additional comments were added up to 550 CE, but after that the Talmud was complete.

The Mishna is written in Hebrew, but the Talmud is a record of discussions that took place entirely in Aramaic, so it is written in Aramaic (both the Palestinian and Babylonian versions). There are all sorts of different material in it, all mixed together. A big part of the Talmud is taken up with discussions of laws and rules. That part is called *halacha*. *Halacha* described what a Jew was supposed to do according to the rabbis, and it covered almost every part of a person's behavior. One of the things that the rabbis who created the Talmud were probably trying to do was to make laws that would keep Jews separate from the non-Jews they were living among. The rabbis also wanted to make rules that would keep the Jews far from the possibility of breaking any of the basic Jewish laws. For both these reasons the *Ammoraim* (meaning, the Interpreters, which is what the rabbis who wrote the Gemara were called), made lots of strict detailed rules about how to live your entire life. For instance, you may have heard about the kosher eating rules. There are only a few sentences in the Bible that these rules are based on. One sentence says you should not cook a baby goat in milk taken from its mother. But from that sentence the rabbis made all sorts of rules about not eating any dairy foods with any meat foods, and not even using the same dishes for dairy and meat, or even eating them around the same time. If you followed this rabbinic rule you certainly weren't going to be breaking the no-goat-in-mother's-milk rule from the Bible. Just as important, it made it hard even to eat with your non-Jewish neighbors, and marrying them would be impossible. In this way the *halacha*, the rabbis' laws, helped keep the Jews a separate people.

The *halacha* wasn't completely cut and dried. The Talmud was a record of discussions and those discussions had lots of disagreements. Both sides of the disagreement were usually reported in the Talmud. For instance, going way back to the early days of the Tannaim, we read about the followers of Hillel and the followers of Shammai. Rabbi Hillel had a less strict approach to understanding the laws of the Torah than did Rabbi Shammai. These two great rabbis disagreed often about what the right rules were. The Talmud tells us about this disagreement.

There is a famous story in the Talmud that tells us about the different approaches of Hillel and Shammai. According to legend, a man came to Shammai and asked him to teach him all of the Torah while he stood on one foot. Shammai thought the man was making fun of him and so he chased him away. The man then went to Hillel with the same request. Hillel is said to have replied "Don't do to others what you hate to have done to yourself. All of the rest are just explanations of this rule. Now go and study the explanations."

The rules that became part of the *halacha* were the ones the majority of the rabbis agreed to. In that sense the rule-making was democratic. But it was also democratic because the minority opinion in the disagreement wasn't completely ignored. It was recorded in the Talmud for future generations to read and consider. Of course, it was only the rabbis making the rules, not all the people, so in that way the *halacha* wasn't very democratic at all. But on the other hand, any Jewish man, if he studied and learned enough could become a rabbi. Most of the more powerful rabbis came from certain families, and the best jobs for rabbis were usually kept in those families; but it was still possible for a smart and hard working poor person to become a leading rabbi. At least if that person was a male. Girls were not taught Torah or Talmud and weren't allowed to become rabbis and help decide on the Law; that is another way *halacha* is very undemocratic.

Besides the Halachic parts of the Talmud, there are parts that contain legends, folktales, funny stories and all sorts of other writings. These parts are called *Aggadah* or *Midrash*. The Talmud, therefore, is a collection of Jewish laws and literature that describes a whole culture and a whole way of life. It was what Jews had in the Diaspora instead of a country.

The Diaspora

The Roman Empire lasted many hundreds of years, and by the time it fell apart there were Jews living in every part of it: in Italy and Spain, Greece and Anatolia (today's Turkey), North Africa and Gaul (today's France), and probably even Britain.

Even though there were bloody wars between Rome and the Jews of Judea during the five hundred years the Empire lasted, the Jews in other parts of the Roman Empire mostly got on fairly well. The Romans thought the Jews' religion and customs were a little strange. They thought it was odd to refuse to work on the Sabbath or to avoid eating pork. But at times the Romans seemed to respect Judaism too; they tolerated and showed an interest in the religion.

Things for Jews in the Roman Empire changed when Christianity became its official religion. At first Romans just thought of Christians as special types of Jews. But Christianity spread among non-Jews of the Empire and became a big problem for the Roman leadership. They didn't like people who were more loyal to their religion than they were to the Empire. The Romans had had problems with the Jews of Judea because they wouldn't give their first loyalty to Rome, and so the Romans had basically wiped out the Judean Jews. The Romans kept an eye on Jews in the Diaspora, but the Diaspora Jews were a small part of the total population of the Empire. The Christian population, on the other hand, was growing rapidly. Sometimes the Romans tried to stop the spread of Christianity by persecuting Christians, but this didn't work. Finally, in a kind of "if you can't beat them join them" move, the Roman leadership became Christian itself. This ended up being a disaster for the Jews.

Christianity's Rise to Power

The Emperor Constantine, who ruled from 307-337 CE, was the first Christian Emperor. He moved the Empire's capital from Rome to Byzantium (renamed Constantinople in his honor), where today's Istanbul is. This move eventually led to the Empire's being split in two. The eastern part, where Constantine had moved, became known as Byzantium. This Byzantine Empire was mostly Greek-speaking and had old and well-populated cities in it. It lasted for another thousand years, and the brand of Christianity that grew up in it was called Orthodoxy.

The western part of the Empire was still centered on Rome. This part of the Empire was Latin-speaking and it didn't last much more than 150 years after Constantine's move. Historians have different opinions about why this part of the Empire fell apart. One of the reasons was that German speaking peoples from northern Europe kept invading the Empire, and eventually the Empire was unable to hold them off. The German tribes finally conquered Rome itself, and in 476 CE a German king made himself Emperor. But the Western Roman Empire didn't really stay one Empire. Different German tribes had conquered different parts of it. Over the centuries there had been Huns and Vandals, Goths, Ostrogoths and Visigoths, Franks and Lombards. Different kingdoms arose throughout the old Western Empire.

But the Western Empire did not completely divide. One thing ended up keeping it together. Throughout the West, the same kind of Christianity became official; what came to be known as Roman Catholicism. The Roman Catholic Church was headed by the top priest in Rome, the Pope. This did not happen all at once. There were religious disagreements and fights among Christians in the West. At first the German tribes seemed to favor a kind of Christianity called Arianism. Arians usually treated Jews better than other Christians treated the Jews, so from a Jewish point of view it is too bad the Arians ended up losing.

By the time Christianity became the Empire's official religion, Jews and Christians had been acting like enemies for centuries. Now that Christians had power, things became bad for the Jews. Christians preached against having anything to do with Jews. They said Jews worked for the Devil or were even children of the Devil. They also blamed the Jews for Christ's death, and because they believed that Christ was God, they said Jews were God-killers. Famous Christian preachers, like John Chrysostom (345-407) would preach about what disgusting evil people the Jews were, and then excited mobs of people, after hearing Jews described as such horrible demons, went out and massacred Jews.

Some of the Christian Emperors tried to protect the Jews from being murdered. This helped the Jews survive in Christian lands. But these Emperors still passed laws that discriminated against Jews and made their lives very hard. The Emperor Theodosius (408-450) and the Emperor Justinian (527-565) both passed Codes, sets of laws, which made it hard for Jews to work and worship. As far back as Constantine, in 329 CE, there were laws that wouldn't let Jews marry non-Jews (gentiles).

Sometimes there were attempts to force the Jews to convert. When this happened, many did convert and many were killed who refused to convert. But some Jews always managed to survive. Usually the policy was to make Jews hated outcasts, people who were not part of society, but still to let them live and remain Jewish. Pope Gregory (590-604) called the Jewish religion vomit, but said that Jews shouldn't be killed and shouldn't be forced to convert. This became official policy in the West. It was a policy that was not always followed. Jews were still sometimes slaughtered, forced to convert or kicked out of an area. But things mostly did settle down for a few centuries, allowing Jews in Christian lands, the Catholic West and the Byzantine East, to get on with their lives.

Persian Rule

Outside of the Roman Empire's boundaries, there were Jewish communities in Southern Arabia, Persia, Ethiopia and perhaps and as far away as India. But as we have seen when we talked about the writing of the Talmud, the most important Jewish community was in Babylonia. It was an old and large Jewish community, going back at least till 586 BCE. At times it must have been very prosperous. Even when Babylonian Jews were allowed to return to Judea, many chose to stay in Babylonia (today's Iraq).

The Jews in Babylonia had been part of the Persian Empire since the days of Cyrus. In 140 BCE, the Persian Empire itself was conquered by peoples from the East called the Parthians. The Parthians had no special single religion and were pretty tolerant of religious differences, so life for the Jews under Parthian rule was good. The Jewish Exilarchs, the leaders of the community in Babylonia, were able to rule the Babylonian Jewish community according to Jewish law without the Parthians interfering much. That began to change in 226 CE, when the Parthian Empire was taken over by a new group of Persians. These Persians were not so religiously tolerant. They followed a religion called Zoroastrianism. Although there were some Zoroastrian Persian kings who treated the Jews well, others persecuted the Jews. At times there were massacres and whole Jewish cities in Babylonia were destroyed. In 470 CE, during the rule of the Persian King Peroz, whom Jewish tradition remembers as Peroz the Evil, the Jewish religion was practically made illegal in Babylonia. That was one of the reasons the Babylonian rabbis thought they had better put the Oral Law into writing at that time. They were afraid there wouldn't be enough rabbis left to pass on the tradition orally.

This brings us to the beginning of what historians of the West call the "Dark Ages." At this point, Jews no longer have a homeland in Judea. Instead Palestine is a mostly Christian land that is part of the Byzantine Empire. There are large groups of Jews scattered across the Mediterranean world and Middle East, mostly under the rule of the Catholic Christian Latin/German

Western Kingdoms or the Orthodox Christian Byzantine or the Zoroastrian Persian Empires.

In some ways, all these Jews were similar to the people they lived among. They spoke the local language and followed the local business and criminal laws. The Talmud even told them that the local law had to be obeyed. Their dress and food was influenced by the local customs. But in many ways Jews were quite apart from the people they lived among. One reason for this is that the non-Jews wanted to keep them separate. We already have seen how in Christian lands hatred and fear of Jews had become part of the laws and traditions. But Jews had their own traditions and laws, described in detail in the Talmud, and following these Jewish traditions also helped keep them apart from the non-Jewish population. In addition it connected them to Jews living in other parts of the world. Each Jewish community, from Spain in Western Europe, to Yemen in Southern Arabia, to Sura in Babylonia, ruled itself. But they were all ruled by the same Talmud and this brought a kind of unity to them, making them, in their own eyes, one people.

Jews had become an unusual kind of people. It was not common territory or language that made them a people but rather a common way of life and common memories of the ancient past. This way of life and memories of the past was what made up the Jewish religion. The Jewish religion had become the religion of one people, one ethnic group. Although in ancient times the Jews used to try to convert others to their religion, ever since the Hadrianic persecutions in 135 CE there had been laws against converting people to Judaism. So even though there have been some converts to Judaism throughout history, mostly it has been a religion that you were born into. Furthermore, even if you stopped believing in Judaism or following its laws, other Jews still considered you a Jew, a bad Jew perhaps, but still a Jew.

Like many other religions, Jews believed that the one God who rules the whole world had given them their religious laws. But unlike most other religions, Jews didn't believe that God had given this religion to everybody. He had given it only to the Jews. God had chosen the Jews to follow the true laws. Eventually the Messiah would come and then all of humanity would recognize the truth of the Torah, but until that happened, Jews thought that Judaism was just for the Jews. So if you wanted to follow the Jewish religion, you had to become part of the Jewish people.

FIGURE 9 – Engraving of Moshe ben Maimon (Maimonides).

FIGURE 10 – Page of a manuscript written by Maimonides, in Arabic written in Hebrew script.

Chapter 6

Under Islam

Mohammed

As we have seen, by the beginning of the seventh century, the conditions that most Jews lived under were bad. So it is not surprising that when a people following a new religion conquered most of the places Jews were living, the Jews welcomed them. Sometimes the Jews even fought alongside them to assist in their conquests. The new conquerors were Arabs and the new religion was Islam.

Before Islam, there were some Jewish and some Christian Arabs, but most Arabs worshipped a variety of local gods. Arabs originally come from the Arabian Peninsula. Like Jews, Arabs are a Semitic people, that is, they speak a Semitic language. Arabic is a cousin of Hebrew. Some Arabs were settled in towns, but most were nomads, like the ancient Hebrew tribes. These nomadic Arabs are called Bedouins, and there are still some nomadic Bedouins to this very day.

In 570 CE, Mohammed was born. He grew up in Mecca. Mecca was an Arabian city that was a major trading center. It was also a holy city to Arabs and had shrines filled with hundreds of idols of the local gods. Mohammed grew up to be a merchant. He married a wealthy businesswoman and so, although originally from a poor family, he became a prosperous man.

Mohammed was not satisfied with the local religion that worshipped idols. He knew Christians and Jews and was influenced by their ideas. According to Islamic tradition, when Mohammed was about 40 years old, the Angel Gabriel appeared to him and dictated to him the words of the one true God, Allah.

This occurred frequently over the following years, and the words Mohammed heard became the Muslim holy book, the Koran.

Mohammed believed that the God who had spoken to him was the same God that had spoken to Abraham, Moses and Jesus. He thought he was the latest in a line of prophets that God used to send messages to the world. According to Mohammed, Christianity and Judaism weren't exactly false religions, they were just outdated. Muslims respected Jews and Christians as people who followed holy books inspired by true prophets. However, Muslims thought these books didn't include God's latest, clearest, and final message. That was the message Mohammed was bringing to the world through the Koran.

The new religion was called Islam, which means "submission," and its believers were called Muslims, obeyers. The religion said there was only one God, Allah, and that Mohammed was God's messenger. Muslims believed that good people would be rewarded in Paradise after they died, wicked people punished in Hell. To be a good Muslim you had to declare your belief in Allah as the one God, and Mohammed as his prophet. You also had to pray five times a day, give charity, fast during the month of Ramadan, and visit Mecca once in your life, if you could. Muslims also believed they should spread the faith about the one true God.

Mohammed's followers at first were family and friends. The Arab businessmen of Mecca felt threatened by Mohammed. They made money from the pilgrims, the religious tourists, who used to come to Mecca to visit the idols in their shrines. So Mohammed's preaching against the idols, saying they were phony gods, was obviously not good for business. In 622 CE, Mohammed and his followers had to run away from Mecca. They went to Medina, another Arabian city. This escape from Mecca marks the first year of the Muslim calendar.

Mohammed was not only a great religious leader, he also was a great political and military leader. Within ten years of the escape from Mecca, Mohammed and his followers had conquered most of the Arabian Peninsula and the Arab people for Islam, so that by the time Mohammed died in 632 he had created a strong new religious community that was ready to take on the world.

The Caliphates

The Arabs wanted to spread their new faith. They were also interested in capturing the wealthy Byzantine Empire to their north and Persian Empire to their east. And capture them they did.

In 635, the Muslims captured Damascus, in 637, Jerusalem. Babylonia, parts of Asia Minor, North Africa, and most of Spain followed soon after. In less than a century after Mohammed's death, the Muslims had created an empire that was one of the largest the world has ever seen. Most of the world's Jews lived in it, and over the centuries the Jewish population under Islam grew and flourished.

The leaders of the Muslim Empire were called Caliphs, which means "ones who come after," because they came after Mohammed. The Caliphs were both the political and religious leaders of the Muslims, just as Mohammed was, but of course they weren't considered prophets. Mohammed was the final one of those.

The empires of the Caliphs were called Caliphates, and in 661 the Umayyad dynasty of Caliphs established its capital in Damascus. The Arab Muslims wanted to force all idol worshipers to convert to Islam, but they allowed Jews and Christians to keep their religion, since the Muslims felt that at least Jews and Christians were worshipping the one true God, if not quite in what the Muslims believed was the right way. Of course, many Jews and Christians became Muslims anyway, because some people always want to become part of the most powerful group, and surely because some sincerely believed in Islam. At first the Arabs tried to keep all of the top jobs in the Empire for themselves, but eventually non-Arab people who had become Muslim also became part of the leadership. In a while, much of the population in the Empire started speaking Arabic, both Muslims and non-Muslims, since that was the language of government and religion. That is why today Arabic is the language of North Africa and most of the Middle East.

The Arabs brought their new faith to the peoples they had conquered, but they also learned many things from the conquered peoples. Out of this mixture of Greek-Roman, Persian, and Arabic cultures one of history's great civilizations was created: Islamic civilization. Islamic civilization at one time stretched from Spain to as far-east as Indonesia and the Philippines. In Islamic civilization we find great art and architecture, poetry and music, philosophy and science. The Caliphates contained rich and large cities as well as great universities.

For their time, the Caliphates were pretty tolerant. If you were willing to become a Muslim, your nationality or skin color was not important. But Jews, Christians, and other non-Muslims did not have full rights. They were *dhimmis*—protected but second-class citizens who had to pay special taxes and wear special clothes. Still, they were usually permitted to go about their own business. Women, even if they were Muslim, had very few rights in Islamic society. But of course at that time women didn't have rights in most societies.

The Umayyad Caliphate lasted until 750 when a new dynasty took over, the Abbassids. The Abbassid Caliphate lasted five hundred years. Its capital was Baghdad. During the Abbasid dynasty Islamic culture reached its peak. The Abbasids were conquered by a Turkish people, the Seljuks, who in turn were conquered by the Mongols, and then came another Turkish people, the Ottomans. All of these conquerors either were or became Muslims and their empires were Islamic. However, after the first Caliphate, the entire Islamic world was no longer part of a single empire. Parts of the Caliphate broke away to form their own Islamic kingdoms. Sometimes these separate kingdoms stayed officially part of the Caliphate, but they were really not controlled by the Caliph in Damascus, Baghdad, or Istanbul. Spain, for instance, became a separate Islamic country very early, and for long periods parts of North Africa were also separate from the Caliphate. But although it did not stay under one ruler, the Islamic world remained united through religion and culture.

The Conditions of the Jews

The Jews, like all people who weren't Muslims, were discriminated against under Islam. At certain times, in certain places, Jews were even severely persecuted by the Muslims. There were forced conversions, massacres, and expulsions. But mostly things were not that bad. Compared to the horrible and almost constant persecution Jews suffered in Christian countries during this same period, life for Jews under Islam was pretty good.

First of all, in many ways, Islamic customs were similar to Jewish ones, so Jews were not such strange outsiders. Islamic law, the *shari'a*, is like Jewish law in some ways. Muslims don't eat pork and they circumcise their boys. Islam and Judaism both don't approve of making images of God. And the holiest thing in each religion was a holy book, the Torah and the Koran.

Second, although Jews had to pay lots of special taxes, their economic situation, that is, their opportunities to work and how much wealth they had, was usually good under Islam. Jews were allowed to work in almost all areas. Jews were famous as doctors under Islam. There were Jewish farmers and artisans. Even though there were some Islamic laws against it, Jews were sometimes government officials.

Since the Islamic rulers depended on the non-Muslims for taxes, they liked them to be rich so they could tax them a lot. The Jews also found the conditions for trade good. The Islamic world was a huge area, all following the same basic rules. The way business was done in Fez, Morocco, was the same as the way it was done in Baghdad, thousands of miles away. And Jews from one part of that world could count on the hospitality and assistance of Jews from any other part. Even if a Jewish trader was captured by pirates, he could usually count on local Jews ransoming him, that is, paying the pirates for his safe return.

Until about 800, Jews were the only go-betweens between the Islamic and Christian world, and, for centuries after that, they were the main go-betweens. For almost a thousand years, Christian Europe and the Islamic world saw each other as great enemies. They didn't have much to do with each other except when they were at war. But Jews bridged the two worlds. Jews from the Caliphate and from Christian Europe could communicate in Hebrew, and since they were of neither religion, they could be considered neutral in the great quarrel between Muslims and Christians. This was a big advantage for Jewish traders. Of course, Jews were such a small part of the population of the Muslim world that even with these advantages they never became the main merchants of the Islamic world.

Exilarchs and Geonim

Soon after Babylonia was captured by the Muslims the great Jewish community of Babylonia began to recover from the persecutions it had suffered under the Zoroastrian Persians. Exilarchs once more ruled the Jewish community. These Exilarchs lived like great princes and were treated that way by the Muslim rulers. The Jewish Academies at Sura and Pumbedita became strong and influential again. The scholars at these schools continued the tradition of studying and interpreting Jewish law. From all over the world, Jews would write letters to these schools asking questions about how best to solve a problem they had according to Jewish laws. The answers they received are called *responsa*, and we still have many of the *responsa* that were written over the years. In fact, sending letters to famous rabbis to get their opinion on a question of Jewish law became a lasting Jewish tradition. There are collections of rabbis' *responsa* from many different times and places, and the *responsa* have become another part of the Oral Law.

The heads of the great Babylonian academies were called Geonim (Excellencies, or Geniuses). The Geonim usually, but not always, came from a few families of rich and famous rabbis. These Geonim became so important that they were rivals to the Exilarchs for leadership of the Jewish community. One particular Gaon, Sa'adia, who actually wasn't from one of the traditional Geonic families but came from Egypt, became head of the Sura Academy in 928. Sa'adia was a very important Jewish thinker and scholar. He translated the Bible into Arabic and also wrote books in Arabic that tried to explain the philosophy behind the Jewish religion. Some religious thinkers try to show that their religion is reasonable, that it makes sense. Sa'adia Gaon was the first Jewish thinker in medieval times to do this so-called "philosophical justification" of Judaism. He was also the first scholar to examine the grammar of the Hebrew language. In addition, Sa'adia was the editor of a prayer book that was used by Jews in Arabic lands for hundreds of year and is still in use among Jews from Yemen.

Sa'adia may have been the greatest single Gaon of the Babylonian Academies and the most influential, but over the centuries there were almost a hundred Geonim, and together they helped shape the rules and customs of Jewish life all over the world. The academies were at times considered almost another Sanhedrin, and Jews around the world looked to them for guidance. But they were never the only Talmudic schools. There were schools of the Talmud throughout the Jewish world under Islam. Some, like the one in Tiberias, Palestine, tried to compete with the Babylonian Academies. And even though Jews all over looked up to the Academies in Babylonia, they still ruled themselves locally and didn't have to listen to the Geonim or the Exilarchs of Babylonia.

The ruler of a local Jewish community was called a Nagid. Some Nagids had a lot of freedom from the Muslim rulers and were able to control their own communities with little interference. Others had less power. But the Jewish communities of Islam were never controlled by a single Jewish center of power. The Babylonian Jewish leadership had a lot of influence over the Jews in Islamic lands, but it never actually ruled those outside of Babylonia.

Karaites

Sometime between 700-900 CE, a group of Babylonian Jews became unhappy with the power of the Exilarch and the Geonim. They thought that this power came from their use of the Oral Law to control people's lives. This group believed that the Oral Law really didn't come from God at all, and that the true Jewish religion should only follow the laws of the Torah. About the Torah law, this group, who are called Karaites, was very strict, but they completely rejected the Talmud. At times there was anger and hatred between the Karaites and other Jews, Sa'adia Gaon was a great opponent of Karaism. Usually the anger was not so great, but Karaism eventually came to be considered by Jews as a separate religion from Judaism.

Karaism grew and at times there were big communities of Karaites in Egypt, Turkey, and the Crimea, (in the southern part of Russia), although we don't know exactly how big. For a while the Nazis were considering whether to kill the Karaites as Jews, but decided not to. Today there are only about 10,000 Karaites left, mostly living in Israel.

The Golden Age

Jews in Islamic countries usually lived in their own communities, but there were often lots of mixing with the Muslim neighbors. When the people mixed, so did their cultures. Nowhere did this happen more in medieval times than in Spain when it was under Muslim rule.

When the Visigoths captured Spain from the Romans and became Christian, they enslaved the Jews of Spain. Naturally, when the Muslims conquered Spain they were very much welcomed by the Jews, whom the Muslims freed. Spain only remained part of the Caliphate a short while before it broke away and set up its own Caliphate. By 900, the Caliphate of Cordoba in Spain became a place where Jews mixing with Arabs entered one of the greatest periods of Jewish culture. It is known as the Golden Age.

Jews lived in many cities in central and southern Spain at this time: Zaragoza, Granada, Seville, Toledo, and Cordova. For most of the Golden Age these were part of one Spanish Islamic kingdom, but at times the Muslims of Spain themselves broke into smaller kingdoms. Jews often were important people in these kingdoms, advising the Muslim rulers or being their personal doctors. One of the first of these important Jews was Hasdai ibn Shaprut, born in 915. Not only did he become an important minister in the court of the Caliph of Cordoba and a diplomat of the Caliph to other countries, he was also a Talmudic scholar, philosopher, and Hebrew poet. Some people consider the Golden Age to have started with his career. It may have reached its peak with Samuel ibn Nagdela—Samuel HaNagid, known as Samuel the Prince. He was a Vizier, the top minister, to the Muslim King

Habbus of Granada. Samuel practically ruled Granada. He was also a poet and a scholar. Maybe no Jew in the Golden Age was quite as successful as Samuel the Prince. But there were many like him who became powerful politicians and also leaders of Jewish art, religion, and community affairs.

More than anything else, what made the Jewish Golden Age in Spain golden was all the beautiful Hebrew poetry that was written then. There were many Hebrew poets at that time, and the best of them, such as Samuel ibn Nagdela, Moses ibn Ezra, Solomon ibn Gabirol, and especially Judah HaLevi, wrote the best Hebrew poems since the Bible. Many of the poems have become Jewish prayers and Hebrew songs.

Often these poets were also scholars and philosophers. Judah HaLevi, born in Toledo in 1085 wrote a philosophical justification of Judaism in addition to his poetry about nature and his religious poetry. Halevi also wrote about the Jewish people's love and attachment to the Land of Israel. When he himself was forced to flee Spain during a period of persecution, he went to North Africa, and then, according to Jewish legend, went to the Holy Land, where he was killed by a Crusader (we will talk about the Crusaders in the next chapter). Whether or not Halevi himself ever did go to Palestine, it is certainly true that his poetry helped keep alive and strengthen Diaspora Jews' longing for the land of Israel.

The single most influential Jew to come out of the Golden Age was Moses ben Maimon, known as Rambam in Jewish tradition, and to the rest of the world as Maimonides. He was born in Cordova in 1135, but his family didn't remain there long. When Maimonides was eleven years old, Cordoba was conquered by the Almohades. The Almohades were fanatical Muslims from North Africa and they were much less tolerant of other religions than the Muslim rulers of Cordoba whom they took over from. The Almohades tried to force people who weren't Muslims, including Jews and Christians, to convert to Islam. As a result, many Jews fled Spain, including Maimonides' family. Maimonides' family lived in Fez, Morocco, for a while, then went to Palestine before they eventually ended up in Egypt. Through all these travels Maimonides continued his studies. He was known as a very great doctor and that is how he earned his living, but his fame rests on his commentaries on Jewish law, religion, and philosophy.

Maimonides wrote a book called the *Mishneh Torah*, a complete code of Jewish law. There are so many Jewish laws in the Talmud that it may be hard to find the right one when you want it. Therefore codes have been written to make it easier to follow Jewish law. The *Mishneh Torah* was one of the first codes of Jewish law ever written. But it is not just a handbook that makes things easier to look up; it is also a discussion of the laws that explains what they mean. Students of Talmud still study Maimonides' *Mishneh Torah* to see what Maimonides' had to say about Jewish law.

Maimonides was also a philosopher, and one of his books, *The Guide for the Perplexed*, written in Arabic, is one of the greatest books of Jewish philosophy ever written. Maimonides tried to show that the Jewish religion was reasonable. He was against all the parts of the Jewish tradition that he considered superstitious. He tried to show that you could believe in the best science and best philosophy of his time and still believe in Judaism.

Besides these two most famous ones, Maimonides wrote other books. He also wrote *responsa*, which are rabbinic opinions on cases of Jewish law. Most of these writings have been preserved, and so not only was Maimonides one of the most influential Jews of his day, but among religious Jews he has remained one of the most influential people of all time. He died in 1204. His body was taken from Egypt to Palestine, where he was buried in Tiberias.

FIGURE 11 - Modern statue of medieval Jewish poet
Judah HaLevi.

FIGURE 12 - Medieval manuscript painting showing a Jewish man
(at right).

Chapter 7

Medieval Christendom

Byzantium

As we have seen, at around the time the Roman Empire became Christian, the Empire had split in two. The eastern part was called Byzantium. We have already spoken of the laws passed in Byzantium that discriminated against the Jews: they were forced to live in separate neighborhoods, they were not allowed into many types of jobs, and sometimes there were riots in which many Jews were massacred. At least four times during the long history of Byzantium, in 640, 721, 873 and 920, there were attempts to force the Jews to convert to Christianity. These attempts never fully succeeded. But the hard life for Jews in Byzantium kept the Jewish population there very small.

Until 950 there probably were no more than 10,000 Jews in all of Byzantium. That means, that in all of Byzantium, which included modern Greece, eastern Turkey and most of the Balkan countries, there were fewer Jews than there are on several streets of New York City today. They were mostly craftsmen and small traders and lived in the big cities. Like the rest of the Byzantines, they spoke Greek, but their Greek had so many Hebrew words in it that it became its own dialect, Judeo-Greek. Something like this happened very often in Jewish history. Jews would use the same basic language as the people around them, but because they usually lived in their own neighborhoods, and because they had their own religious language, Hebrew, Jews ended up speaking the local language in their own special way. Later we will see how this led to the development of some very important Jewish languages.

Early Western Europe

The Jews in the western part of the Roman Empire also suffered with the coming of Christianity, but at least they remained Roman citizens with certain rights. However, when the Western Roman Empire broke up into different Christian kingdoms, the Jews were treated like foreigners in most of the places they lived; they had to get special permission to continue living where they were living.

In the early Middle Ages, things weren't as bad as they eventually became. The German tribes that conquered the Roman Empire weren't fully Christian themselves at first, and so they didn't have all of the built up Christian hatred of Jews. In the early Middle Ages, the Jewish population was also very small in Western Europe, so they were hardly noticeable. In addition, there were very few Christian merchants. So Jews, many of whom were merchants, were very useful to have around.

Gradually, Jews began to spread throughout Western Europe. They emigrated north where, at the time of the Roman Empire's collapse, there were very few Jews. By the year 1066, there were Jewish communities in France, England and Germany as well as the ones in Spain and Italy. As the number of Jews grew, as the lands they were in became more and more Christian, and as more Christians went into trade (which made Christians resent Jewish traders and not need them as much), the situation of the Jews in Western Europe became more troubled. Finally, when the Crusades—holy wars that we will talk more about a little later—began in 1096, the Jewish experience in Christian Europe became full of catastrophes. These catastrophes forced the Jewish communities to move constantly and seek new places to live. But even though the Jews were pushed from place to place, Jews never had to leave Western Europe altogether. Sometimes they would only have to move to a nearby town. To understand why this is so, we need to understand something about European society in the Middle Ages.

Feudalism

Medieval Europe, that is, Europe during the times of the Middle Ages, developed a way of life that we call feudalism. Our stories about knights and castles are drawn from Europe during feudal times. Most people were farmers then, but they did not own the land they lived on or grew crops on. The land was owned by someone called a lord, the lord of the land. The lord was a kind of military leader. He usually would live in a castle, and he and his soldiers were supposed to protect the farmers who lived on his land. In return the farmers spent much of their time working for the lord. They would have to give him a large portion of the crops they grew or the other things they made. These farmers were not allowed to leave their jobs and move to another place. We say that they were "tied to the land," forced to spend their lives working for the lord of the land. These farmers, who in many ways were just like slaves, were called serfs. The serfs belonged to the land and the land belonged to the lord.

Depending on the country they were in and on how much land they owned, a lord might be called a knight, a baron, a count, an earl, a duke or even a king. The king of course, was usually the greatest lord in a country. Some lands belonged to the Church, and in those cases bishops, that is, head priests, were the lords of the land.

This land-owning group of lords was called "the nobility." They first became lords by conquering some land in war and making themselves boss of it. After that, their children would inherit the land and the serfs on it. The only way to become a noble was to be born one or to be part of a conquest and win some land. In general, serfs stayed serfs and nobles stayed nobles.

But some nobles, called vassals, belonged to other nobles, whom I will call overlords. Of course the vassals wouldn't actually work their overlord's land like a serf, but they might have to give to their lord some of the things their own serfs grew or made. Also, in time of war, which was almost all the time in the Middle Ages, these vassals had to provide soldiers that they led into battle for their overlord. In return, the overlord granted the vassal lordship over some piece of land. People pretended that every lord in a country was a vassal of the king, but really most lords ruled their lands any way they liked. Some lords even went to war against their own kings. In a way, moving from one lord's land to another's was like moving to another country.

One way of looking at feudal society is that it was one big "protection racket." A protection racket is when someone offers to protect you if you pay them, but if you don't, they are the ones who will harm you. It is a little like paying off violent criminals to leave you alone. Of course, like some criminal protection rackets, feudal lords might try to offer protection from other criminal gangs. So a feudal lord was supposed to protect serfs from each other as well as from other feudal lords. Unlike modern criminal protection rackets, in medieval Europe feudalism was considered legitimate and the right way to do things. Medium-size lords paid off big lords, little lords paid off medium-size lords, and the serfs paid off everyone. The Church said this was the way God intended things to be, and probably most people accepted the system.

Feudal Europe consisted of thousands of these "protection" relationships. The serfs lived on manors, very small farming villages that not only produced their own food but also made almost all their own clothing, work tools, and all their other necessities. The lord lived in the manor house or castle on the manor. The lord was the ruler and protector of the manor, which was like his own little kingdom.

Although most people lived on manors, there were some medieval towns. They were very small compared to modern cities, but they had a lot more people than a manor would. These towns were filled mostly with craftsman—artisans who made the few fancier products that were available in medieval Europe—and with the merchants who bought, sold, and transported these products. The towns were part of the feudal system too. A whole town might be under the protection of some lord, and within the town different groups might be under the protection of the lord. The lord might offer the town, or a group in a town, a charter. This charter was a written contract that explained what the lord was allowing the town or the group to do and what the lord expected from them. It also promised the town or group the lord's protection.

The Jewish Condition

While some Jews at some times and places in medieval Europe were farmers, mostly they were townspeople who were under some lord's protection. That is why when they lost the protection of one lord, or that lord was unable to protect them, they could pick up and move to another lord's land—that is if they could find another lord willing and able to protect them. Sometimes a king, the top overlord, would kick Jews out of a whole country. This happened in England in 1290, France in 1306, and Spain in 1492. But often they would only be kicked out of a local lord's land and were able to move to a town not far away. Whether it was a whole country or only a piece of it, these expulsions, as they are called, helped create the idea of "the wandering Jew"—the idea that the Jews were a people with no permanent home.

Christians thought this Jewish homelessness was a punishment from God that the Jews suffered for not believing in Jesus and killing him. Jews also thought it was a punishment from God, but not for anything having to do with Jesus. They thought it was a punishment for not obeying the Torah, God's laws, carefully enough. They believed that when they did follow the Torah faithfully enough and when they had suffered enough for past disobediences, then the punishment of exile, homelessness, would end. Then the Messiah would come and he would lead the Jews back to the land of Israel.

In the early Middle Ages, there were still a fair number of Jewish farmers. Often they were vintners, people who grew grapes and made wine from them. But even in those days, most Jews were artisans, such as goldsmiths or jewelers, or merchants. As time went on, fewer and fewer Jews in Europe were allowed to keep their land. In addition, as more Christians became artisans and merchants, those jobs started to be closed to Jews too. For instance, if there were enough Christian silversmiths in a town, they would form a club, called a guild. This guild would get protection, a charter, from the town's lord. Nobody who was not a member of the guild was allowed to work as a silversmith. The guild members wanted this rule so there would be more work for them. Of course, Jews would almost always not be allowed to join the guild, so they couldn't work as silversmiths in that town.

Money-Lending

As more and more guilds arose, in different types of occupations, there were fewer and fewer ways that Jews could earn a living. There were even merchant guilds, so Jews had to leave the business of trade, which had been one of their main occupations. One thing that was left to the Jews, because Christians were not allowed to do it, was being a sort of one person bank, a moneylender. Christians believed it was sinful to charge interest. If you lend somebody $100 dollars but they have to pay back $110 dollars, that extra $10 is interest. In medieval Europe, charging interest was called usury and was thought of as a sin. That means that if someone borrowed $100 dollars from someone else, they should only pay back $100 and not any extra money. The problem is that if people are not allowed to charge interest, they won't have any reason to lend others money, except among friends. If you lend someone money you can't use it while they have it and there is always a chance that they won't pay it back. So people won't lend money unless there is some reward, some profit in doing so. If charging interest were outlawed, there would be no legal borrowing or lending.

But even in medieval Europe, where most people used only things they or their neighbors grew or made themselves, there were times when people needed to borrow money. Sometimes the crop failed and money was needed to buy food. Sometimes a tool unexpectedly broke and needed to be replaced. A lord might need extra money to pay for fighting expenses. So the problem was how to provide this necessary service, which the Church officially said was sinful.

Jewish money-lenders became the answer. While there were always Christian money-lenders in medieval Europe (in fact, in the early Middle Ages the Christian monasteries had a monopoly on money-lending!) as time went on, the Christian belief that charging interest was sinful drove most Christians out of the business. At the same time, Jews were being forced out of most other ways to earn a living. So the money-lending business was largely taken over by Jews. The money Jews had gotten from the businesses and trades they were no longer allowed to practice got them started in the money-lending business.

The odd thing was that Jews also thought that usury, charging interest, might be sinful. But since there was almost no other way to survive, the rabbis found a way to make charging interest, at least to non-Jews, acceptable in Jewish law. The rabbis even created a whole set of instructions for how Jews should behave in business with non-Jews. They encouraged strict honesty because if Christians got angry at one Jew it could cause a disaster for the whole Jewish community. The rabbis also made a rule called *ma'arufia*, that no Jew could take a Christian customer away from another Jew. In that way more Jews could make a living and Jewish trade and businessmen didn't have to fear that they would lose a customer to another Jew charging lower prices or less interest.

Even though Jewish money-lending provided a service medieval Europe really needed, Jews were disliked for doing it. First of all, Christians considered money-lending a sinful activity. In addition, unlike today when people borrow money to buy a home, pay college tuition, or start or improve a business, in medieval Europe people usually had to borrow money in times of trouble. And since so many didn't pay the loans back at all, moneylenders had to charge a very high interest to stay in business. So instead of seeing the moneylender as someone who was helping make their lives better, the way an honest and helpful banker might be seen today, the medieval moneylender was seen as someone who was taking advantage of someone else's troubles. So the business of money-lending that the Jews were forced into, and that the Christians very much needed, actually added to Christian hatred of the Jews.

Of course, not all Jews were moneylenders. Many Jews remained small merchants, peddlers, going from manor to manor selling goods. In southern Europe, Spain and Italy, many occupations remained open to Jews and so Jewish moneylenders were less common there. But in general, the idea of the Jewish moneylender became fixed in the mind of medieval Europe. In

England, being a Jew and being a moneylender were almost thought of as being the exact same thing. The idea of the greedy Jewish moneylender, who doesn't do honest work, but instead just "sucks the blood," that is, lives off of the work of non-Jews, was an idea that would remain for a long time and cause much suffering for Jews.

To live in a town Jews had to get the protection of a lord and be granted a charter. Lords granted the Jews charters because they needed their services, either as artisans, merchants, or moneylenders. In addition the lords taxed the Jews heavily for the privilege of living and doing business in that town. Often the lord would be the king himself. In many places Jews weren't considered the king's vassals, but rather his property, with which he could do whatever he wanted. In England, Jews were called the king's "sponges," because whenever he needed money, he would "squeeze" them and the money would drip out. A lord would sometimes expel Jews from his lands when he thought there was no more money to be squeezed out of them or when he wanted to take all of their money and property at once.

Religious Hatred

While the economic arrangements added to the dislike between Christians and Jews and helped keep the hatreds alive, the basic cause of the problem was the way medieval people's religious beliefs made them look at the world. To medieval Christians, Jews weren't simply people of another religion who didn't understand or never learned about the true religion, Christianity. Instead, Jews were people who came from the same faith Christians came from but stubbornly refused to admit that Jesus was the messiah and son of God. Why should Jews deny the truth, which they could see as easily as Christians? The Christians believed that Jews must be against truth itself, against honesty and goodness, even against God. Maybe Jews weren't even human. Maybe they worked for the Devil, were assistant devils, demons. For Christians, Jesus Christ came to save people's souls and would come again to save the whole world. If the Jews were against Christ, perhaps they were the ones preventing him from saving the world. Some Christians thought of the Jews as the "anti-Christ,"—the great enemy of Jesus and his saving work.

These ideas about the Jews were found throughout medieval culture. It was a culture where religion was very important and entered every part of life. People heard Jews described as devils in sermons at church. The paintings and sculptures they saw decorating their churches often showed Jews as demons and monsters. The plays they saw on Easter were often about how the Jews killed Jesus.

The Church had a big say in how medieval Europe was ruled. To show that God disapproved of the Jews the Church wanted to make sure the Jews were kept separated from Christians and were considered below them. The Church also didn't want the Christians mixing with the Jews because there was a fear that Jews might try to convert Christians to Judaism. To keep Jews separate, recognizable, and humiliated, a Church council in 1215 ordered that Jews wear a yellow badge on their clothing. This law wasn't always and everywhere enforced, but it was another medieval form of persecution that was around a long time and came back to haunt Jews in modern times.

Although the medieval Christian religion and its Church was the source of the Jews' persecution, it was also the Jewish communities' main protectors, making it possible for Jews to exist in medieval Europe. Of course, as we have seen, individual lords and kings offered Jews protection for financial reasons. Sometimes these lords were bishops, high priests in the Church, who were acting for the same financial reasons as any other lord. But the Church also protected Jews for religious reasons: the Jews served as an example of the sorry state of people who did not believe in Jesus and did not belong to the Church. Christians also believed it was part of God's plan to convert the Jews, so Jews had to be kept around for God to do his work. In 1120, the Pope even issued a law that said the Jews should be protected throughout Christendom. The law wasn't always obeyed, but without it, and other protections the Church and individual bishops tried to give Jews, it is hard to see how Jews would have survived in medieval Europe at all.

Although they didn't have the power to do much about it, medieval European Jews didn't think well of their Christian neighbors either. Of course, part of Jewish dislike of Christians was caused by the persecution Jews suffered at the hands of the Christians. But another part was based on Jewish religious beliefs. Christianity was viewed as a rotten and false child of Judaism. They felt that Christians pretended to believe in the main Jewish holy book, the Bible, but they didn't follow any of the laws Jews believed were written there. Worse, to Jewish eyes, Christians broke the two most important religious laws: they worshipped idols and they believed that there was more than one God. Even though Christians said they believed in one God that had three parts, the Father, the Son and the Holy Ghost—to Jews, this sounded like they believed in three gods. And all the pictures and statues of Jesus, his mother Mary and the hundreds of saints that Christians prayed to, looked to the Jews like idolatry, the worst of sins. God had said in the Bible not to make or pray to "graven images", and Christian religious art sure looked like graven images—idols—to the Jews. Finally the Jews believed that they were a "chosen people" selected by God to follow his law and eventually show the whole world the right way to live. All in all, the Jews considered themselves superior to non-Jews. Although they must have hated the Christian persecution, medieval European Jews were probably pleased to be separated from Christians. That way they could lead their separate, and they thought better, religious life.

The Crusades

While life was never entirely safe in medieval Europe, and got gradually worse with the rise of Christian merchants and spread of Christianity, the most terrible sufferings and disasters began with the start of the Crusades in 1095.

Palestine was holy to Christians because that is where Jesus was born, lived, preached, and died. Jerusalem was considered especially holy because that was where Jesus was executed and buried. Palestine had been under Muslim control for hundreds of years, and even though Christian travelers—pilgrims—were usually allowed to go and visit the Christian holy places, Pope Urban II thought it wrong that it wasn't controlled by Christian rulers. So in 1095 he called upon the Christian nobility in Europe to conquer Palestine, the Holy Land. Thus began the First Crusade, a holy war to conquer Palestine.

Nobles from all over Europe responded to Urban's call. Overlords gathered their vassals, who in turn gathered *their* vassals, to form troops in order to "liberate" the holy land from the infidels, that is, the Muslims who didn't believe in Christianity. But as these Crusaders gathered, they turned their attention to the Jews living among them. Thinking of Jesus' grave in the Holy Land naturally made the Crusaders think of his execution and the Jews they blamed for it. Why, they asked themselves, should we go off to fight the enemies of God so far away before we deal with God's enemies here at home? Some preachers, such as Peter the Hermit of Amiens in France, made speeches to get the Crusaders and the local crowds angry at the Jews. (A hermit is someone that keeps all to himself, but obviously Peter had stopped being a hermit by this time). With all of the religious excitement and war fever around, it is not surprising that violence against the Jews broke out. There were massacres in many parts of Europe—in France the Jews of Metz and Rouen suffered greatly; in Germany, in the towns of Cologne, Mainz, and Worms the Jewish communities were almost completely wiped out. Sometimes the Jews would be locked in their synagogue and then the synagogue would be burned down. Very often the local bishop would try to protect the Jews. Sometimes, as in the German towns of Speyer and Trier, the bishops were able to limit the violence, but in other towns, they weren't able to control the crowds. It is impossible to know the exact numbers, but certainly many thousands of Jews were slaughtered during the First Crusade.

Besides murdering the Jews, the Crusaders sometimes forced them to convert to Christianity. In the town of Ratisbon, all of the Jews were dragged down to the Danube River and baptized—dunked in water and made to become Christian. Once you had become a Christian, you had to stay a Christian or you could be executed as a heretic, someone who had belonged to but then left the true faith. The Church didn't approve of these violently forced conversions, and sometimes a bishop or lord would let these forcibly converted Jews return to Judaism. In fact, the King let the Jews of Regensberg go back to Judaism. But often those forced to convert were never allowed to practice Judaism again.

Faced with massacres and forced conversions, medieval Jews developed a custom they called "sanctification of the name," that is, dying for the sake of Judaism. Instead of converting, the Jews would say prayers and commit suicide. Of course many Jews converted to save their lives, but many killed themselves rather than convert.

The Crusaders eventually arrived at and conquered much of the holy land. But when Muslims reconquered part of Palestine 50 years later in 1146, the Pope called for a second Crusade. Once again, as the Crusaders gathered in Europe and Christians' religious feelings got excited, Jews were killed. Peter of Cluny, another Jew hating preacher, made speeches against the "Christ-killers." In general, during the Second Crusade, the Church did a better job of protecting the Jews than it did in the First Crusade. Bernard of Clairvaux, an important Church leader of the time, did much to protect Jews. Some priests even helped Jews escape to safer lands. But still many Jews were killed or injured in the violence of the Second Crusade.

In 1187, the Muslims reconquered Jerusalem itself and a third Crusade was announced. This time the Church and the nobility in France and Germany did a better job of protecting their Jewish communities than they had in the earlier Crusades. But in England, the Third Crusade was horrible for the Jews. This is odd, because in the first two Crusades little harm came to English Jews. But in 1189 King Richard the Lionhearted left for the Crusades and Jews were attacked in Norwich, Lynn, Stamford, and most terribly in York. When the Jews of York realized something bad was going to happen, they went to the castle and locked themselves in. For a good while the Jews held out in the castle. But when all hope was lost, the Jews of York burned all of their things and then killed themselves. Again an entire Jewish community was wiped out.

One interesting thing about the York massacre was that when the Christian crowd finally got into the castle, one of the first things they did was destroy the official records of who owed money to whom. It looks like the Crusade massacres weren't only about religious hatred, but may also have been caused by people trying to get out of having to pay the money they owed.

In the next fifty years there were a number of smaller Crusades, and Jews were hurt in each one of them. Jewish communities that the Crusaders traveled through on their way to Palestine were often victims. For instance, there was a Crusader riot against the Jews of Constantinople in 1204 and the French Jews of Normandy were slaughtered in 1236.

The Crusaders arrival in Palestine was also a disaster for the Jews there. On the way to Jerusalem, the Crusaders killed Jews in Haifa and Hebron. When Jerusalem itself was conquered, the Jews of the city were locked in the synagogue and burned to death. For the almost one hundred years that the Crusaders ruled Jerusalem, no Jew or Muslim was allowed to live there. Jews only returned to Jerusalem when Muslims reconquered it under the leadership of Saladdin in 1187.

Still, outside of Jerusalem, some Jewish communities in Palestine managed to survive in the kingdoms the Crusaders set up. When the last Crusader-held city, Acre, fell to Muslims in 1291, there were still Jews living through much of Palestine.

Blood Libel

The start of Crusades were not the only times Jews had to worry during this period of European history. There were many things that Jews were accused of that often caused Christians to riot against Jews and kill them, one accusation being that they killed Christian children as part of the Jewish religion. Sometimes it was said that Jews used a Christian child to pretend they were killing Jesus again. Sometimes it was said that Jews needed Christian blood to make medicine needed to cure special diseases that God had cursed the Jews with. Usually it was said that Jews needed the blood of a Christian child to make *matzah*, the unleavened bread eaten by Jews at Passover.

These false charges against the Jews are called "blood libels," and they continued to be made in some places right into the twentieth century. But they were most common in medieval Europe. In Norwich, England in 1144; in Bloise, France in 1171; in Zaragoza, Spain in 1182; and in Fulda, Germany in 1235 there were blood libels that led to the death of Jews.

Jews were also accused of poisoning the wells. Although this lie had started hundreds of years earlier, it was especially harmful to Jews during the Black Death. The Black Death was an epidemic of the Bubonic Plague, a contagious disease caused by germs carried by rats. This disease killed a tremendous number of people in Europe in the years 1348-49. Medieval people didn't know what caused the disease. One popular explanation was that Jews had poisoned the wells. Naturally, this lie also led to the killing of Jews.

FIGURE 13 – Engraving of Jews being burned to death in medieval Europe during the Black Death.

Another sin Jews were charged with was called "desecration of the host." In some types of Christianity, including the Christianity of medieval Europe, a wafer is used during the Church service. During the service the wafer is believed to miraculously change into the body of Christ. This wafer is called "the host." Jews were accused of robbing this wafer and torturing it to cause pain to Christ. Sometimes Jews were accused of stealing paintings of Jesus and torturing the pictures. Everyone knew how much Jews hated religious images, so it was easy to believe Jews might want to hurt Jesus through the paintings and the statues.

All of these things Jews were accused of—the blood libel, poisoning of the wells, and desecration of the host—often led to the destruction of an entire Jewish community. Even if only one Jew was believed to have done the act, the entire Jewish community was held responsible. So whenever a Christian child was missing or found dead, whenever disease broke out in a village, whenever it was Passover or Eastertime, or whenever a Christian had a grudge to settle with a particular Jew, the Jews of medieval Europe had cause to worry.

Conversions and Disputations

Although the Church was officially against forced conversions, it did put pressure on the Jews to convert. One way of doing that was to make Jews come and argue with Christians about which was the true religion, Judaism or Christianity. These debates were called "disputations." Sometimes these disputations were reasonably friendly. But usually they were frightening and dangerous for the Jews. If the Jews lost the debate (and since the judges were Christian, they always did lose), they might be forced to convert. Jews also had to be careful in these debates not to say anything that the Christians felt was insulting to their religion. Of course, it is hard to prove that a religion is false without saying anything bad about it, but that was what the Jews were supposed to do. When the great Jewish Rabbi Nachmanides did too well in his disputation, he was forced to flee Spain to save his life.

Sometimes the Jews would be required to defend their religious books. Jews who had converted from Judaism to Christianity would report that the Talmud was insulting to Christianity. And in fact the Talmud does say some harsh things about Jesus and Christians. In a trial of the Talmud held in Paris in 1240, the Talmud was found guilty. It was condemned. Thousands of Jewish books, not just the Talmud, were burned in

Paris two years later. There were also book-burnings of Jewish books in other parts of Europe.

The Medieval Jewish Community in Western Europe

The period we call medieval times, or the Middle Ages, lasted hundreds of years. Western Europe has many different countries in it, and naturally there were lots of different Jewish communities living there in lots of different ways during the Middle Ages. But we can still describe what a typical medieval Jewish community in medieval Europe was like.

As we have seen, merchant, money-lender and peddler were the most common occupations, but there also were plenty of artisans in some places (in southern Europe there were even some Jewish artisan guilds) and even a few Jews who worked the land. The Jews, of course, were under the authority of the king or local lord and had to obey all of the laws of the land. But for all matters that just concerned the Jewish community, the Jews in each town ruled themselves.

The Jewish community at that time called itself the *kehillah*. The *kehillah* had many jobs. It was first of all in charge of collecting taxes from the Jews and deciding how much each Jew would pay towards the total amount of money the *kehillah* needed. Lots of this money would also need to be paid to the king or local lord as protection money. The remainder would go to take care of the needs of the community. The *kehillah* decided how much went to helping the poor, or the sick, or widows. It decided how much went for taking care of the cemetery or the synagogue, and paid the salaries of anyone who worked for the *kehillah*. It was also concerned with the education of children.

Most people in medieval Europe, even many nobles, didn't know how to read. Usually only the priests and monks did. But the Jewish religion said that all of its boys should read so that they could fulfill the commandment of studying the Torah and the Talmud. Not all of the boys were always taught. Sometimes those that were taught learned only a little. But still, compared to the communities around them, the ability to read was very widespread in the Jewish community. This was one of the reasons Jews were able to be money-lenders and merchants; they could keep the books.

The *kehillah* did feel it was its responsibility to provide education, but it didn't always do this well. Poor boys seldom got the same opportunity to learn as wealthier ones. Girls, of course, were completely excluded. But we do know that a few girls managed to study anyway and became great scholars. And it was scholars, people that knew a lot about the Jewish religious books, who were most respected in the *kehillah*.

The *kehillah* was more democratic than the Christian communities of the time. In some small kehillot (plural of kehillah), many decisions were made by a meeting of all the Jewish men of a community, where everyone could have his say. But usually a *kehillah* was governed by a council of the leading men in the community. The leading men were those who were rich or those who were scholars. In other words, rabbis and rich merchants or rich moneylenders were the rulers of the community. These were really not two completely separate groups. Rich people had a better chance of giving their sons a good education than poor people. The rich would also marry their daughters to important rabbis or into families that had a tradition of great rabbis. In this way, wealthy families and scholarly families got mixed together. Sometimes a poor boy managed to become a great scholar, or a person who was not from a wealthy family did become rich. When that happened they were accepted into the ruling families. But usually leadership of the kehillah was kept among a closed group of families.

Since they were part of the same group, it was natural that the rabbis who decided what Jewish law was usually decided in such a way so that they and their wealthy relatives could remain wealthy and powerful. This did not mean that they didn't worry about the whole community. There were certain religious laws that made them responsible toward the whole community and the Christians held them responsible for what any Jew did. We must remember that the real rulers of the *kehillah* were the Christian nobility, and they could keep all the Jews as poor and powerless as they wished.

Most Jews, like most people in most places, followed most of their communities' rules because they were brought up to respect and believe in those rules. Besides this natural human habit, the kehillah's main tool for making sure that its members followed its rule was the threat of *herem*—banning. If you were put in *herem*, it meant you were thrown out of the community and no Jew would have anything to do with you. In the medieval world, where everyone had to be part of a group, this was a very serious threat. You would have to leave your whole way of life, family and friends, and become a Christian—or die.

There were Jews throughout the Middle Ages who did convert to Christianity. Christians were the rulers and the majority and it was always tempting to join them. And of course, some Jews may have sincerely come to believe that Christianity was the true religion. Any Jew who converted voluntarily to Christianity, for whatever reason, was considered a traitor by other Jews. Some Jews even hated Jews who were *forced* to convert. They thought the threatened Jews should have chosen to die "sanctifying the name." But usually the rabbis and the community accepted these forced converts back to Judaism if the Christian rulers would let them go back.

Some Christians converted to Judaism during the Middle Ages, but this was very rare. Jews were not allowed to teach Judaism to Christians and if Christians stopped being Christians they were heretics—people who had left the true faith. Heresy was a crime punishable by death.

So while the medieval Jewish community had lots of economic dealings with the surrounding Christian community, in all other matters it was in its own world. Jews usually lived together in their own part of town—sometimes called Jews' Street. Near Jews' Street would be the synagogue, the Jewish school, the *mikvah* (ritual Jewish bathhouse), and the Jewish inn. When business was over, Christians and Jews had nothing to do with one another. They prayed separately, played separately and had their own schools, law courts, charities, and customs.

Medieval Jewish Religious Life

Jewish energy in Europe during the Middle Ages went into two areas. One was surviving in a poor and dangerous world. The other, like their Christian neighbors, was their religion. And for medieval Jews, religion meant study of the holy books. The Jewish communities of medieval Europe didn't have any central authority. A rabbi or small group of rabbis in each town decided on their own what Jewish law was. In a certain sense, the Talmud itself became the only central authority for the Jews of Europe. Some rabbis, such as Gershom ben Judah, known as Rabeynu Gershom, tried to make rules for all of European Jewry. Jews throughout Europe were interested in what he had to say. But they wouldn't necessarily follow his rules if they didn't agree with the reasons he gave for them. Solomon Ben Isaac lived in the generation after Rabeynu Gershom, from 1039-1105. He was known as Rashi and wrote some of the most influential Jewish commentaries and explanations of the Bible and Talmud of all time. Today, when people study a page of Torah or Talmud, it is still usually surrounded by the comments Rashi made on those passages almost a thousand years ago. But even Rashi never became a central authority for European Jews did. They didn't have an Exilarch or a Gaon as the Babylonian Jews did. And they certainly didn't have a Pope, as did European Christians.

The rabbis who followed Rashi, including his two grandsons, Samuel ben Meir (known as Rashbam) and Jacob ben Meir (known as Rabeynu Tam), are called the Tosafists (the Adders), because they added additional commentaries and explanations on the Bible and Talmud. What they were actually doing was continuing the tradition of rabbis making new Jewish law. Like all the contributors to Jewish law before them, they tried to show how their new laws were really just the logical continuation of the old laws, the laws God gave to Moses. By writing questions to other Jewish communities about the law, and getting answers, *responsa*, Jewish law in Europe remained a common tradition even though there wasn't a central authority laying down the law.

While only a few Jews became rabbis or Talmudic scholars, all Jewish men had a religious duty to study the holy books as much as possible. So besides going to the synagogue to pray mornings and evenings, Jewish men were supposed to find the time to learn Torah and Talmud every day. Women were excused or kept out of this part of the Jewish religion. Very often they would be the ones to run the family business, and were forced to earn the family living. But since they had no opportunity to become experts in Jewish law, women were kept out of the leadership of the Jewish community. Of course there were many laws about keeping a proper Jewish home. Women had to know and apply all of these laws, so they were still very involved in one part of the Jewish religion.

Ashkenazic Emigration to Eastern Europe

At first only the Jews living around the Rhine River between France and Germany were called Ashkenazim ("German Jews"), but soon all the European Jews outside of Spain were called Ashkenazim. The Jews of Spain were called Sephardim ("Spanish Jews"). The Ashkenazim of medieval Europe did not have a Golden Age like the Golden Age of the Sephardim. There were poets and philosophers among the Ashkenazim, but nothing to compare to Judah Halevi or Maimonides. David Kimchi, an Ashkenazi scholar did write one of the first books that tried to explain the Hebrew language, and the Tosafists contributed to Jewish law and religion as much as Sephardic scholars did. But overall, the Ashkenazi contribution to Jewish culture in the Middle Ages was much poorer than the Sephardic contribution. This is not surprising. The Ashkenazim couldn't freely mix with another culture as could the Sephardim, so they didn't have new ideas come from the outside. Also, Ashkenazi life was frequently disrupted by persecutions. Those circumstances made it difficult for Ashkenazi culture to develop as fully as it might have.

The persecutions of the Ashkenazi Jews in medieval times eventually moved most of them out of France, Germany, and England and into Eastern Europe. Jews were expelled from all of England in 1290 and all of France in 1306. Germany in the Middle Ages was a collection of many little countries without a common ruler that had any real power over its many parts, so the Jews were never kicked out of all of Germany. But they were expelled from some parts, and as we have seen, most of the Jews of medieval Germany were often treated very badly. So, over the years, medieval Jews moved east into such countries as Poland, Hungary, and Bohemia. There had long been some Jews in some of these countries. In Bohemia, Jews had successfully fought alongside other Bohemians against the First Crusaders. And not all Western Jews went east. Some remained in Germany. Farther south, under the protection of the Popes, there remained a good size Jewish community in Italy. But most Ashkenazim were moving or had moved east by the end of the Middle Ages.

The countries of Eastern Europe were welcoming to Jews at this time. They had only recently started to become Christian so the tradition of Christian Jew-hatred was not very well established. In the late Middle Ages, East European countries didn't have many merchants or artisans yet. The population was almost all nobles and peasants. It was like Western Europe in the early Middle Ages. So the Jewish skills as craftsmen and businessmen were badly needed. The nobility of Poland and Hungary invited Jewish communities to settle on their lands. They promised them protection and freedom to run their own affairs. They believed that Jews would help their lands prosper.

As the Ashkenazim came east, they brought with them their devotion to the Talmud. They continued to base their lives on what the rabbis told them the Talmud said was the law. They also brought the language that many of them had spoken in Western Europe. This language was based on one type of German, but it had a lot of old French words in it too. In addition it had a great many words from Hebrew and the Jews wrote it using the letters of the Hebrew alphabet. When they brought this language to Eastern Europe, they started to include words from East European languages, such as Polish. This language developed and is called Yiddish. Yiddish became the language of Ashkenazi Jewry for almost a thousand years. It was in Yiddish that Jews eventually created another Golden Age of Jewish culture.

The Khazars

Although most East European Jews probably came from Western Europe at the end of the Middle Ages, there is a possibility that some came from a very different place—Khazaria, a kingdom south of Russia. We do not know much about Khazaria, but we do know that sometime between 750 and 900 the nobility of Khazaria and at least part of the population converted to Judaism. There is a legend that the Khazar King Bulan wanted to know what religion to believe, so he invited a Muslim, Christian, and Jew to explain their beliefs. After hearing what each had to say, he chose to convert to Judaism, because the Muslim and the Christian each said that Judaism was the closest religion to the truth after their own. There might be a kind of truth in this legend. Khazaria was right between Christian Byzantium and the Muslim Caliphate. Picking a neutral religion might have helped Khazaria stay independent.

The Khazars were a nomadic, Turkish speaking people. At first they may have been Karaites, the kind of Jews who did not follow rabbis or accept the Talmud. In 800 the Khazar King, Obahdiah, invited Jewish scholars to his kingdom to teach the standard form of the Judaism of the rabbis.

Somewhere between 980 and 1200 Khazaria was conquered by Russia. We don't know for sure what became of the Khazars. Some historians believe they went north into Eastern Europe and settled there. If they did, then when the Jews of Western Europe moved east, they and the Khazars completely mixed together to become a single Yiddish-speaking people following and continuing the Ashkenazi tradition of Judaism.

FIGURE 14 - Medieval synagogue in Sopron, Hungary.

FIGURE 15 - Sephardic couple from the city of Sarajevo,
around 1900.

Chapter 8

The Sephardim

Sephardim and Ashkenazim

Starting in the eleventh century, there began to be more and more differences between the Sephardic Jews living in Spain and the Ashkenazi Jews living in France and Germany. There began to be different prayers and melodies used in the service, different holiday traditions, and different everyday customs. In fact, the situation of the Jews of Spain was in many ways very different from the situation of Jews of the rest of medieval Europe. In the early Middle Ages, as we talked about before, all Spain was ruled by Muslims. In the eight century Christians began to reconquer Spain, but it took hundreds of years for Christians to reconquer all of Spain. When they did, they found a Jewish community that was more involved with the non-Jewish society than any other Jewish community was in the rest of Europe. Like the Spanish Muslims, the Spanish Christians at first made use of the talents of the Spanish Jews and tolerated them. Some Jews even helped the Christians reconquer Spain when the intolerant Muslim Almohades came to power in much of Muslim Spain. So the Golden Age of Spanish Jewry, which we talked about before, didn't end all at once when the Christians took over Spain. But the Christian re-conquest did eventually lead to Spanish Jewry, the Sephardim, being faced with the same problems as Jews in other parts of Europe.

The Persecution of the Sephardic Jews

It took the Christians hundreds of years to reconquer Spain from the Muslims. Many Christian kingdoms were established in the reconquered lands. The Christian Spanish kings introduced into their new kingdoms the feudal system and the anti-Jewish laws that were common in the rest of Christian Europe. But at first these anti-Jewish laws were not very strictly enforced. Officially Jews became property of the king, just as they were in the rest of medieval Europe. For a while, Jews from the great Sephardic families, like the Abulafias and the Abravanels, continued to be wealthy and to advise and serve the rulers. There remained Jewish doctors, lawyers, poets, and scholars under the Christians.

But things gradually became worse under the Christians. Sometimes the Jews would side with one Christian king against his enemy, and if their side lost, the Jews would suffer. This happened when a friend of the Jews, King Pedro of Castile was defeated by his brother Henry. Under Henry's rule, in the 1390's, thousands of Jews were massacred.

Hatred of the Jews had been spreading throughout Christian Spain from the beginning of the re-conquest. Anti-Jewish preachers, like the monks Brother Martinez and Brother Ferrer, would travel from town to town making speeches against the Jews and encouraging people to attack them. Jews often had to move from one part of Spain to another. Spanish Christian kings and bishops demanded more and more disputations, which usually led to trouble for the Jews. As time went on, the only way Jews could keep their good position in Spanish society was to convert. Sometimes converting was the only way for Jews to save their lives.

Many more Spanish Jews converted than did the Ashkenazi Jews when they were faced with the same situation. The practice of "sanctifying the name," dying rather than converting, never caught on among the Spanish Jews. Maybe it was because they had better lives and were more worldly than the Ashkenazi Jews. But whatever the reason, many did convert. During the massacres of the 1390's, there were mass baptisms and thousands of Jews were converted.

New Christians and Marranos

The converted Jews were called "New Christians." One interesting historical question is whether the New Christians really became Christians or whether they secretly continued to be Jews, practicing the Jewish religion behind closed doors. We know that some certainly remained secret Jews. For a while, many historians thought that most of the New Christians remained secret Jews. But now it is believed that probably most New Christians really accepted their new religion.

Many of the old Christians believed that the New Christians remained secret Jews. They called the New Christians "Marrano," which means pigs. Even though it started as an insult, the word "Marrano" came to mean a secret Jew, and there were Jewish families who were proud to be Marranos. For hundreds of years there were Marrano families in Spain and Portugal. They would secretly pass on the Jewish traditions from generation to generation. Over time, many of the traditions were lost. But to this very day you can find families in Portugal or Spain who seem just like their Christian neighbors, except that they have some private, family traditions that show that these are Marrano families, such as lighting candles on Friday nights,

But most New Christians probably weren't Marranos. On the whole the New Christians did very well in Spanish society. Now that they were free of the rules keeping Jews down, these Jews were able to get, or get back, important jobs in government and wealth in business. Their children married the children of the Spanish nobility, and by the end of the fifteenth century, most Spanish nobles had at least some Jewish ancestors.

The success of the New Christians made many old Christians angry and jealous. As a result two things happened. One was that for the first time among Christians, even after Jews converted to Christianity they were still hated and treated differently. Some Spanish towns expelled Christians who had "Jewish blood" in them, that is, Jewish ancestors. This was the first time "Jews" were persecuted not for their religion, but for their ancestry. It didn't matter what they believed or did. All that mattered was who they were born to. This kind of racist Jew-hatred would continue and cause Jews their greatest catastrophe ever almost five hundred years later.

The second result of old Christian jealousy and suspicion of the New Christians was the establishment of the Inquisition.

The Inquisition

In 1474, Isabella became Queen of Castile, a kingdom in Spain, and in 1478 she asked the Pope if a special organization could be set up in Spain called the Inquisition. Its job would be to investigate the faith and activities of Spanish Christians to see if they were being true to the Catholic religion. If the Inquisition had doubts about people's faith, it would investigate them, and perhaps put them on trial. If they were found guilty of being untrue to Catholicism, they would be convicted of heresy. The punishment for heresy was being burned to death.

If people didn't like someone, or suspected their neighbors, or wanted to get rid of some business rival, they might report them to the Inquisition. The Inquisition also encouraged people to report on anyone they thought might be a heretic, and threatened to punish people who didn't report secret Jewish activities they knew about. Tomas de Torquemada became head of the Inquisition in 1483. He told people what to watch for to catch secret Jews. Did they wash their hands before meals? Did they avoid work on Saturdays? These might be signs that people were Marranos. The Inquisition also had its own spies and officials out looking for heretics.

When the Inquisition questioned suspects, it often tortured them. People sometimes confessed to heresy even if they weren't heretics. Some sincere Inquisitors may have thought they were doing their victims a favor by getting them to confess. They thought if heretics didn't confess, they would go to hell when they died and suffer hell-fires forever. The Inquisitors would kill their victims even if they did confess, but they thought that they were saving their victims from having to go to hell by getting them to confess before they died.

Of course, the people who got most of the Inquisition's attention and suffered most from its work were the New

Christians. They were the ones that many people wanted out of the way. They were also the ones whose faith in Christianity was most doubted. In Seville in 1481, six New Christians were accused of being secret Jews and were burnt alive. Their execution was called an *auto-de-fé* (meaning an Act of Faith, in Spanish). It was the first of many *auto-de-fé*s that took place in Catholic lands where the Inquisition had power. Thousands of New Christians would be burnt at the stake for the crime of being secret Jews.

Maniera di bruciare quelli che furono condannati dalla Inquisizione.

FIGURE 16 – Print of Jews burned at the stake in an *auto-da-fé* during the Inquisition.

Although most *auto-de-fé*s took place in Spain and Portugal, the Inquisition executed people in Italy and the Americas too. In 1528, only a few years after Spain conquered it, there was an *auto-de-fé* in Mexico City. The Inquisition had some punishments less than death, but burning people alive was its most dramatic punishment. Probably over 30,000 people were killed by the Inquisition over the years. Some, who really were Marranos, probably died saying the Shema, the prayer Jews traditionally say at the moment of death. Others were sincere Christians and probably died with Jesus' name on their lips. The Inquisition lasted in Spain and Portugal for hundreds of years.

Expulsion from Spain

One odd thing about the Inquisition is that it didn't bother Jews. Its job was to fight heresy. Heresy was the crime of not being true to the Christian faith *if you were supposed to be a Christian.* But Jews who had not converted weren't supposed to be Christians. They were infidels—people without Christian faith—but they weren't heretics. Of course Jews were persecuted at this time in all sorts of ways, but they weren't punished for following the Jewish religion and the Inquisition had no power over them. This put the Inquisition in a funny position. It would torture and burn to death a family it accused of secretly doing Jewish things, like lighting Shabbat candles in its home, while the family's Jewish neighbors would be left alone for openly doing the same thing. In addition, the Inquisition concluded that it would be impossible to wipe out the Jewish activities of the New Christians as long as there were Jews around to teach them and influence them. So the Inquisition convinced Queen Isabella and her husband King Ferdinand of Aragon, who together ruled most of Spain, to expel all of the Jews from their kingdoms.

There is a story that just before the king was about to sign the expulsion order, the Jewish leaders Abraham Senior and Isaac Abravanel offered a huge amount of money to him to let the Jews stay in Spain. The king was about to accept the bribe when Torquemada burst in holding a crucifix, a little statue of Jesus on the cross. Torquemada put the crucifix in front of the king and queen and said that Christ had been betrayed by Judas for thirty pieces of silver (that was a story from the Gospels) and if the king and queen wanted now to betray Christ again, this time for 30,000 pieces of silver, here was the crucifix for them to sell. At that point, they turned down the Jewish leaders' offer and signed the expulsion order. The story probably isn't true, because

Ferdinand and Isabella knew they would be getting lots of the wealth the Jews would have to leave behind anyway.

On March 30, 1492, the law was signed that all Jews would have to leave Spain and any territory owned by Spain by the end of July the same year. After over a thousand years of Spanish Jewish culture, the Jews had only four months to pack up, sell what they could, and leave. From one to two hundred thousand Jews left Spain that spring and summer. When Christopher Columbus sailed from Spain that year on his first voyage to America, he surely saw many Jews boarding ships to flee from Spain. Most Jews at first went right next door to Portugal, but Portugal expelled its Jews five years later. It was in Muslim countries that the Jews of Spain, the Sephardim, found places they could settle down.

The Dispersion of the Sephardim

The closest lands that would accept the Jews that were expelled from Spain and Portugal were the Muslim lands of North Africa. There had been Jewish communities in these lands since Roman times, and they had remained throughout the Caliphates. For hundreds of years before 1492, some Sephardim had come to North Africa to escape persecution in Spain. Maimonides' family had lived for a time in Fez, Morocco. Now these old Sephardim, and even older, original Jewish communities of North Africa, were joined by the Sephardic refugees of 1492 and 1497.

Getting to these lands of refuge was dangerous. Jews were killed, kidnapped, or robbed during the sea voyages escaping Spain. But once settled in these Muslim lands, they were usually pretty safe. There was certainly some discrimination against Jews. A few occupations were not open to them. They had to pay special taxes. They couldn't officially hold certain government jobs. They had to live in a special section of town (in Morocco called the *mellah*). There were even some anti-Jewish riots, where Jews were killed. But in general these were tolerant countries. Many Sephardim settled in for a long stay in North Africa, where they built strong and sometimes wealthy communities.

The lands that were most welcoming to the Sephardic refugees were part of the Muslim Ottoman Empire. The Ottoman Turks had captured most Muslim lands and also the Christian lands of the Byzantine Empire. By 1492, the Ottomans had established an Empire that included most of the old Caliphate and most of Byzantium. It included Palestine, Greece, Turkey, the Balkans, Syria, Egypt, and Iraq. The Ottomans themselves were Muslims, but they were very tolerant of the different religions and peoples in their Empire. The Ottoman capital city of Constantinople was the most international city in the world. There were Greeks, Turks, Arabs, Slavs, Armenians and even some Ashkenazi Jews there. The Sephardic Jews settled in the Ottoman Empire and built large and strong communities. Constantinople, of course, attracted many Sephardim, but so did other cities such as Izmir(then called Smyna). Salonika eventually became the city where Jews were the largest group.

These Sephardim did many things to earn a living in the Ottoman Empire. They were miners, fishermen, and metalworkers. Many who had been doctors in Spain continued to be doctors under the Ottomans. Some even became advisers to the Sultan, who was the ruler of the Ottoman Empire. Many of the Sultan's best diplomats were Jews. But the Sephardim's most valuable contributions to the Ottomans were as merchants. The Sephardim had contacts with other Jews all over the world. They usually spoke many languages and understood foreign, Christian customs. They also had business experience. The Sephardim's business in international trade brought wealth to themselves and the Ottoman Empire. The Sultan is supposed to have said "How can you call King Ferdinand a wise ruler if he throws out of his kingdom so many skilled people, making himself poorer and me richer?" Today there is still a Jewish community in Istanbul (Constantinople's name after 1922) that is descended from the Sephardim who came there five hundred years ago.

In Palestine: Kabala and Shulchan Aruch

It was not surprising that when they were expelled from Spain some Jews wanted to live in Palestine, the Land of Israel. There were a few small Jewish communities already there. But the Sephardim's arrival made the Jewish population much larger. A few of them settled in Jerusalem. More went to Hebron. But the town most affected by the arrival of the Sephardim was in the Galilean hills, Safed. In 1492, only a few Jews lived in Safed. Less than 100 years later it had 21 synagogues and 18 *yeshivot*, Jewish colleges. Safed became a center of Jewish learning and religion, especially that part of the Jewish religion which is called *kabala*.

Kabala is the "mystical" tradition in the Jewish religion. Some religions are almost completely mystical and most have some mystical traditions. In general, mystics believe that God fills the whole world and that if you know how to pray, or meditate, or act in the right way, you can experience being with God here on earth. Mystics also believe that the knowledge you need to experience God is secret and that only a few people really understand it. They often also believe that mystical knowledge tells about the future and what will happen to the world at the end of time. All the parts of the Jewish religion that have these kinds of beliefs are known as *kabala*.

The main book of *kabala* is the Zohar, the Book of Splendor. The Zohar turned up in the thirteenth century and people said it had been written by Shimon Bar Yochai over a thousand years before that. While some parts of the Zohar may go back that far, most of it was probably written or put together by Moses de Leon, who lived in the thirteenth century.

For a couple of hundred years no one paid much attention to the Zohar. But when the Jews were expelled from Spain many became more interested in mysticism. They wanted to experience God to overcome their suffering. They wanted to know the future to find out when the Messiah would come. They thought that now must surely be a good time for it.

Safed became the center of study of the *kabala*. One rabbi in particular, Isaac Luria, known as HaAri, the Lion, was the great teacher of *kabala* in Safed. Born in Jerusalem in 1534, Luria himself came from an Ashkenazi family, but his students who filled the Yeshivot and synagogues of Safed were mostly Sephardim. Luria wrote no books, but his student Chaim Vital wrote down his teachings, which are one of the most important sources of Jewish mysticism.

Another important rabbi who lived in Safed at this time was Joseph Caro. Caro was interested in *kabala* and spent much time studying and teaching it. In his long life he wrote many things. His writings that had the most influence on Jewish life weren't mystical at all—they were explanations and codes of Jewish law. Most important of these was his book, the *Shulchan Aruch*, the Set Table.

The *Shulchan Aruch* was a handbook of Jewish law. There were many books of Jewish law. Besides the Torah, there were the many volumes that made up the Talmud and all the commentaries on the Talmud. There were also all of the collections of *responsa*, rabbis' letters that made decisions about Jewish law. The law in these books would be mixed together with folktales, legends, history, and details of the discussions and thinking that led up to the law. These books were not well organized to use as law-books. They didn't have all the laws on one topic in one place, so it was very hard to find out what the law was on a particular matter unless you were willing to do some research, which might take a lot of time. Even if you had the time, you might not be able to do it unless you had a good Jewish education and knew your way around the Jewish legal books. So there was a great need for handbooks of Jewish law to collect all the laws and organize them by topic.

The *Shulchan Aruch* was not the first handbook of Jewish law. Maimonides' *Mishneh Torah* had been written over three hundred years before Joseph Caro lived and there had been other handbooks as well. But Caro's *Shulchan Aruch* became the most influential handbook of Jewish law ever written. It was easy to use, thorough and based on Caro's great knowledge of all of the Jewish law-books and legal traditions. It became very popular as soon as it was published in 1567. Everyone used it, even learned rabbis who had to make a legal decision and who didn't want to take the time to research the original law-books. Soon short versions of the *Shulchan Aruch* were written that were even easier to use. Some of these short versions were translated for people who couldn't read Hebrew. The *Shulchan Aruch* became the standard of Jewish law. Throughout the Jewish world it was accepted that if the *Shulchan Aruch* said something was a law, it was a law. Moses Isserles of Cracow, Poland wrote an Ashkenazi appendix to the *Shulchan Aruch*. He added the Ashkenazi legal traditions that the Sephardi Joseph Caro had not included. Today, over four hundred years after it was written, there are still Jews who base their lives completely on the rules of the *Shulchan Aruch*. The expression "a Shulchan Aruch Jew" came to mean a Jew who followed every detail of the traditional Jewish law. It was Joseph Caro's book that decided which details would become the traditional Jewish laws for centuries to come.

Ladino

When the Sephardim left Spain, one of the things they took with them was their language. It was mostly Castilian Spanish, but it had many Hebrew words and it was written using the Hebrew alphabet. Sometimes this language was called Judezmo, but it is usually known as Ladino. The Sephardic Jews continued to use and develop Ladino wherever they settled. Ladino took new words from the languages of the peoples the Sephardim were living with, such as Arabic, Greek and Turkish. But still it stayed so close to the Spanish of 1492 that if Queen Isabella came back to life in the early twentieth century, she could understand a Jew in Salonika, Greece, who spoke Ladino better than she could understand a Catholic in Madrid who spoke modern Spanish.

Over the centuries, wherever Sephardic communities could be found, Ladino could be heard. Business was done in Ladino, poems were written in Ladino, and songs were sung in Ladino. Most Sephardic communities were in the countries surrounding the Mediterranean Sea, such as Palestine, Turkey, Greece, and Morocco. But Sephardic communities were also established in Holland and the Americas. Ladino became one of the long-lasting and great languages of Jewish culture.

FIGURE 17 - Drawing of an 18th Polish Jewish boy.

Chapter 9

In Eastern Europe

At about the same time that the Jews of Spain were going into exile, the Jews of Eastern Europe were entering their own Golden Age. We have seen how in the late Middle Ages Jews were badly treated in Western Europe. They were massacred and forced to convert. They were not allowed to earn a living in the usual way. Lies were told about them so that they were hated, beaten, humiliated, and killed. Of course, these thing did not happen all of the time and in every place in Western Europe. But they happened often enough in the centuries between 1000 and 1500 to make many Jews want to leave the Western European countries. And even if they didn't want to leave, Jews were expelled, that is, thrown out of many places in Western Europe. When they left England, France and Germany, they or their descendants mostly ended up in Eastern Europe, especially Poland.

Poland was just beginning to become Christian at this time. It was a country of landowners and peasants who farmed the land. There were almost no middle classes of people between these large landowners and poor peasants. There were few towns, few craftspeople, not much manufacturing, and less trade than there was in the West. The rulers of Poland believed that their lands would become richer and more powerful if they could develop their lands economically the way Western Europe had. They welcomed the Jews fleeing Western Europe, who had just the sorts of skills needed in Poland for economic development. Also, because Christianity was so new in Eastern Europe, the traditional Christian hatred of Jews was not yet so great there. And so it was that during the medieval persecution of Jews in

Western Europe the rulers of Poland began inviting Jews to settle in Poland.

In 1264, King Boleslav of Poland promised to protect the Jews of Poland, to let them earn a decent livelihood and to let them live according to Jewish customs. Eighty years later King Casimir made the same promise. Still, by 1492 there were probably less than 30,000 Jews in Poland. But by the time those 30,000 had grown-up grandchildren, there were over 150,000 Jews in Poland. Not only had the Jewish population become larger, in the 1500's the Jews of Poland created a rich culture and strong community. The power to rule themselves that the Polish Kings had given them was used by the Jews to create a form of Jewish life that would have great influence on the way most Jews lived for the next five hundred years.

How Poland's Jewish Community was Organized

The Jews in Poland settled in towns in the countryside. These towns were called *shtetls*. These *shtetls* were very different from the ghettoes of Western Europe. The ghettoes of Western Europe, which we will read about in the next chapter, were crowded streets and neighborhoods that the Jews were forced to live in. They weren't allowed to live in other parts of town. But the *shtetls* of Eastern Europe were often whole towns of Jews doing business with the Christian peasants who lived in the surrounding countryside. Even if the whole *shtetl* wasn't Jewish, a big part of it was. Unlike the West European ghettoes, in the *shtetls* Jews lived together voluntarily.

Most Jews wanted to live near other Jews because they needed special things to lead a Jewish life, and those special things were only available where there was a group of Jews. They needed a synagogue to pray and study in. They needed a school to teach their sons Torah and Talmud (girls were still not given an education). They needed a ritual bathhouse, called a *mikvah*, to bathe in at certain times when their religion told them they must bathe. They needed a rabbi to explain Jewish law to them and decide how Jewish law should solve problems that came up. They needed a special butcher, a *shochet*, who knew how to kill animals in a kosher way so that the meat would be kosher. And they needed the other Jews themselves. Many Jewish prayers and rituals can only be said if there are ten adult Jews, a *minyan*, present (in those days, and even among some Jewish groups today, only men would count toward the *minyan*). Jews only married other Jews, so a Jewish community was needed to have brides and grooms for the children.

The Jewish communities in the *shtetls* were usually run by a council called a *kahal*. This *kahal* was chosen by and made up of rich and learned men. It was their job to keep up the Jewish institutions, such as the synagogue and school. Often they also organized welfare funds for the needy in the community. This might include a fund to educate poor boys, a fund to support advanced Torah study, a sick fund for people too sick to work, a widow's fund for women left poor and alone after the death of their husbands, a fund to help bury the poor, and one to help poor brides have a wedding. To pay for these things, the *kahal* taxed the community and received contributions from it. One of the most important jobs of the *kahal* was collecting money from Jews and giving it out to the common Jewish institutions and community welfare needs.

These local councils made most of the decisions that ruled their own communities. But there were many decisions that it was best to coordinate with all of the other Jewish communities in Poland, such as how Jewish communities should relate to the rulers of Poland. And so the local councils would send delegates to higher councils that represented more than one community. The highest council, the one which made decisions for all of the Jewish communities in Poland was called the Va'ad Arba Artzot, the Council of Four Lands. It was called this because it had representatives from the four different parts of Poland. This Council usually met twice a year, once in the town of Lublin and once in the town of Yaroslav. Great fairs were held in those cities. At these fairs people came from all over to buy, sell and trade. At local fairs, held once a month or once a week, peasants from the countryside came into town to sell their animals and crops and to buy things the townsfolk made that the peasants needed. But at the great fairs, such as those held in Lublin and Yaroslav, merchants came with their wares from great distances to do business. These fairs were very convenient places for the Council of Four Lands to meet. People were travelling to them from all over and the town was prepared to receive travelers. Lublin and Yaroslav also had large Jewish communities to host the Council.

The Council of Four Lands was like a combination of a Supreme Legal Court and a Legislature. A legal court decides how a law applies to a particular problem or situation. If some of the people who have brought the problem to the court don't like the decision that the court makes, they can often "appeal" that decision to a higher court, that is, they can ask another court that has more power to see if it agrees with the lower court's decision. The Council of Four Lands was used by the Jews as their highest court. It was given the final say in on how to apply the law.

It was also a legislature. Courts apply the law, but legislatures *make* the laws. In other words a court says whether a rule has been broken, but a legislature makes the rules. The Council of Four Lands was a legislature for Polish Jews, but it did not think of itself as a legislature, because all rules were supposed to come from God, and their mission was just to figure out God's rules and how to apply them. But, of course, just as in the days of the making of the Talmud, the Council faced new situations for which they needed to make new rules. They tried to follow the spirit of the old rules and they never admitted, probably not even to themselves, that they were making new rules.

In the almost two thousand years between the end of Herod's rule and the founding of the State of Israel in 1948, Jewish communities never had as much power to rule themselves as they did in the days of the Council of Four Lands. It was the closest Jews came in the Diaspora to having their own government. The Polish Kings weren't much interested in how the Jews lived among themselves, so they left almost all those decisions up to the Jewish Councils. But even so, the Jews did not completely rule themselves. They still had to obey the Christian Polish rulers in any matters that the rulers cared about. In fact, one of the most important jobs of the Council was representing the Jewish communities of Poland to the Polish rulers. If the Polish King was considering a law, or tax that would affect Jews, or if there was something, like protection, that Jews needed from the King, it was the Council of the Four Lands that talked with the King.

Although the Council of Four Lands was strongest in the 1500s and 1600s, it lasted until 1764. In that year, the Polish Kings started a new tax system. For the Polish rulers, the most important job of the Council of Four Lands was that it collected taxes from the Jews to give to the King, so when they didn't need the Council for that anymore, they got rid of it.

Economic Life

Jews brought to Poland the skills they had developed in Western Europe. First among these was money-lending. An economy cannot grow without a system of "credit," that is, a way to borrow money to produce the things that will increase wealth, like new tools and new roads. Many of the first Jews who came to Poland were moneylenders. They provided the credit that the Polish nobility understood was needed to make their lands richer. Jews also became merchants in Poland. In almost every type of trade at that time—cattle, cloth, dyes, lumber—we find Jews. Jews also practiced many of the crafts.

In the mid-1500s, when the Polish rulers began to expand their rule into the neighboring lands of Lithuania and Ukraine, another job became important for Jews: estate agent. The Polish nobility would own large farmlands and villages of peasants—estates. Often they did not live on these estates, and even when they did, they were not interested in doing the work it took to manage the estates. So they would hire someone to do it for them. This was the estate agent and the job of estate agent in the Polish kingdom became almost completely a Jewish job. The estate agents would manage the estate. This meant collecting rent and other fees from the peasants. It also meant that Jews would have shops on the estate where the peasants would have to buy the things they needed. One type of Jewish business often found on the estate was the tavern, the place where liquor was sold and people came to drink. Jews, in fact, pretty much had a monopoly on the liquor business in Poland, that is, they were the only ones allowed to sell liquor. Tavern-keeper became an important Jewish occupation.

The jobs of estate agent, shop-keeper and tavern-keeper did not make the Jews popular with the Christian peasants. It was always a Jew that these poor peasants had to give their money to: taxes, rent, payment for goods, even to get drunk. When the landowner became greedy, which was not unusual, he would demand more money from the estate agent. This forced the estate agent to demand more money from the peasants. To them it was the Jewish agent who was being greedy. Not only greedy, but sometimes in control of their lives. The peasants might be forced to pay a fee to use their church. Imagine how the peasants would feel going to the Jewish agent to get the keys to their church!

Of course, in shtetls many Jews worked serving the needs of other Jews in town. There were teachers, butchers, milkmen, vegetable growers, tailors, cobblers, hat-makers, synagogue custodians, matchmakers, and dealers in all sorts of goods. But when Christians thought of Jews, it was often the landlord's agent they thought of.

Daily and Religious Life

There were religious rules and traditions that told the Jews of Eastern Europe how they should behave in almost every matter. Of course not everyone paid the same attention to the rules. Some people followed the rules more closely than others; they were more "observant" or "pious." But just about all Jews followed some of the rules and agreed that it would be best if everyone followed all of the rules. In other words, no Jew questioned the idea that Jews should live according to Jewish law. So the Jewish community as a whole was governed by these rules, even if some of its members weren't very pious.

The Jewish law came from the Torah and the Talmud and all of the commentaries on them that rabbis had been writing for centuries. For almost everything you did there was a law that told you how it must be done or at least how best to do it. Going to sleep and waking, eating and drinking, working and praying, doing business and getting married, giving birth and getting buried, all had Jewish laws to guide you. It was every Jew's duty to know the laws for everything that they regularly did. People would greatly admire the "learned," that is, those who knew a great deal of law. Whenever anything even a little unexpected happened, if you weren't sure of what the law said to do in that situation, you'd have to go to the rabbi, who was the expert on the law. He would give you his opinion on what the law said to do. Because he was the rabbi, his opinion was more than just advice-it was a decision that you were supposed to be guided by.

Every part of Eastern European Jewish life was thoroughly affected by Jewish religious beliefs and practices. Boys, often as young as three years old, went off to school to study the Torah. The community provided free schools for students from poor families, but usually families paid for their sons' school. The school, called a *cheder*, kept most boys studying Torah and Talmud till they became Bar Mitzvah at thirteen. The better students would continue their studies at Yeshivas, schools for advanced religious studies, well beyond their thirteenth birthday. These *yeshiva bochurs* (yeshiva boys) would often go to another town and live with host families to continue their studies. There they would spend long days studying the Talmud and discussing all the possible meanings of all its laws. Yeshiva students were trained to argue about the correct way to understand the Talmud. These arguments often became very detailed and complex. You needed a sharp mind to be good at these arguments, which is why the arguments were called *pilpul* (pepper), because it has a sharp taste. The very best students would become rabbis and spend their whole life studying. But even boys who had stopped school before they became Bar Mitzvah were expected to try to find some time in their day or week to continue their religious education for the rest of their lives.

Studying and being learned in Jewish law was the most respected and honorable activity a man could do. The graduates of the Yeshivas became the leaders of the community. These rabbis would often marry into rich merchants families. Together, the learned and the rich ruled the Jewish communities. The local Jewish community was called the *kahal*, and the *kahal*'s officers, the *gabbaim*, and its president, the Rosh HaKahal, were usually the richest and most learned men in town.

Although a good number of men spent their lives studying the law, most had other jobs. But that didn't mean the Torah wasn't a big part of their life. They would get up in the morning and wash the way the law told them to. There were morning prayers to be said, both at home when you got up, and at the synagogue before starting work. The fringed undershirt they wore, tsitsits, was required by Jewish law, and all men followed the custom of keeping their head covered. In many cases there were laws affecting work, such as how to treat your animals and what were fair ways of doing business. Whenever you stopped to eat, there were before and after prayers, and of course what you ate had to be kosher. After work it was back to the synagogue for evening prayers.

A woman's life wasn't filled up with as much praying but her tasks were also ruled by Jewish law. Most women were involved in helping the family make a living, by tending to the animals at home, growing vegetables to sell, or going to the market to sell them. If her husband was a scholar busy studying all day, chances were that she was the main "breadwinner," for her family. But in addition to helping earn a living, the women had to take care of the children and the housekeeping. Housekeeping in a Jewish home had to follow Jewish laws. There were many laws: the laws of kashrut, concerning the preparation of food and clothing; laws about how to make the house ready for a holiday, such as cleaning all the *chometz* (yeast products, bread and cake) from the house for Passover; laws about what housework wasn't allowed on Shabbes and laws about when to light Shabbes candles. In addition, there were many laws about a woman's personal life; there were rules about when she had to attend the community bath-house, the mikvah, rules about her hair (covered outside the home if she was married) and even rules about how and when she and her husband could make love.

Jewish laws and traditions told the Jews of the *shtetl* what they were supposed to do in most situations. When a boy baby was born, at eight days of age he was to have a *brit milah*, a ritual circumcision. At three he was to get his first haircut and to start *cheder*, religious school. When parents felt it was time for a child to marry, they went to visit the *shadchan*, the matchmaker (if the matchmaker had not already visited them) to find a suitable bride or groom for their child. The law told them what to do when invited to a neighbor's wedding or bar mitzvah, as well as what to do at their own celebrations.

Holiday preparations marked the seasons: building a *succah* in the fall, lighting Chanukah candles in winter, making the house *Pesahdik* (Passover-ready), in spring, mourning the Temple's destruction in summer. When someone died, everyone understood how and when she or he should be buried (as soon as possible, in a plain wooden coffin) and how the dead person should be mourned, both for the week immediately following the death, when the grieving family received visitors while sitting *shiva*, and the month and year after the death when certain prayers were said and certain activities, such as going to parties, were not allowed.

Those are only a small sample of the rules, customs, holidays and traditions that made up a *shtetl* Jew's life. If we wrote down all of them, you would see that for a *shtetl* Jew almost everything they did they did in a special Jewish way, a way that reminded them they were Jewish. This made the Jews think of themselves as a separate nation, a different people than the Christians of Eastern Europe. The Christians thought so too. But more than anything else, having their own Jewish language, Yiddish, kept the Jews of Eastern Europe a people apart.

Yiddish

In Chapter 7 we learned that when the Jews of Germany came to Poland they brought the Germanic language they spoke with them. Besides Germanic words, their language had words from Old Italian and Old French, for among the Jews were many peddlers and traveling merchants who picked up and used words from all the lands they visited. When they came to Poland they added many Polish words. But the biggest addition of words to the basic Germanic language of these Ashkenazi Jews was from the Hebrew language.

Even though Jews had not used Hebrew as their language of daily life for well over a thousand years, they had not completely stopped using it. It was the language most of their prayers were in. It was the language of boys' education. It was the language of most Jewish holy books and scholarly books. All the words that best described the Jewish people's religious life and feelings were in Hebrew. So while most of the words for everyday life in Yiddish are Germanic words, many of the words for holidays, rituals, and spiritual ideas are from Hebrew. And since Jewish education was in Hebrew, when Jews wrote down their Yiddish language, they used the Hebrew alphabet to represent the Yiddish words. That is why written Hebrew and Yiddish look the same (*if* you can't understand either language!), even though they are very different languages.

The same Yiddish language, with some differences of pronunciation, was spoken by Jews throughout the lands of Eastern Europe. Christian peasants from Hungary, Lithuania, and Ukraine were not able to understand each other's language, but Jews from each of the areas had no trouble talking to each other. In fact, while there were differences of local customs, these Jews from the many lands of Eastern Europe led quite similar lives.

One thing that helped make Yiddish such a widespread language among the Jews of Eastern Europe was the printing press, which was invented at about the same time Jews were settling in Eastern Europe. Although most of the first Jewish books printed were in Hebrew, some early ones were in Yiddish and were used throughout Eastern Europe. One important one was the *Tsena Urena*, a version of the Hebrew Bible that was translated into Yiddish for the use of Jewish women. Remember— girls did not receive an education in Hebrew. If they were going to become familiar with Jewish scripture, it had to be in the language spoken by all the Jewish people, men and women, children and adults, educated and uneducated, rich and poor. That language was Yiddish. The Jews of Eastern Europe felt so close to the Yiddish language that they simply called it "Jewish." That is what "Yiddish" means in Yiddish. No other language used by Jews, not even Hebrew, ever got that honor.

For a thousand years, from its early formation in the Rhineland in the Middle Ages, until the mid-20th century, Yiddish was the language of Eastern European Jews. Assimilation in America, Nazi mass murders, and Stalinist persecutions—all of which we will read about later—have led to the near disappearance of people whose first language is Yiddish. During the past five hundred years, those Ashkenazi Jews were the vast majority of the world's Jews, and Yiddish recorded and helped to shape their experiences, thoughts, and feelings. In the late 19th and early 20th centuries, Jews used Yiddish to write stories, plays, and songs. They had Yiddish newspapers and schools. We shall read of that later too. Yiddish is no longer widely spoken. Only a few very religious Jews use it as their everyday language, but for a long time, having Yiddish as your mother tongue, as much as anything else, made an Ashkenazi Jew feel like a Jew.

FIGURE 18 – Print of Sabbatai Zevi

FIGURE 19 – Painting of the Vilna Gaon

Chapter 10

Massacres and Mysticism

When the Jews first came to Eastern Europe anti-Semitism was not very strong. But it grew. One reason was the growth of Christianity in the East, which brought the traditional Christian dislike and fear of Jews. Another reason was the arrival of German merchants in Eastern Europe. These merchants were business competitors of the Jews. The Jews were a threat to their livelihood. In 1572, the great Polish landowners replaced the strong Polish kings who had ruled much of Eastern Europe with much weaker kings. The strong kings had been able to protect the Jews throughout the kingdom. Now the Jews had to depend on the protection of the local Polish nobleman. Sometimes that local protection was given and sometimes it wasn't.

In the last chapter we read how Jews became estate agents for the Polish nobility. Jews managed the large farms owned by Polish landowners and so became the bosses of the peasants in the villages who worked on these farms. This caused hatred of the Jews. The hatred was especially strong in the part of the Polish Kingdom called Ukraine. Poland conquered more and more of the Ukraine in the late 1500s. The Ukrainian religion was Christian, but not the same kind of Christianity as that of the Poles; Poles were Catholic and Ukrainians Orthodox. Many Ukrainians were nomadic people before the Polish conquest forced them to settle in one place and farm the land. Ukrainians hated being ruled by these rich Polish foreigners and they hated the local Jews who seemed to them the main helpers of the Polish landlords.

Bogdan Khmelnytsky was a Ukrainian who ran away from the part of Ukraine controlled by the Poles. There were still unconquered parts where nomadic Ukranians, called Cossacks, continued to live independent lives riding their horses on the open plains. In 1648 Khmelnytsky organized these Cossacks to attack the Polish controlled parts of Ukraine. To Ukrainians Bogdan Khmelnytsky is a national hero who fought to free Ukraine from Polish rule, but in Jewish tradition he is remembered as Khmel the Wicked. Wherever they went Khmelnytsky's Cossacks, joined by the local Ukrainian peasants, killed Poles and Jews. Jews could sometimes save their lives by converting to Christianity. But often they preferred to be killed rather than convert. Sometimes, if they were caught by the Tatars, who fought with the Cossacks against the Poles, Jews were sold into slavery. But most Jews in Ukraine in 1648 and 1649 didn't convert or become slaves. They either fled the advancing Cossacks and became refugees or were caught by the Cossacks and murdered, usually cruelly. During the attacks Jews gathered in towns and tried, along with the Poles, to defend the town from the Cossacks. But the towns were overwhelmed and then the slaughters began. Women were raped, towns burned down, children drowned. In the end, hundreds of communities were completely destroyed. There were great massacres of Jews in Tarnopol, Narl, and Nemirov. The Nemirov massacre was remembered and mourned as a fast day among Polish Jewry for hundreds of years after. Many tens of thousands of Jews were killed during the Khmelnytsky massacres. Jewish tradition put the number at over 100,000.

This disaster had a lasting effect on the Jews of Poland. There were refugees and widows everywhere. There were thousands of Jews to be ransomed from slavery. Whatever wealth the Jews had before Khmelnytsky was mostly destroyed. And only a few years after the Khmelnytsky massacres, Swedes invaded Poland from north. The Swedes did not kill Jews, but Poles thought that the Jews welcomed the Swedes, and so Poles killed Jews. By 1660, the Jewish people of Eastern Europe had become poor, frightened, and miserable. They felt that their suffering could get no greater.

Because their suffering had become so great, the Jews of Poland were open to the idea that it was a good time for the Messiah to come. Pious Jews believed that the Messiah was the person that God would send to lead the Jews out of exile, back to

Palestine to establish a Jewish kingdom. It would be a righteous kingdom that would lead the whole world to God and justice.

Jews in Poland also became very interested in the mystical Jewish ideas, *kabala*. As we said in Chapter 8, these ideas had been given new life in the 1500s by the Sephardic Jews of Palestine. Mystical ideas emphasize the magical and mysterious parts of religion. Mysticism describes the secret ways of quickly feeling close to God. Jews felt that there must be a religious mystery to explain their suffering and they wanted a magical way of getting close to God to feel better. The mystical ideas of the time said that the world was just about ready to receive God's anointed one, the Messiah. All of this helped create the amazing reaction of the Jews to Sabbatai Zevi.

Sabbatai Zevi

Sabbatai Zevi was born in Smyrna on the western coast of Turkey, in 1626. When he was born, Smyrna was part of the Ottoman Empire, an Empire ruled by an Islamic King, the Sultan. The Empire was large. It covered most of the lands surrounding the eastern Mediterranean Sea and much of the Middle East. Most of its people were Muslims, but it also had many Christians and Jews.

Sabbatai Zevi was the son of a wealthy businessman, and Sabbatai received a good Jewish education. He was good looking and had a fine singing voice. But as a young man he began to act strangely. Sometimes he was very sad. But at other times he would get very excited and enthusiastic. Today many people might say he was mentally ill. Even in his own day many people thought he was crazy. He left Smyrna and traveled about the Empire, leading an ascetic life, that is, a life that avoided all pleasures and comforts. Sabbatai sometimes thought he was the Messiah and would act as though he were the Messiah. He did things, such as say the name of God out loud, that only the Messiah was supposed to do. This would get the rabbis in the towns he visited angry, because they thought he was just a sacrilegious madman. They chased him out of town. Sometimes

Sabbatai thought he was possessed by demons—evil spirits inside him who controlled him—and he wanted to be cured.

Nathan of Gaza was a rabbi in Palestine who had a reputation as a healer of souls. In 1665 Sabbatai went to Nathan to be rid of his demons. Nathan convinced Sabbatai that he wasn't possessed by demons but that he was actually the Messiah. Nathan began to preach that Sabbatai Zevi was the Messiah. The news spread quickly among Jews in Palestine, then the entire Ottoman Empire, and then throughout Europe. Many rabbis didn't believe that Sabbatai was the Messiah and were angry at his followers, but other rabbis accepted him as the Messiah. And among all sorts of common Jews, rich and poor, belief in Sabbatai was very widespread. Throughout the world Jews prepared for the Messianic age. They did special religious rituals to repent, that is, to wipe away their sins. They had celebrations welcoming the messianic age. People sold their belongings so that when the Messiah called for the return to Palestine, they would be ready to follow him. There was great excitement throughout the Jewish world. Not since the days of Bar Kokhba, 1500 years earlier, had so many Jews believed that the Messiah was among them.

The disruption all this excitement caused in the Empire concerned the Sultan's officials. When in 1666, word spread that Sabbatai Zevi would become king of the Empire, the officials decided to arrest Sabbatai. After a few months under arrest, he was given the choice of converting to Islam or being executed. Sabbatai converted.

When Sabbatai left Judaism most of his followers were disappointed and heartbroken. Becoming a Muslim seemed to prove he wasn't the Messiah. But some of his followers refused to stop believing in him. People like Nathan of Gaza tried to explain how Sabbatai's conversion was part of the mysterious plan to bring about the Messianic age. Even after he died in 1676, some Jews continued to believe that Sabbatai Zevi was the Messiah, in much the same way that some Jews continued to believe Jesus was the Messiah after his death. When things don't work out the way people expect and want them to, they will often come up with new ideas to keep their hopes alive. It is less painful than admitting a big mistake and accepting a deep disappointment.

Unlike Christianity, the Sabbatean movement did not go on to become a separate world religion. But it did not die out completely. Those faithful to Sabbatai Zevi continued to be a sect, that is, a small group with special beliefs, within Judaism. The rabbis were very much against the Sabbateans, so usually, but not always, the Sabbateans operated as a secret sect. Belief in Sabbatai Zevi among Jews slowly died away in the century after his death, but occasionally there would be a burst of energy in the movement. In 1756 a Polish Jew, Jacob Frank, became the leader of some of the Sabbateans and declared that he was a reincarnation of Sabbatai Zevi, that is, he was Sabbatai come back to life, and he was the Messiah. Frank taught that Jews did not have to follow Jewish laws, or for that matter almost any laws, anymore. Naturally the rabbis were very much against Jacob Frank and his followers. They did what they could to suppress his followers. The rabbis treated the Sabbateans and the Frankists as a shameful episode in Jewish history, best not spoken of. When it was spoken of, these movements were used as examples of how Jews could go terribly wrong. Sabbatai Zevi, Jacob Frank, and others Jewish leaders of sects rejected by the rabbis came to be called "false Messiahs" in Jewish tradition. rabbis not only denounced these "false Messiahs" of the past, but they warned about future false Messiahs. In fact they started to frown on all mystical beliefs in Judaism. The rabbis said that what being a real Jew was all about was studying the Talmud and following every detail of its law, as the rabbis saw the law.

The Rise of Hasidism

The failure of the Sabbatean movement made most Jews suspicious of anyone who said he was the Messiah. But they weren't fully satisfied with the rabbis' Judaism of all-study-and-rules either. Not everyone had the time to study, and not everyone felt his spiritual feelings satisfied by following lots of detailed rules. These were hard times for East European Jews and they wanted a religion that would comfort them. After the Khmelnytsky massacres and the wars that followed them, the Jews of Eastern Europe were very poor. The Gentile rulers made more and more laws that prevented the Jews from certain businesses and certain jobs. Hatred of Jews was also on the rise. The old medieval blood libel, the accusation that Jews killed Christian children as part of their religion, became more common. Sometimes, especially around Easter, there would be violence against Jews. Poor, often hated and abused by their neighbors, ruled by an elite of scholars and merchants, common Jews were ready for something which would help them get through their everyday lives. Hasidism was to be that something.

Israel ben Eliezer was born in the southeast of Poland around the year 1700. We know of him mostly through legends, so we cannot be too sure of the facts of his life. He probably had a decent Jewish education, but he does not seem to have been a great scholar. He was very pious, following all the Jewish laws, and seemed to have a calm and comforting personality, one which people found very attractive. Living with his wife in the rural Carpathian Mountains, Israel became a *Ba'al Shem*, a Master of Names. A Ba'al Shem was a sort of practical magician and faith healer. He used magic prayers, charms, and formulas to help solve people's problems, especially their health problems. These men were called Ba'al Shems because it was thought that their power came from the knowledge they had of the names of angels and demons. They were able to call on the angels to help you and call away the demons who were harming you. Most common Jews (just like most of the Gentile people they lived among) were very superstitious then, and a Ba'al Shem, like magic healers in many societies, gave them the hope and confidence that would sometimes help them get better.

Israel ben Eliezer became known as the Ba'al Shem Tov, the Master of the Good Name. He went beyond the normal healing activities of a Ba'al Shem. He spoke of making God a part of your daily life. He taught people to see God in everything about them and everything they do. He said prayer should not just be mumbling the right words; prayer should be said as if you really meant it, with passion. He said all of life should be lived joyously, with a feeling that God was always present. Although the Besht (short for <u>Ba</u>'al <u>Shem</u> <u>To</u>v) never said that studying Talmud and following Jewish law wasn't important, he did say that feeling close to God and taking pleasure in God's presence was more important. He also taught that some men, *tzadikim*, were so close to God that they could help others become close to God.

The followers of the Besht became known as Hasidim, pious or righteous ones. During his life the Besht gathered some disciples about him in the town of Medzibozh. But it was after his death in 1760, that one of his disciples, Dov Ber, organized Hasidism into a powerful religious movement. Dov Ber was a very learned *magid* (preacher). From his base in the town of Mezirech he trained the Hasidic leaders who brought the Besht's ideas to all parts of Poland. These leaders would settle in a town and become the local *tzadiks*, the Hasidic guides to God.

This Hasidic form of Judaism had great appeal and spread very rapidly. You didn't have to be a scholar to be a good Jew. You didn't have to be studying in a Yeshiva to be near God. You could be a poor laborer, and if you took joy in your work and thought of God, that was even better than unfeeling Talmud study. Instead of just following rules, you were supposed to sing and dance to be a holy Jew. In addition, you weren't all on your own, the local *tzadik*, who was called the *rebbe*, could help you. The rebbe helped not only in your religious life, but, as part of the Ba'al Shem tradition, he helped with all sorts of life's problems. If you were sick, you might seek the rebbe's help, or if you were poor, or if you couldn't have a baby, or if you couldn't find a husband for your daughter. The rebbe became the focus of Hasids' lives. His followers would gather at his house for Shabbes and holidays. They would feast with him and sing with him and dance with him and pray with him. In fact, the singing and dancing were considered a kind of Hasidic prayer. It is easy to see Hasidism's appeal to the poor Jews of Eastern European. But it also seemed to attract some of the rich and middle class Jews of Poland too. With Hasidism, the dry religious life of East European Jews became filled with emotion and energy.

In a few generations most of the rebbes' homes became like the courts of minor kings. The different local Hasidic groups didn't recognize a single leader of the whole movement. The *local* rebbe was the highest Jewish authority to his followers. Different Hasidic groups would argue with each other over who had the greatest rebbe. Each rebbe's closest disciples were like court officials and the rebbe's subjects would come from the surrounding area to seek his advice and help or just to enjoy his company and the excitement of being at court. Rebbes also became like kings by passing their position down to their sons and sons-in-law. There began to be Hasidic dynasties, just as there are royal dynasties. Usually the dynasty was named after the town it was located in: Satu Mare (Satmar), Lubavitch, Belz, Gur. Many rebbes also became very wealthy, and lived in great luxury, and paid less attention to the well-being of their followers' bodies and souls than they did to their own power, fame, and wealth. But other rebbes did act saintly and deserved their reputations for wisdom and kindness.

Misnagdim

Although Hasidism spread quickly among East European Jews, its rise made some Jews, especially some rabbis, very unhappy. These opponents of Hasidism were called "Misnagdim," which means "opponents" in Hebrew. There were many things the Misnagdim didn't like about Hasidism. They thought its emphasis on emotional prayer led Jews away from study and the law. They did not like the noisy style of Hasidic prayer. Misnagdim thought all of that wild singing and dancing was undignified. And they didn't like the role of the rebbes. Traditional rabbis were respected for their religious knowledge. But the Misnagdim felt that Hasidic rebbes presented themselves as special spiritual beings, with souls closer to God. Worse, the rebbes claimed that their high spirituality could earn other people credit with God. The Misnagdim believed that no person should be a go-between between people and God. They thought that was idolatrous. Finally the Misnagdim feared that Hasidism was the beginning of a new religion that would divide the Jewish community, leading many Jews away from the true path.

There were probably other, more selfish reasons, that some rabbis opposed Hasidism. Rabbis were the keepers of Jewish law. Their knowledge of the law, and their right to decide what the law meant, gave them a great deal of power over other Jews. But that power was reduced if Jews stopped believing that following the law was the key to being a good Jew and receiving a heavenly reward. Hasidism never said that Jews should not follow Jewish law, but it did say that heartfelt prayer and the favor of the rebbe was even more important. This was a threat to the scholarly rabbis' authority and power.

The Vilna Gaon

The leader of the Misnagdim was Elijah ben Solomon Zalman, one of the greatest Jewish scholars of all time. Elijah was born near Grodno in 1720 to a family of respected rabbis. When he was very young, people recognized that Elijah was a genius. He grew up devoting himself completely to study. He would study by candlelight during the day so he could close the window shutters and not be distracted by activities outside his house. He would only sleep a few hours a day, so that he would have more time to study. It is said that he even put his feet in cold water so that he would not fall asleep while studying.

As a young married man, Elijah settled in Vilna, in the Lithuanian part of the Polish kingdom. He became known as the Vilna Gaon, the Genius of Vilna. Elijah wrote over 70 books. He wrote commentaries on all of the important Jewish holy books. To better understand the Jewish holy books, he even wrote on some non-Jewish subjects, such as mathematics, and astronomy. Elijah believed it was important to have an accurate and complete knowledge of *halacha*, Jewish law, because he thought that there was nothing more important for a Jew than strictly observing the law, down to its smallest detail. Elijah wasn't against Jewish mystical knowledge—he himself was a master of the *kabala*, but he felt that nothing should interfere with the full observance of the law. Elijah felt that because all of Jewish law was given by God it was all of fundamental importance.

The Vilna Gaon was admired and respected by all of the Jews of Europe. Not only was he recognized as a great scholar of Jewish learning, people also knew that he led a very modest and pious personal life. He did not try to use his fame to become rich and powerful. He was never boastful. Outside of his family and small group of close followers, he even avoided seeing people. So when the Vilna Gaon, at age 50, started to oppose the new Hasidic movement, he didn't do it because it was a threat to his wealth or position (he was not rich and had no official position). He didn't do it because the Hasidim treated him like an enemy. They didn't. Like all the Jews of Europe, they revered the Vilna Gaon. The Vilna Gaon was a Misnaged because he believed Hasidism was a threat to *halacha* and Jewish unity.

Elijah, the Vilna Gaon, was very strong and extreme in his opposition to Hasidism. He said Hasidim should be fought by all good Jews, that their writings should be burnt, and that they themselves should be excommunicated. The dispute between the Hasidim and the Misnagdim became so bitter that it sometimes led to violence. The two groups even tried to get each other in trouble with the Gentile authorities. The Vilna Gaon himself spent a couple of months in jail because of the quarrel with the Hasidim. Largely because of the Vilna Gaon's opposition, Hasidism never became very strong in Lithuania and nearby regions. Lithuanian Jews, Litvaks, got a reputation as scholarly and un-superstitious, but also as unfeeling and cold.

After the Vilna Gaon's death in 1797, the bitterness of the disagreement between the Misnagdim and the Hasidim gradually lessened. There were a number of reasons for this. One was that the Misnagdim saw that Hasidim were different from Christians, Sabbateans and other new Jewish movements from the past: the Hasidim did not want to forget about any of the traditional Jewish laws. For their part, the Hasidim began to lay more stress on study and observance of *halacha* than they had in their earliest years, and the study and knowledge of the Talmud plays an important role in today's Hasidic Jewish life.

But the major reason for the peace between Misnagdim and Hasidim in the first years of the 1800s was the rise of a common enemy. This enemy made the differences between the Hasidim and Misnagdim look small. Compared to this new threat, Misnagdim and Hasidim both looked like defenders of the same basic traditional Eastern European Ashkenazi Judaism. The new enemy was the *Haskalah*, the Jewish Enlightenment. The Haskalah was the movement among European Jews to change

Jewish traditions so that Jews could become part of the modern world. We will discuss the *Haskalah* in more detail later. But for now the important thing to say about the *Haskalah* is that it brought all traditional Jews together in opposition to it. Eventually the *Haskalah* made all of its opponents, Misnagdim and Hasidim, into a small minority of the world's Jews, as they remain today.

The Partition of Poland

During the rise of Hasidism, events in non-Jewish politics were taking place that would have a big effect on East European Jewry. Most East European Jews lived in the lands of the Polish kingdom. Now that kingdom was being taken over by other countries. In 1772, parts of Poland were taken over by Russia, Austria, and Prussia. More was taken in 1793. What was left of Poland was divided up in 1795. The Jews of Eastern Europe were now living in three separate countries. Each of these countries was ruled by a strong central government: the Czar in Russia, the Emperor in Austria, and the King in Prussia.

At first this did not change the Jews' lives much. But over time there were important effects. Although Poland had had a weak central government and the local noblemen-landowners had had lots of independence, conditions throughout Poland for Jews had been pretty much the same. But after partition the Jews lived in different countries with different laws and government policies. They also could not travel to or communicate with the other regions as easily as they had before. The strong central governments of their new nations were better able to force their policies on the Jewish population than could the weak old Polish government. Gradually this drew the regions of old Polish Jewry somewhat apart in the way they lived and thought. However, eastern European Jews remained culturally very similar to each other until the catastrophes of the twentieth century.

FIGURE 20 - A street in the Jewish ghetto, Frankfurt, Germany.

Chapter 11

From Ghetto to Emancipation

We now turn our attention from the Jews of Eastern Europe back to the Jews of Western Europe. We have already seen that in medieval times many countries in Western Europe, such as France and England, expelled all of their Jews. These expulsions had different reasons in different countries. But in general there were two groups that wanted to throw the Jews out. One group was made up of *some* members of the Catholic clergy. These priests, bishops, and monks thought that having non-Christians around would have a bad influence on the people, giving them un-Christian religious ideas. They also thought that Jews were evil: killers of Christ and helpers of the Devil. It would be better, they thought, not to have such people as your neighbors.

Another group that wanted to get rid of the Jews was Christian businessmen. In early medieval times there weren't many Christian businessmen, but in late medieval times the feudal economic system began to come apart. It was being replaced by ideas and ways of doing things that encouraged more profit-making businesses. More Christians became businessmen —mostly merchants and bankers. The Jews, some of whom had been merchants and bankers all along, were competition for this new group of Christian businessmen. Naturally, the new Christian businessmen were happy to see the Jews go. Finally, in 1492 and 1498, even Spain and Portugal expelled the Jews.

But there always remained some Jews in some parts of Western Europe. This was especially true in Italy and Germany. Italy and Germany had not yet become unified countries ruled by a single government. Germany was made up of many different countries, such as Saxony, Hesse, and Prussia. The same was true of Italy; Venice, Naples and the Papal States (the area around Rome) were separate countries with their own independent rulers. These are only some of the many states that made up Italy and Germany. Some of these German and Italian states did throw out their Jews. But not all did, although the ones that didn't expel the Jews felt some of the same anti-Jewish pressures as did all of the countries in Western Europe.

By the 1500s, these pressures to expel the Jews had grown very great. By then feudalism was really falling apart and business competition was on the increase. The recent expulsions of Jews from Spain and Portugal brought new Jewish refugees to those towns in Europe that still allowed Jews to live in them. But these Jewish refugees were not very welcome. In addition, in the 1500s important religious changes began among Christians in Europe. These changes affected attitudes toward the Jews. The changes are known as the Protestant Reformation.

For a long time some Christians had been unhappy with the way the Catholic Church practiced Christianity. In 1521, a Catholic monk in Germany named Martin Luther publicly "protested" against the Church and started the Protestant movement, a movement that wanted to reform the Christianity of the Catholic Church. Others, such as John Calvin, also disagreed with the Catholic Church and began their own branch of the Protestant movement. In the long run, the Protestant Reformation was good for the Jews. Once Protestant Christians and Catholic Christians became used to living with each other peacefully, even though they had religious disagreements, it became easier to accept and tolerate Jews. But that took a while. The immediate effects of the Protestant Reformation mostly increased the Jews' problems. On the Protestant side, Luther became angry when the Jews weren't willing to accept his new brand of Christianity. He preached against the Jews, calling them monsters and wolves He said their synagogues should be burnt and their rabbis not allowed to preach. He wrote a pamphlet called "The Jews and their Lies," and he urged Christians to hate Jews and have nothing to do with them. The Catholic Church reacted to the Protestant Reformation by becoming very strict about religion. The Church was more worried about Jewish influence than ever. The Catholic struggle against Protestantism, called "the Counter-Reformation," would often fight against Jews as it was fighting against Protestants. All of these excited religious feelings among Christians were trouble for the Jews. One trouble was a strengthened desire to expel them.

But the Jews were a good source of money and so some rulers were very reluctant to throw the Jews out of their lands. These rulers could tax the Jews as much as they wanted and no one else cared. They didn't want to lose this money sponge, which was so easy to squeeze. A way of satisfying those who wanted to throw out the Jews without actually throwing them out, was by forcing them to live separately from everyone else. That is how the ghettos came into being.

The Ghetto Laws

The first ghetto was created in Venice in 1516. Long before the creation of ghettos, Jews had usually lived together in their own parts of town. But ghettos were something different. The ghetto laws in most cities said that all the Jews had to live there—they had no choice in the matter. The ghettos were completely walled off from other sections of the city, with only a few gates leading in and out of them. At night, the gates were locked, with all the Jews inside, as if they were prisoners. They were only allowed out of the ghetto during the day, and then only if they had business outside of the ghetto. In some ghettos Jews had to pay a tax every time they left the ghetto. And they were forced to wear special clothes, usually a yellow badge, or a funny pointed hat, so that people could make fun of them and hate them. Sometimes the Jews of the ghetto were required to come to a Church where they heard a Christian sermon that insulted Judaism and tried to convince them to convert to Christianity.

The ghettos were in the oldest or worst parts of town. In Venice, an industrial district was made the ghetto. It was the Foundry District (where iron is made). The Venetian word for "foundry" is "getto," and that is where the word "ghetto" comes from. In Rome the ghetto was set up near the Tiber River where the dirty river water would frequently overflow. The neighborhood smelled bad and conditions were unhealthy.

The ghettos were always crowded. And they were dark. The ghetto wasn't enlarged no matter how big the Jewish population of a town grew. This forced the Jews to build upward, adding stories to their wooden homes. The high buildings, pressed right up against each other along the narrow ghetto streets blocked out the sun. Windows facing outside of the ghetto were ordered boarded up so Jews couldn't look at the Christians. This blocked out another source of sunlight (remember, this was long before any electric lights).

The ghettos were also poor. Laws were made that kept Jews out of most professions, and often even business activities as bankers or merchants were forbidden. Many Jews became peddlers, buying up second hand clothes and trying to resell them. They had to make sure that they would get back to the ghetto before the gates were shut for the night. Other Jews became pawnbrokers, a kind of poor person's banker. A pawnbroker gives a small loan to a person. The borrower gives the pawnbroker something to hold, such as a ring, or a coat, until the loan is repaid. If it is not repaid in time, the pawnbroker can sell the thing left by the borrower. The poor Christians benefited from the services of the poor Jewish peddlers and pawnbrokers, who provided cheap goods and loans they couldn't get elsewhere. But these poor Christians often did not see it that way. It just seemed to them that it was the Jews who were always taking their money and taking advantage of their poverty. And because these Jews were poor themselves, they did try very hard to get the best price they could from their Christian customers.

There were some wealthy Jews in the ghettos. Over the centuries, a very small number of ghetto Jews became very rich. The famous Jewish banking family, the Rothschilds, had its start in the ghetto in Frankfurt, Germany. Some ghetto Jews had money because they were doctors to Christians (even though it was usually against the law for a Christian to have a Jewish doctor, it was a law rich Christians were quick to break when they were sick). Some Jews became rich by being financial advisers to the local prince or duke. Others, through a combination of luck and intelligence, managed to save enough as peddlers or pawnbrokers to become merchants or bankers (if they were allowed to).

A number of Jews acquired great wealth during the Thirty Years War. This war took place in Germany in the 1600s. It was a religious war between Protestants and Catholics. Most Jews suffered from the war, being taxed, or even slaughtered, by both sides. But some Jews made money by supplying the armies with food, clothing, and other things an army needs. As neutrals in the war, Jews were in a better position than Catholic and Protestant businessmen to be suppliers. They could travel more freely across war zones to make trades and find supplies.

These rich Jews were a small minority in the ghetto but they were its leaders. Only people who paid enough taxes were allowed to be or choose the leaders, so naturally only the rich became leaders. The ghettos were taxed very heavily by the Christian authorities. Getting money from the Jews was the only reason Christian rulers permitted them to stay in the first place. When the Jews were protected from mob violence, it was because the ruler wanted them to keep making money so they could be taxed. The taxes weren't for any services that the prince gave the Jews, they were just "protection money." Of course in those days most taxes were just that. It is not as though the Christian subjects were getting a great school system or garbage pick-up. But at least the Christians weren't being taxed nearly as heavily as the Jews were.

And ghetto Jews also taxed themselves to pay for all the Jewish community services within the ghetto. Like the earlier medieval Jewish communities, and like the *shtetls* of Eastern Europe, the ghetto had schools to run, officials to pay, and synagogues to maintain. So the community had to collect money for these things as well as tribute money to pay off the Christian rulers. The rich Jewish leaders, as the rich usually do everywhere, tried to get the poor to pay as much as possible, however, since the community's very survival, including the survival of the rich families, required that the Christian rulers get their money, the rich often paid great amounts of taxes and thus becoming the rescuers of the community.

Even in towns where there were no official ghettos, ghetto-like laws and conditions were common. There might be a "Jew Street," where Jews were expected to live. Jews had to pay special taxes and wear special clothes. There were occupations forbidden to them. And Jews always had to worry about anti-Jewish violence.

Nowhere in Western Europe where Jews completely free of laws against them. But in some places the laws were much lighter than in other places. Even in some cities with official ghettos, there were times when the ghetto laws weren't strictly enforced. There are reports that in Rome, which had a ghetto, Jews could be seen on the Jewish Sabbath strolling all dressed up, outside of the ghetto along the banks of the Tiber.

Jewish Life in the Ghetto

It is easy to see the terrible parts of ghetto life. But even though ghetto life was often terrible for most people who lived there, it had some advantages for the Jews of the time. Living together in a walled neighborhood did provide some protection from mob violence. It also made it easier to celebrate Jewish holidays as a community and to organize Jewish schools, courts, slaughterhouses, baths, and synagogues. Jewish life in the ghetto was very intense. The schedule of Jewish events, from the daily prayers each morning and evening, to the weekly Sabbath, and on to the yearly holidays, such as Rosh Hashanah, Chanukah, and Passover, gave a familiar and comfortable rhythm to ghetto Jews' lives. Weddings became community festivals.

The religious atmosphere of the ghetto helped Jews not despair over the poor ghetto conditions. Of course they frequently had to worry about money, but they could also think about the ancient kings of Israel, and the scholars of Babylon. In their minds at least, Jews were often not in the ghetto. They were in the desert with Moses, or Jerusalem with King David, or with Rabbi Akiva in Lydda. Of course this ability to escape the ghetto mentally was easier for people who had more time to pray and study—the better off men, rather than women and poor men. But everyone in the community had some opportunity to escape the ghetto in spirit through Jewish life.

Not only did the Christian rulers prevent Jews from doing much of what they wanted, so did the rules and traditions of the Jewish community. Worried that the whole ghetto would suffer from the behavior of individual Jews, the ghetto community kept a tight control over the lives of its members. This tight control also helped maintain the power of the rabbis and rich families. There was not much room for individuality, for living differently from other Jews. Ghetto Jews probably rarely even wanted anything that the community did not approve of. People did not think of themselves as individuals, with a life independent of the life of the community. The ghetto was not a place where there was much freedom.

Hundreds of years in the ghettos of Europe and of expulsions left a lasting mark on the Jewish people and on how others saw the Jewish people. It created a picture of Jews as timid, pale, and always seeking money. The Jewish peddler became the symbol of the Wandering Jew. The myth of the Wandering Jew became very strong at this time; the Wandering Jew was described as, a homeless peddler condemned to travel forever for his crimes against Christ. Some Christians claimed to have seen the actual Wandering Jew. Jews also were thought of as very "clannish," that is, as a people who stuck together and kept others out. And being in ghettos really did strengthen Jewish togetherness and Jewish concern about the behavior and opinions of other Jews.

Ghetto Jews were also very superstitious, as poor suffering people often are. They believed in all sorts of demons and spirits. There is the tale of Rabbi Judah Loew of the Prague ghetto who made a statue out of clay. He wrote the Hebrew word for truth, "Emet" on the statue and by saying the secret name of God, Rabbi Judah brought this statue, the "Golem," to life. Rabbi Judah gave the Golem superhuman powers to protect the ghetto. But the Golem went wild; the "e" from "Emet" was erased, leaving "Met," the Hebrew word for death. The Golem became a bogeyman to the ghetto Jews.

The harshness of ghetto life also increased belief in and hope for the coming of the Messiah. It is easier to live through bad times if you have faith that good times will come. And the centuries in the ghettos were mostly bad times. The people needed hope that the messianic age and the end to Jewish sorrows was at hand. There were all sorts of legends about how and when the Messiah would come. Belief in the coming of the Messiah was strong in many periods of Jewish history, but the false Messiahs of the 1600s and 1700s, such as Sabbatai Zevi and Jacob Frank, got more attention than others who claimed to be the Messiah at other times.

Capitalism and the Enlightenment

In the same centuries that the ghetto Jews of Western Europe were poor, superstitious and mistreated by the Christian rulers and population, there began changes in Western Europe that would eventually lead to a great growth of wealth, knowledge, freedom, and equality. It took a while before those changes affected the conditions of the Jews. But when they did affect Jews, they changed Jewish history as much as anything has since the beginning of the exile from Palestine.

What were these developments that so affected the Jews? First there was the growth of a new economic system. People, of course, had always wanted wealth, and some people had always tried to become wealthy through business. But now there was more buying and selling than ever. Artisans used to make things alone to sell, or with the help of a few apprentices. Now businessmen owned huge shops producing thousands of items to sell. These huge shops employed large numbers of people. These people had to work for these new bosses because, when feudalism ended, peasant farmers were often thrown off their farmland. They had no other way to make a living than by working in these new workplaces. There was more borrowing to start businesses, and more banking to make loans. Lots of traditional ways of making a living and trading goods and services were replaced by the single activity of buying and selling. Everything was for sale: land, money, labor, natural resources from around the world, and goods produced by the thousands of workers in new factories.

At first all of this economic activity hurt the Jews. The new Christian businessmen wanted Jewish business activity shut down. But eventually opportunities were created for Jews.

Christian society, especially the rulers, realized that their nations' wealth was increased by giving the Jews the freedom to take part in the new business activity. In the beginning it was only a few Jews that were permitted to leave the ghettos. These were often the ones who became financial advisers or bankers to the prince or king (in German lands they were called *Hofjuden*, Court Jews). But eventually many Jews became part of the new economic system, "capitalism."

There were also great scientific changes in the 1600s. Galileo, Copernicus, and Newton explained the movements of the stars in the sky and things on the earth using new ideas. There were important new discoveries in chemistry and biology. And philosophers tried to understand the world without relying on God to explain everything. All of these thinkers told themselves that knowledge should be based solely on "reason," clear thinking about what people can observe with their own senses. They did not want to use magic or supernatural forces to understand the world.

The importance placed on reason made these societies less religious and more *secular*, that is, more concerned with the natural world. People were still religious, including most of the new philosophers and scientists, but when they were engaged in science, philosophy, or even everyday activities, they used non-religious ideas to guide themselves. Religion became less important in everyday life.

When this new style of thinking was applied to politics and society, many old traditions were questioned. Why are some people given more rights than others? Who gives kings and princes the right to boss others around? Why should some people force their non-scientific religious ideas on others? The new thinkers concluded that people are born with equal rights, that rulers should be allowed to rule only as long as the people agree to let them rule, and only as long as they rule for the good of all. Moreover, not only every group but every individual person has a right to believe and worship anyway she or he wants.

Together, all of these ways of thinking about science and politics are called Enlightenment ideas. These enlightenment ideas, along with the rise of the new economic system called capitalism, (which we will describe more in a later chapter) led to the Emancipation of the Jews of Western Europe. (Emancipation means to be set free from restrictions.) Jews were let out of the ghettos, allowed to work in any job, free to worship as they wished, free to mix completely with the non-Jewish population, and eventually, free to help to select the government and even become officials in the government. But this emancipation didn't come all at once. Nor did it come at the same time in every part of Europe.

Glimmerings of Freedom

The first steps toward emancipation of the Jews came in the far west of Western Europe, in the Netherlands and England. In the 1500s the Netherlands had been a province of Spain. The Netherlands was Protestant and Spain was a strict Catholic country. To prevent having Catholicism forced on them, the Dutch people of the Netherlands rebelled against Spain and became an independent country.

At the time of its independence there were many Marranos, secret Jews, living in the Netherlands. These Marranos had left Spain and Portugal to escape the Inquisition. With Spain out of the Netherlands, these secret Jews slowly began to live openly Jewish lives. Although the Dutch people had some doubts about allowing Jews to live among them, they came to accept them. The Protestant Dutch had been persecuted by the Catholic Spanish for their Protestant religion, and so they didn't feel very comfortable with religious persecution of Jews. In addition, the Dutch were becoming a thoroughly capitalist, business-like people, and they quickly saw that their Jewish population could add to the nation's business activity and wealth.

The Jews of the Netherlands made good use of their increasing freedom. Many became prosperous merchants. The Jewish community built great and beautiful synagogues. We know from the portraits that the Dutch artist Rembrandt painted of them that the Jews of the Netherlands began to dress and live very much like other Dutch people. The Jews still kept their separate Jewish community and didn't have full citizenship rights in the Netherlands for over a hundred years more, but in the 1600s they began to become part of the general life of the Dutch nation.

FIGURE 21 – Painting of the interior of Portuguese Synagogue in Amsterdam

Spinoza

One Dutch Jew, Baruch Spinoza, became an important thinker of the Enlightenment. Spinoza, born in 1632, was brought up as a traditional Jew, studying Torah and Talmud. But he questioned the idea that the Bible was written by God and even the idea that God was something other than all of nature taken together. Spinoza wrote that everything could be understood through human reason.

The Jewish community excommunicated Spinoza. They said no Jew should have anything to do with him, because his ideas made people question traditional religious beliefs. Spinoza didn't seem to be too upset. He spent his life peaceably grinding lenses for a living, and continuing to teach that the world is best understood as a completely natural place, a place that is explained through reason. Over the next two centuries, more and more Jews of Western Europe would start to think like Spinoza.

The Jewish population of the Netherlands grew. The first Jews there were Sephardim, Jews originally from Spain. They were joined by Ashkenazim, Jews from the East. The Ashkenazim, who were fleeing the ghettos of Germany and the Khmelnytsky massacres of Eastern Europe, were not welcomed by the Sephardim. They were poorer and less familiar with Christian European manners and ways than the Sephardim were. The Sephardim feared that Christian dislike of the newcomers would cause problems for all of the Jews of the Netherlands. The Ashkenazim and the Sephardim maintained separate communities. In time they got along better and even began to marry each other. But that took time.

England

One Dutch Sephardic Jew, Manasseh ben Israel, even tried to convince England to let Jews into the country so that the Ashkenazi refugees wouldn't all stay in the Netherlands. England had expelled the Jews in 1290. We know that in the late 1500s some Marranos were living in England. One Marrano, Dr. Rodrigo Lopez, was charged with trying to kill Queen Elizabeth and was executed. In the early 1600s the few Jews in England were trying to avoid being noticed. But in the 1640's there was a great change in English politics: a civil war was fought and it was won by the side that gave more power to Parliament than to the king, and more power to extreme ("Low Church") Protestants than to "High Church" Protestants (the High Church Protestants wanted to keep their religion close to Catholicism, but without being part of the Catholic Church.) For a while in the 1650s, there wasn't even any English king or queen. Instead, Oliver Cromwell, who was a general in the Parliaments' Protestant Army, led a military dictatorship.

Manasseh ben Israel thought that Cromwell's government would welcome Jews. It was a government friendly to the rising new business spirit and it hated the Spanish Inquisition. Manasseh thought that Cromwell might be sympathetic to victims of the Inquisition, such as Jews. Also Cromwell-type Protestants loved the "Old Testament," the Hebrew Bible, and were sympathetic to Jews for that reason.

The Cromwell government never officially let Jews back into England. This disappointed Manasseh. But the English government didn't stop Jews from coming in. Even after Cromwell, when England brought back the monarchy, that is rule by kings, and when the High Church Protestants again had the most power in England, Jews were tolerated. As in the Netherlands, Jews became part of the economy and began to live an English style of life. It would still take many years before the Jews of England were allowed full political rights. Only in 1866 could a Jew become a Member of Parliament. And for a long time anti-Semitism made some parts of English society unfriendly to Jews. But from the 1600s onward, the Jews of England have been protected from violence and allowed to worship and work in freedom.

While the Dutch and English Jews were tasting freedom, most Jews of Western Europe were suffering in the ghettos. But in 1791, in France, there was a dramatic change.

The French Revolution

The Enlightenment ideas we spoke of earlier had a great influence in France throughout the 1700s. French thinkers thought it was unreasonable to have a government that was not good for the entire nation and did not have the approval of the people. Also, the new group of business people in France (they were called the "bourgeoisie"), did not want to be ruled by a king and the landowners. In 1789 there was a revolution in France. The leaders of the revolution said that they believed in "The Rights of Man." The slogan of the French Revolution was "Liberty, Equality, Fraternity." The new revolutionary government said everyone should be free (liberty), have equal rights (equality), and support and be friendly to others (fraternity).

But often people don't at first see the full meaning of new ideas. So it was with the leaders of the Revolution. The French Revolution did not give women equal rights, and women still could not vote. Even after the Revolution, France continued to conquer and rule nations in Africa, Asia, and America. There was no change in the French effort to create colonies, treating non-European people as inferior. And the Revolution did not immediately apply its ideas about "The Rights of Man" to Jews either. Some of the Revolution's supporters said that the Jews shouldn't be treated as equals because they were superstitious, backwards, and money grubbers. Others agreed with this nasty description, but said that Jews were like that because they were mistreated by Christians. The argument was won by those who wanted to free the Jews. On September 27, 1791 the Jews of France were given full citizenship. The ghetto walls were torn down and laws against Jews were done away with.

The other countries of Europe felt threatened by the French Revolution. The kings and aristocratic landowners were afraid that the Revolution would spread to their countries and that they would lose their power, wealth, and special privileges. They were right to be afraid. Soon the French Revolutionary armies were on the march. They spread the spirit of the French Revolution throughout Europe. Even when Napoleon became the ruler of France and made himself emperor, his armies carried revolutionary ideas with them. Wherever Napoleon's armies went Jews were emancipated. In 1798, the ghetto in Rome was abolished. Even countries not conquered by France began to change their treatment of the Jews. They saw the new spirit of the times.

Some in the Jewish community were not so sure the freedom offered by the Revolution was a good thing. The ghetto may have been like a prison, but within the prison of the ghetto Jewish life was controlled by Jews. The Revolution said that the Jews were free to live in France as equals, but only if they gave up being a separate community. In 1789, in a famous speech to the revolutionary French National Assembly, Comte de Clermont-Tonnere said that Jews should get nothing as a nation, but everything as individuals. In 1806, Napoleon called together the leaders of the French Jewish community. The gathering was called "The Assembly of Notables." The Assembly, with some reluctance, decided to accept the terms for Jewish Emancipation. This was the beginning of the end of the Jews as a separate nation in Western Europe. It would also present Jews with a new problem: how could they remain Jewish and also participate fully in the life of their country? How could they be French and Jewish? English and Jewish? German and Jewish? This was a problem because, up till this point, being Jewish in Europe was not just having a different religion from the general population; it also meant having a different way of life: different holidays, different sabbaths, different dress, different diets, different educations and different languages. How Jews responded to the new situation is the subject of our next chapter.

Napoleon's armies conquered much of Europe, bringing emancipation to many Jews. But in 1814 Napoleon and his revolutionary French armies were defeated. All of the old kings of Europe came back to power. They tried to undo the changes the revolution had brought. These governments were called "reactionary." A reactionary government tries to reverse progress made toward a free society. Such governments want to go back to the old ways of doing things. One old way of doing things, was keeping the Jews poor, separate, and without equal rights. But the reactionary governments of Europe that came after Napoleon's defeat were not able to fully and permanently reverse the emancipation of the Jews. It was possible to defeat the French armies, but it was not possible to defeat the liberal ideas they spread. Although attempts were made, most West European Jews were not put back in the ghettos. The ghettos that were re-established did not last long. One of the last, the Rome ghetto, was torn down in 1848. So the emancipation of the Jews continued even in the reactionary Europe of 1814 to 1848. Now we must see what the Jews of Western Europe made of this freedom.

FIGURE 22 - Poolstrasse Reform Temple Synagogue in Hamburg,
around 1850.

Chapter 12

Jews Enter the Modern World

Jewish life changed throughout history. Ways of making a living changed. Ways of dressing changed. Ways of speaking, ways of organizing the community, ways of relating to non-Jews—all changed. Religious beliefs and customs changed too. Some religious laws stopped being followed (such as stoning disobedient children to death) and new ones would start to be followed (such as men limiting themselves to one wife.) New prayers were added to religious services and some traditional prayers were forgotten.

In some periods of Jewish history, in some places, the changes were so slow and gradual that no one noticed that there were any changes. But there were also times of great and dramatic change. Often those changes were caused by disasters: expulsions or massacres. But some of the deepest changes came when Jews had an opportunity to mix with a great non-Jewish civilization. When Jewish civilization met Greek civilization in the ancient Mediterranean world, or when Jews met Islamic civilization in medieval Spain, the result was a new form of Jewish civilization. The emancipation of the Jews of Western Europe was another time of great change caused by Jews mixing with another civilization. Not since the Jews were thrown out of Palestine in ancient times had there been such big effects on how Jews lived, what they believed and how they practiced Judaism, nor had there been such an outburst of Jewish creativity since the Golden Age in Spain. In a way, the changes that came after emancipation are still being worked out today.

Historians call the civilization met by the emancipated Jews of Western Europe the "modern" world. We have already spoken about some of the things that made the modern world. The new economic arrangements called capitalism and the rise in scientific thinking were important. So was the decreased part religion played in public life. Finally, the spread of the belief in individual freedom and political liberty helped make the world modern. These things had affected some Western European Jews for centuries. But with emancipation and the political liberation of the Jews, the entire Jewish community had to face the modern world. For many the freedom was exciting and wonderful. For others it was a frightening threat to Jewish tradition. But for all Jews the modern world raised questions that had to be answered. The central question was this: could Jews become full members of this modern world and still remain Jews? The Jewish people created many different answers to this question.

One answer was "no," that Jews could not become members of the modern world and stay Jews. Many traditional religious Jews believed that Jews who lived in the modern world and tried to lead a modern life would find it impossible to follow Jewish laws and customs. For them, all of their traditions were a necessary part of being Jewish. If you stopped following some traditions, you weren't being a real Jew. Jewish traditions came from God, and Jews had to follow all of God's orders. Even the traditional Jews who believed that perhaps some traditions didn't come from God were afraid that if Jews picked and chose which traditions to follow, eventually they would stop following all of them. So it was important to keep all of them. But you couldn't keep all of the traditions if you mixed in the modern world. The traditional Jews decided that it would be best to keep to themselves. They would continue to do business with non-Jews, as Jews had long done and had to do to stay alive, but in no other way would they become part of non-Jewish society.

The Misnagdim and the Hasidim were both groups of traditional Jews. Their bitter feud started to end with the emancipation. They saw that the temptations of the modern world were the major threats to their beliefs. Comparing themselves to a new group of Jews, called Maskilim, the Misnagdim and Hasidim found they had a lot in common.

Maskilim is the word used for Jews who became interested in Enlightenment ideas and the non-religious, secular learning of the modern world. There had been a few Maskilim throughout the 1700s, but none of them had an influence on Jewish society until the career of Moses Mendelssohn. In a way, Moses Mendelssohn became the founder of many of the different modern Jewish movements. Mendelssohn was a German, and it was in Germany that these modern movements got their start. Although most Jews of the 1800s lived in Eastern Europe, Germany was the home of the Jewish thinkers and leaders who led Jews into the modern world.

Moses Mendelssohn

Moses Mendelssohn was born in 1729 in Dessau, Germany. He had a good traditional Jewish education. One rabbi he studied with was a Maskil, and he got Moses interested in secular subjects. Moses followed him to Berlin, and there continued his secular studies. He began to write philosophy books, and his knowledge, along with his honest and sweet character, impressed non-Jewish Germans. A famous German playwright, Gotthold Lessing, wrote a play based on Mendelssohn, called "Nathan the Wise."

Mendelssohn believed that Jews could become full and equal members of German society and still stay Jews. He believed that the Jewish traditions that kept Jews separate (and the ones that made the Germans want to keep them separate) weren't part of the Jewish religion. He said there were Jewish laws and Jewish customs. The laws God gave to the Jews, and these laws Jews were bound to keep, but the customs could and should be changed. Moses Mendelssohn wanted Jews to continue keeping kosher, but stop speaking Yiddish. He wanted them to continue to circumcise their sons, but wear modern European clothing. He wanted Jews to study Talmud, but also to study math, science, and secular German literature. Mendelssohn believed that if Jews made these changes and others like them, they would return to the pure Jewish religion, improve Jewish life, and become more acceptable to the gentiles.

Mendelssohn did his part to create the changes he wanted. He persuaded his many non-Jewish friends to request that the Prussian government (the main one in Germany) give Jews full political rights. He translated the Hebrew Bible and Psalms into German. These translations helped turn the Jews of Germany from Yiddish to German speakers. Going back to Maimonides' opinions, Mendelssohn tried to explain to gentiles and Jews that Judaism is a completely reasonable religion, one that reasonable modern people could proudly follow.

Mendelssohn's influence led to new movements within Judaism, but although he didn't intend it, his influence also ended up leading some Jews, including members of his own family, completely out of the Jewish religion and the Jewish community.

Assimilationism

Traditional Jews were not the only ones who thought it was not possible to join the modern world and remain Jews. But unlike Traditional Jews, these others decided it was better to give up Judaism than give up the modern world. They thought that, in the modern world religion would become very unimportant. It was no longer very important to them. Their plan was to stop being Jews and just assimilate, that is, mix in with the rest of the population. These assimilationists thought it was well worth giving up being Jewish if that was what it took to enjoy European culture and be accepted in European society.

Unfortunately for the assimilationists, it was not enough to just give up Judaism to gain full acceptance into European society; you also had to become Christian. Some people who would have liked to assimilate, didn't mind not being Jewish, but didn't want to become Christian. Others, even though they mostly didn't really believe in Christianity, were willing to officially become Christian. In the 1800s, many German Jews were baptized. Most of Moses Mendelssohn's grandchildren, including the famous composer Felix Mendelssohn-Bartholdy, were brought up as Christians. Many of these Jews who had become officially Christian became important contributors to European civilization. The great poet Heinrich Heine was born a Jew. Karl Marx, the political philosopher was the grandson of rabbis and came from a recently converted family. For a while it looked as though all of German Jewry would eventually be baptized. Some feared that the Traditional Jews were right—Moses Mendelssohn's advice to the Jews to join the modern world would lead to the disappearance of the Jewish people.

Reform Judaism

Not all Jews thought it was impossible to join the modern world and remain Jews. Some Jews believed that Mendelssohn had shown that it was possible, but only if some Jewish traditions changed. They thought that Mendelssohn had not gone far enough with the changes. Mendelssohn was only willing to change customs but not religious laws, but these Maskilim said that the laws themselves were only customs, and that they too had changed in the past. These Jews said it was time for another change, a change that would get rid of all the laws that were out of date. They said the important thing about Judaism was its basic religious ideas. For them these basic ideas were that there is one God who asks us to be just and kind to each other. Jews were people who tried to serve this idea. Modern Judaism should be "reformed" so everything that had nothing to do with being a good person would no longer be a religious law.

The first Reform Jews were mostly wealthy people who wanted a Jewish worship service that looked and sounded "civilized." For them, this meant that it should look and sound like a German Protestant service, with organ music, choral singing, a sermon in German, and rabbis dressed like Protestant ministers. Friday night services were preferred to Saturday morning services. That way, Jews could treat Saturday as a regular business day, as their gentile neighbors did. The first Reform "temple" opened in Hamburg, Germany, in 1819. (Reformers didn't like the word "synagogue"—it reminded them too much of old-fashioned traditional Judaism. That's why they called their houses of worship temples.)

Soon a number of serious religious thinkers became Reformers. Some of these, such as Samuel Holdheim, wanted to quickly get rid of many Jewish traditions. Holdheim said that circumcision, the kosher laws, and services in Hebrew had no place in modern Judaism. Other Reformers, such as Abraham Geiger, were much less radical. They agreed with Holdheim that moral values were the most important part of Judaism, but Geiger felt those values were packaged with traditions that should not be thrown away too quickly. For instance, Geiger was very unhappy with Reformers who wanted to completely forget about Hebrew. He felt that Hebrew had an important role to play in modern Judaism. So there were important disagreements among Reformers. Still, all Reformers agreed that much of traditional Judaism was no longer valuable to Jews. Jews should become Germans (or French, or British, or whatever). They should be full German citizens and live their life like all other Germans did, except that they would have different religious beliefs; they would be Germans of the "Mosaic" faith.

The Reformers believed that besides making Judaism a religion fit for the modern world there would be other benefits from the creation of Reform Judaism. First, many of the Jews who might assimilate because they didn't want to be traditional Jews might become Reform Jews instead. This would prevent a large part of the Jewish population from leaving the Jewish people. Second, Reformers believed that if the old-fashioned backward looking style of Judaism was done away with, Jews would become more acceptable to Christian society.

The Reform movement had good success in Germany, but its greatest success was in the United States. The first large Jewish immigration to the United States was mostly German Jews, who started to come in the 1840s. With Reformers prominent among them, Reform Judaism became the main type of Judaism in America for the next fifty years. The first American Reform congregation was formed in South Carolina in 1824; the first school to train rabbis in America was a Reform seminary, the Hebrew Union College. It was started in Cincinnati in 1875 by Rabbi Isaac Mayer Wise, the German immigrant who became the most important Reform leader of nineteenth-century American Jews.

Orthodoxy

Some Maskilim were very unhappy with Reform Judaism. They agreed with Mendelssohn that Jews should study secular subjects and that Jews could be part of the modern world. They even agreed that some Jewish traditions were only human made customs and that those traditions could be changed. But Jewish law, they felt, was given by God to Moses at Sinai. The laws were passed on and explained by the Talmud sages. Those could not be changed. Those laws every Jew should obey in all their details. That was the main idea of Modern Orthodox Judaism.

It is easy to confuse Modern Orthodox Judaism with Traditional Judaism. Both believed in unchanging Jewish law. But there were big differences: Traditional Jews wanted nothing to do with gentiles and the modern world, while Modern Orthodox Jews did want to be part of the larger society; Traditional Jews barely distinguished between customs and laws, while Modern Orthodox Jews made that difference a major part of their philosophy. Modern Orthodoxy, like Reform Judaism, is a Jewish movement of the last two centuries.

Samuel Raphael Hirsch was the main thinker of Modern Orthodoxy. He was born in Germany in 1808, and for many years was the Orthodox rabbi in Frankfurt. Hirsch founded schools that were models of what he thought a proper Jewish education should be. These schools taught mathematics, German, and science, as well as Hebrew, Torah, and Talmud. Hirsch thought that the Jewish studies were the most important part of the school program, but he didn't think that the secular subjects conflicted with the Jewish subjects. Instead he believed a good understanding of history and the natural world would lead to a better understanding and appreciation of Judaism.

The Science of Judaism and the Historical School

Jews had always studied Judaism from a religious point of view. But there were Maskilim, enlightened Jews, who wanted to study Judaism from what they considered a "scientific" point of view. This, of course, did not mean that they wanted to put Judaism in test tubes and shake it, or to look at it under a microscope. It meant they wanted to study Judaism the way a modern scholar would. They would use the modern methods of history, literary criticism, economics, psychology, and sociology, all of which were being developed in the nineteenth century (1800s). The idea was to get an "objective" understanding of Judaism, that is, an understanding that wasn't based on religious faith or personal feeling. These Maskilim called their approach the Science of Judaism.

Leopold Zunz was the main founder of the Science of Judaism. His first book came out in 1818 and he remained an active scholar until 1872. In his books, which covered many topics in the Jewish past, Zunz demonstrated that Judaism had changed throughout history. Heinrich Graetz, another important member of the Science of Judaism movement, wrote a long, detailed history of the Jewish people. Graetz's history showed how Jews and Judaism had changed through the centuries. This was the kind of evidence that supported the Reformers' opinions, but most members of the Science of Judaism didn't fully support the reformers. Instead, their point of view was represented by still another approach to Judaism, which was named the Historical School.

The Historical School agreed with the Reformers that Jewish law and tradition were not God-given commands that should never be changed. Scholarship had shown that Judaism was created through change and kept alive through change. But who should make the changes? The Historical School did not think that a group of rabbis or scholars should just decide that a Jewish tradition was out of date and then throw it out. That, they complained, was what the Reformers were doing. Instead, the Historical School said that the entire Jewish people does and should decide what stays in Judaism or gets added to Judaism. The Historical School believed that Judaism gradually changes because the Jewish people reject or forget about some old traditions and gradually accept and create new traditions. That is how it had worked in the past and this was how it should work in the future. If the Orthodox said that God created and should guide Judaism, and the Reformers said that an idea of Justice created and should guide Judaism, then we can take the Historical School as saying that the Jewish people created and should guide Judaism.

The Historical School never became very popular or important in Western Europe. Most Jews who didn't assimilate became Orthodox or Reform. But in the United States, in the last part of the 1800s, there arose a new movement called Conservative Judaism that became the most popular kind of Judaism in America. Conservative Judaism was very influenced by the Historical School. The rabbis who started Conservative Judaism were from Europe and were educated in the Historical School kind of Judaism. Conservative Judaism had the same basic idea as the Historical School: the Jewish people were the center of Judaism. In the next chapter, when we discuss the first part of the story of Jews in America, we will return to Conservative Judaism.

Emancipation Continues in the West

The story of the Jews of Western Europe in the 1800s is a story of increasing civil rights and acceptance. Popular hatred and prejudice against Jews did not disappear, nor did the civil rights come all at once. And as we said before, there were even some backward steps on the road to full civil rights, especially when reactionary governments came to power after Napoleon's defeat. But gradually, in country after country, the laws that discriminated against Jews were done away with one by one. Take Denmark for example: in 1814 Danish Jews were allowed to enter the professions. Jews could become doctors, lawyers, and teachers; they could go into any business that a Christian Dane could. In 1837, Danish Jews were allowed to vote in city and town elections, but not national ones. Finally, in 1849, Danish Jews were granted full and equal citizenship.

The full emancipation of Danish Jews was a little earlier than the emancipation of other Western European Jews, but the pattern it followed was typical. Economic freedom and acceptance usually came first. Jews were allowed into new jobs and businesses. This led naturally to mixing with their non-Jewish neighbors on equal terms. Not only did non-Jews get more used to the Jews, but the Jews picked up the customs of the non-Jews and became more like them. All this led to more social acceptance of the Jews, that is, people not only did business with Jews, but they also shared other activities, such as artistic performances, education, parties, and even marriage.

Soon civil rights followed, giving the Jews the same rights others had. The final right Jews gained was usually the right to hold public office. By 1874, when Switzerland fully emancipated its Jews, all the Jews of Western Europe were free and equal citizens. England allowed Jews to sit in Parliament—they no longer had to take a Christian oath to do so. A Jew could be President of the French Republic, and there were no laws discriminating against Jews in Prussia. Many gentiles may have still been personally anti-Semitic, but government policy wasn't. And even the anti-Semitism of the people of Western Europe seemed to be lessening in the first 75 years of the 1800s.

Jews used this freedom to go into many different types of jobs. They entered the professions. There were Jewish musicians and writers. Jews even had military careers. But the majority of Jews were independent business people of one sort or another. Artisans and peddlers became shopkeepers. All sorts of goods were bought and sold by Jews. Through business, Jews became a solid part of the European middle class.

A few Jews became very rich. They were only a small minority of the Jews, but they are important for two reasons. First, their wealth made them leaders of the community. They were the ones who would represent to the governments what the Jews needed and wanted. Second, even though they were a tiny minority of the Jews, many non-Jews thought of these few wealthy and powerful Jews whenever they thought of Jews. Anti-Semites would use these families as examples of rich Jews who secretly controlled the world.

Some of these wealthy Jewish families came from the old Hofjuden, Court Jews, who used to advise European royalty on financial questions. Some were merchants who were very successful. Banking activity is what created many of the greatest fortunes. The Warburgs, Oppenheimers, Seligmans, Montagues and Sassoons were wealthy Jewish families known throughout

Europe. But the wealthiest and most famous Jewish family, a family whose story became a legend, was the Rothschilds.

Mayer Amschel Rothschild was a coin dealer in the Frankfurt ghetto in the 1700s. Through arranging loans and the finances for a local ruler, the Landgrave of Hesse, Rothschild acquired lots of money. He sent his sons to some of the main cities of Europe to start branches of the family business. There was a Rothschild bank in Paris, London, Vienna, and Naples as well as Frankfurt by the early 1800s. The Rothschild banks' business was mostly with governments. They found people to lend money to governments and charged a fee for the service. Governments even came to depend on the Rothschild's money. During the Napoleonic wars, the Rothschilds were the main financial backers of the alliance against Napoleon. Because they were spread out all over Europe, the Rothschilds had an advantage in the international banking business. Having international connections was an advantage that other European Jewish banking families also had.

By the middle of the 1800s, the Rothschilds were not only fantastically rich, they were also part of the highest society in Europe. They were made part of the nobility in France and England. Like some other wealthy Jews, the Rothschilds fought for the rights of Jews. Mayer Amschel Rothschild himself fought for the end of the Frankfurt ghetto.

The influence of some wealthy and respected Jews was seen in 1847 during the Damascus affair. A group of Jews in Damascus, Syria (which was still part of the Ottoman Empire then) had been falsely accused of killing people as part of a Jewish religious ritual. The arrested Jews were tortured and forced to confess. Their case became famous. Rich and respected Jews, such as Sir Moses Montefiore in England, took up the cause of these Damascus Jews. They were able to get their governments to protest the treatment of the Damascus Jews. This was evidence that European Jews were no longer completely powerless, outsiders in European society.

The Montefiores and the Rothschilds were very proud of their Jewish heritage. In those families few of the members abandoned Judaism. But this was not true of all of the rich Jews. Like many of the middle class Jews of Western Europe, some wealthy families forgot about their Judaism. But as the century progressed there seemed to be less reason for Jews of Western Europe, whether they were rich or middle class, to pretend to become Christian. In the days of Heine's and Marx's youth there were still many things Jews were not allowed to do, so ambitious Jews who weren't religious anyway were willing to get baptized to officially become Christian. But by the second half of the century, Jewish emancipation had triumphed throughout Western Europe. Jews could officially stay Jews and still be full citizens. The rush to baptisms stopped.

Jewish emancipation in nineteenth century Europe was part of the fight of the European peoples for a freer, what historians call a more liberal, society. Jewish emancipation was only one cause in this fight for liberty. Ethnic groups fought to have their own national governments. Workers fought for better working conditions and fairer pay. Citizens fought for control of their governments and freedom of expression. There were even the beginnings of the women's rights movement. In 1848, there was a wave of revolutions throughout Europe demanding more of these freedoms. Those revolutions were defeated, but it was a temporary defeat. Not only were Jews emancipated during the 1800s, but throughout Western Europe great progress was made toward an overall more liberal society.

Jews had been key fighters in this struggle for liberalism—not only for the equal rights for Jews, but for all of the liberal causes. The worker's rights movement, the movement for democratically elected governments, the movements for national freedom—all had a high number of Jewish participants. So nineteenth century liberal Europe was in part created by Jews. And if we remember the important part played by Jews in the new capitalist economy, we see that Jews helped to make the entire modern world. It was a world they, very reasonably, thought that they could safely and comfortably live in as Jews. They would be Jews, not as a separate nation living in exile among gentiles as their ancestors had done, but as full Germans, or French, or English, or Italians, who just were of the Jewish faith. Being Jewish would not make them different from their neighbors, except in their religious beliefs. In this way they would fit in. But as we shall see, in Europe, things did not work out that way. However, there was a place where something like that did happen. We now turn to the coming of Jews to America.

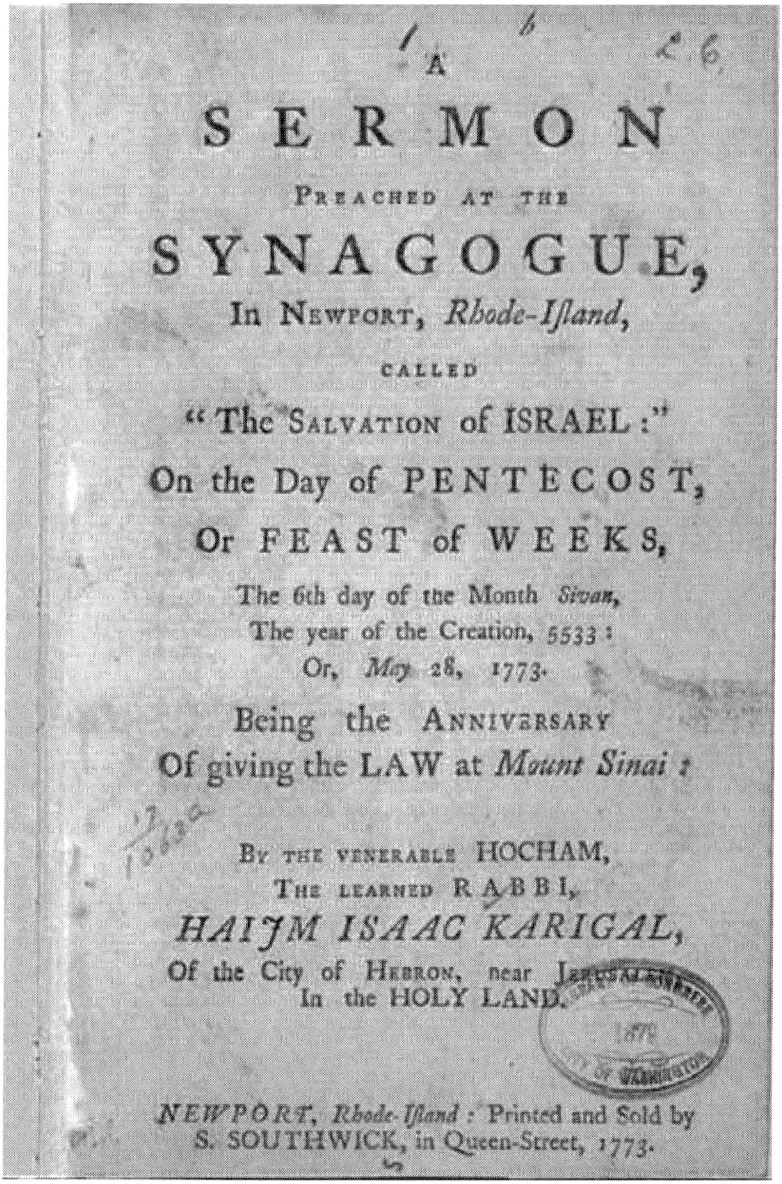

A

SERMON

PREACHED AT THE

SYNAGOGUE,

In NEWPORT, *Rhode-Island*,

CALLED

"The SALVATION of ISRAEL:"

On the Day of PENTECOST,

Or FEAST of WEEKS,

The 6th day of the Month *Sivan*,

The year of the Creation, 5533:

Or, *May* 28, 1773.

Being the ANNIVERSARY

Of giving the LAW at *Mount Sinai*:

BY THE VENERABLE HOCHAM,

THE LEARNED RABBI,

HAIJM ISAAC KARIGAL,

Of the City of HEBRON, near JERUSALEM,

In the HOLY LAND.

NEWPORT, *Rhode-Island*: Printed and Sold by

S. SOUTHWICK, in Queen-Street, 1773.

FIGURE 23 - The first Jewish publication in the Americas.

Chapter 13

The First Jews in the Americas

In 1492, Christopher Columbus sailed across the Atlantic Ocean seeking a water trade route from Europe to India. Columbus was Italian but he was working for the Queen of Spain. He did not reach India, but instead landed on a Caribbean island. That began the European conquest and colonization of the Americas. As you know, this had a big effect on the lives of the people who were living in the Americas. Many were made into slaves or near-slaves. Many more died of European diseases that were new to them. Some were killed in battles with the European conquerors or were outright massacred by the Europeans. The conquest of the Americas had a big effect on Europe too, making nations and many individuals rich, and eventually providing a place for all kinds of Europeans to come to try and build a new life. In this way it also had a big effect on Jewish history, for it led in time to the largest, most powerful, and most prosperous Jewish community ever. It is therefore interesting that Jewish American history begins in the same year that final disaster struck another once great Jewish community. For, as you may recall from Chapter 8, 1492 was the year the Jews were expelled from Spain.

Latin America

Some of the men who sailed with Columbus were New Christians, that is, Jews or the descendants of Jews who had converted to Christianity. There may have been some Marranos (New Christians who were secretly still practicing Judaism) among them. Certainly many Marranos hoped that they would be able to come to America and be able to practice their religion openly, far away from the persecution of the Inquisition. But it did not take long for the Inquisition to set itself up in the Americas. Most of the Americas were conquered by Spain within less than a hundred years after Columbus' first voyage. One large exception was Brazil, which came under the control of Portugal. Both Spain and Portugal were devout Catholic countries where the Inquisition was very strong.

In fact, Jews were not allowed in America, and officially neither were New Christians. But, as we have said, some New Christians arrived with Columbus. Throughout the three hundred years of Spanish and Portuguese colonial rule there were New Christians that came to Latin America. Sometimes they were able to get in because exceptions were made for groups or individuals. More often officials just ignored the rules. Many New Christians were merchants and their skills were wanted in colonial Latin America.

The Inquisition was on the lookout for any New Christians who were secret Jews. They called them "Judaizers." There were times, when the Inquisition thought that it had caught a group of secret Jews, that it would hold a mass execution. These suspected Marranos were publicly burned to death. The ceremony was called an *auto-da-fé*, an act of faith. Infamous *auto-da-fé*s were held in Mexico in 1593 and in Peru in 1639. Some of the people executed probably were secret Jews. Others were probably sincere New Christians, punished because people had grudges against them or because of prejudice against them for having Jewish ancestors.

The Jewish community in the Americas had its start in Brazil, in the town of Recife. From 1630-1654 Recife was controlled by the Dutch. The Inquisition had no power there, so some Sephardic Jews who were Dutch citizens settled in the town, the first openly Jewish people in the Americas. But when the Portuguese reconquered Recife, the Jews had to leave. They travelled to another Dutch controlled city in the Americas, along the North American Atlantic coast. The city was called New Amsterdam.

Colonial America

When this shipload of Jews from Brazil arrived the chief magistrate of New Amsterdam was Peter Stuyvesant. He was no friend of the Jews. Stuyvesant didn't even want to let the refugees from Recife into New Amsterdam. But Jewish merchants back in Holland had influence with the Dutch company that controlled New Amsterdam. The company ordered Stuyvesant to let the Jews settle in the city.

Stuyvesant let them in, but he didn't want to give the Jews equal rights. Under the leadership of Asher Levy, the Jews of New Amsterdam fought for their rights. They wanted to be able to have communal worship services, to have a kosher butcher, and to lead full Jewish lives. They also wanted to have normal citizen rights and duties. They wanted to stand guard like other citizens of New Amsterdam and pay the same taxes. Eventually, in spite of Peter Stuyvesant, and with more help from the Jews back in Holland, they won those rights. In 1664, the British conquered New Amsterdam. Now these Jews were part of the British colonies in North America. The British renamed the city New York, and Asher Levy's community became the first New York Jews.

During the next hundred years of British rule, other Jewish communities were formed in its North American colonies. Synagogues were built in Charleston, South Carolina; Philadelphia, Pennsylvania; Savannah, Georgia; Montreal, Quebec (which the British took from the French in the French and Indian Wars); and New York, where the first synagogue in the colonies was built in 1729. In 1760 a synagogue was built in Newport, Rhode Island. That beautiful synagogue can still be seen there today, the oldest standing synagogue in the United States.

These first American Jewish communities were Sephardic (although Ashkenazim joined them by the 1700s). Their members were primarily people who owned small businesses. There were many craftsmen among them. Bakers, silversmiths, and candle-makers were well represented. The merchants were shopkeepers who dealt in dry goods, hardware, and liquor. In Canada, many Jews were in the fur trading business.

A few Jews were in the slave trade, in which kidnapped Africans were transported to the Americas in horrible conditions and then sold into slavery. Jews were a tiny minority of slave traders and slaveowners though; most slave traders and slaveowners were Christians.

The first American Jewish congregations were religiously observant, but because their communities were small they could not form their own self-contained societies. So there were many intermarriages—Jews marrying people who were not Jews. In addition these small Jewish communities could not put as much pressure on their members to stay observant as could the larger, more self-contained communities of Europe. So many individuals in these early communities relaxed their strict observance of traditional Jewish law.

The colonial American Jews had greater freedom than European Jews of the time had, but they were still usually second class citizens. Conditions were different in each colony, since each colony could make its own rules, but in most places Jews didn't have the right to vote. Colonial Jews were very seldom the victims of anti-Semitic violence, so even if they didn't have equal citizenship they were usually left in peace. Moreover, there was often a sort of respect for Jews in colonial America. The non-Jewish Europeans were mostly Protestants who loved the "Old Testament" (the Christian version of the *Tanakh*, the Hebrew Bible). They identified with Jews, hated the Inquisition, and thought of America as their promised land. They also often thought of themselves as coming to America to avoid religious persecution, and that made them a little hesitant about persecuting others for *their* religion.

By the time of the American Revolution, the war of the colonies to be independent of Britain, there were probably around 3,000 Jews in America out of a total population of 3,000,000—around one tenth of one percent. Most Jews supported the Revolution. The Revolution was fought in the name of freedom. The words of the Declaration of Independence, that "all men were created equal" and had certain rights that couldn't be taken away from them, naturally appealed to the Jews, who had been long denied most rights in Europe. And as American businessmen,

Jews also favored the Revolution, which in part was fought to free American business from British control.

The United States

In 1789, a few years after they won their independence from Britain, the American colonies, now the United States, formed a new government with a new basic set of laws for the nation, the Constitution. Part of that basic law was that in the United States there would be what we now call a "separation of church and state." This idea was something new in the world. People still disagree about what exactly a separation of church and state means, but almost everyone agrees that, at least, it means that the government can't favor one religion over another. In other words, the Constitution said that the United States couldn't treat Jews differently than it treated Christians. Emancipation of the Jews was written into the basic law of the country.

Although George Washington said in his famous letter to the Jews of Newport "to bigotry, no sanction"—America would not approve of prejudice—it took some time before that emancipation became a reality in the lives of all American Jews. At first it wasn't clear that the United States laws overruled all of the local laws. Maybe the United States government had to treat Jews as full citizens, but did that mean that each state had to do the same? Each state of the new country had its own state laws, and it took a while before Jews were emancipated in every state. But by 1826, the year Jews were finally allowed to be government officials in Maryland, Jews were equal citizens throughout the United States.

Part of the reason Jews obtained full freedom in the United States before they did in other countries was surely that the United States was built on the idea of freedom. But another part may have been that Jews were not needed to play the part of the hated, feared and persecuted outsider that they played in Europe. The American idea of freedom and equal rights for all was not applied to the millions of African-American slaves or to the American Indians. Maybe Jewish freedom came a little quicker in America because all those of European origin were bound together in denying freedom to the non-Europeans they lived near and with.

In the first half of the 1800s, the Jewish population of the United States grew rapidly from the immigration of German Jews. Lots of Germans were coming to the United States and Jews were among them. They came for economic opportunities. They also came as a result of political upheavals in Europe. In 1848 there were uprisings of workers, liberals, and national groups throughout Europe against the reactionary governments that came to power after Napoleon's defeat. When these 1848 uprisings were put down, lots of German Jews decided it was time to make their way to America. By 1860, right before the Civil War, there were 50,000 Jews living in America.

These German Jews not only settled in large cities, they also spread across the entire country. Many became travelling peddlers. These peddlers would bring essential goods to isolated towns. Many opened dry goods stores in the South and the West, where they might be the only Jewish family in town. Though the immigrants were poor at first, eventually these shops led to prosperity for many of the families that came from this generation of German Jewish immigrants. The Civil War in particular was, as wars often are, a good business opportunity. Great Jewish companies and retailers started in this period: Levi-Strauss, Neiman-Marcus, Abraham and Strauss, Filene. Throughout the country, the name on the local clothing merchants shop was likely to be a Jewish name.

These German Jews brought with them the attitudes of the Reform movement that was gaining popularity in Germany. In 1854, Rabbi Isaac Mayer Wise, an immigrant from Germany, settled in Cincinnati. He became the organizer of the Reform movement in America. In 1875 he founded a seminary to train rabbis in America, the Hebrew Union College. By that time, Reform Judaism had become the dominant form of Judaism in the United States. Almost all American Jews who belonged to a congregation were Reform Jews. Like the Reform Jews of Germany, they called their synagogues "temples" and believed that it was not necessary to follow all of the traditional laws as long as one remained loyal to the Biblical teachings on justice and morality. Judaism for the Reformers was largely about struggling for a better world. Like the German Reformers, American Reform Jews didn't think Jews were a nation. To them, Jews were a religion. Their nationality was 100% American and Judaism was just their faith. In 1885, the American Reform movement wrote down all its basic beliefs at a meeting in Pittsburgh. That document is called the Pittsburgh Platform, and it was the official position of American Reform Jews for over 50 years. It said that Jews believed in democracy, social justice, and equality, and that many traditional Jewish laws were not appropriate for modern times.

In 1861, Abraham Lincoln became President of the United States, and in April of that year the Civil War began. The immediate cause of the war was the attempt of some southern states to leave the United States (the Union) to form their own country, the Confederate States. But the underlying cause of the war was slavery. The southern states were afraid that the northern states, which were trying to keep slavery out of the new western states, would eventually try to end slavery. The northern states didn't want the south to leave, but they wouldn't let slavery into the new states, even if that was what it took to satisfy the South. If either the North or the South had not cared about the future of slavery there would have been no civil war.

In general, Jews were not prominent in the abolitionist movement, but some were; Ernestine Rose who came to America when she was 26 years old and was the daughter of a Polish Rabbi—although not religious herself—became an activist against slavery (and for women's rights). Not as actively anti-slavery as Rose, still Jews were mostly sympathetic to the Union side. First of all, more Jews lived in the North. But in addition, every year for thousands of years, Jews had celebrated their own release from slavery. Passover taught Jews about the evils of slavery and the need for freedom. On a practical level, Jews understood that a free society with equal rights for all was the safest situation for Jews, who, after all, were also a minority in America.

Still, there were Jewish supporters of the Confederacy. Around three thousand Jews fought in the Confederate Army (around seven thousand were in the Union Army) and hundreds of Jews died in the war. One Jew, Judah Benjamin, became a high government official in the Confederacy. Lincoln said Benjamin was an Israelite who sided with the Pharaohs. Some Confederates doubted Benjamin's loyalty, but there doesn't seem to be any evidence that he wasn't a faithful official of the slave states. Nonetheless, the North's victory in 1865 was welcomed by most American Jews.

By 1881, the German Jewish immigrants and their descendants were well established in the United States. They were increasingly prosperous businessmen, mostly middle-class retailers, but also with some wealthy bankers and industrialist. Their religion was the modern Reform Judaism, which fit in very nicely with the hopeful, forward-looking attitude of American democracy. But that year things happened in Eastern Europe that would lead to major changes in American Jewry. The settled, modern, comfortable, and rather small American Jewish community was about to be joined by a huge immigration of very different Jews. To pick up the story of those Jews, we must return to Europe, to the Czarist Empire.

FIGURE 24 - 19th century American Jewish anti-slavery and women's rights activist Ernestine Rose.

Figure 25 - Jewish family, Eastern Europe, 1909.

Chapter 14

In the Czarist Empire

At the end of the Eighteenth century, the Czars were the all-powerful rulers of a large empire centered in Russia. It was an empire that had undergone few of the changes that were making Western Europe modern. There was not much industry and only a very small middle class. Most people still earned their living on the land. Many of these were serfs, peasants-farmers who were owned by the local landowner. The Russian peasantry was horribly poor and completely illiterate. Throughout the empire, political rights and freedom were unknown. The religious toleration of different kinds of Christianity, by this time common in Western Europe, had not come to Russia. The Czars were Eastern Orthodox Christians and they wanted all of their subjects to be Eastern Orthodox Christians. It troubled the Czars that their big empire contained peoples who were different from the Russians in religion, language, and culture. They hoped that they could "Russify" all their subjects. Even the Czars that wanted Russia to be more modern, more like western Europe, such as Peter the Great and Catherine the Great, hoped that their subjects would become Russified.

With few exceptions, the Czars had kept Jews out of their lands. But when Russia took over much of Poland in 1795, the Czars suddenly found themselves with a large Jewish population. Most Polish Jews lived in Ukraine, Lithuania, and eastern Poland, lands that came under Russian rule when Poland was divided up and taken over by Prussia, Austria, and Russia. Living under the rule of the Czars turned out to be a serious misfortune for the Jews.

The Czars wanted the Jews they now ruled to become Russian. Although the Czars discriminated against most of the many non-Russian peoples in their empire, the Jews seemed to them an especially foreign and difficult minority. They did not live in one place, but were scattered throughout the western parts of the empire. They spoke their own language, Yiddish, and kept to themselves. Jews had their own local governing institutions. And they weren't even Christians, let alone Orthodox Christians. Among Russians, medieval prejudices against Jews were still very strong. Jews were considered infidel killers of Christ. The Czars wanted the Jews to disappear by blending in with the rest of the population. They called this policy "amalgamation."

The Jews had no interest in amalgamating. They were poor, but the Russian peasants were even poorer. Russians were as superstitious and almost as oppressed as Jews. Russian society did not tempt Jews to leave traditional Jewish ways.

For the next hundred years, the Czars' policies toward the Jews swung back and forth between trying to attract the Jews into amalgamating by being welcoming to them and trying to force the Jews into amalgamating by being harsh to them. Sometimes the Czars tried both strategies at once. More often the harsh approach was followed. Even when they tried, the Czars and their advisers didn't seem to know how to be very welcoming. They thought that being a little less harsh would make Jews want to amalgamate. When that didn't work, they would return to intentionally cruel policies to force Jews to amalgamate.

The Pale of Settlement

Russian policy toward the Jews was confused from the start. They wanted Jews to amalgamate, but the first thing they did was to restrict where Jews could live. Jews were not allowed to live wherever they wanted, but instead were required to live in certain parts of the western provinces. The area where Jews were permitted to live was called the Pale of Settlement. It was illegal for Jews to be outside the Pale without special permission.

Throughout the years under the Czars, there were additional rules about where Jews could live and travel. The Pale itself was continually made smaller, crowding the Jews more and more. Sometimes they were expelled from whole villages. Although the authorities wanted Jews to blend with the Russian population, they wanted Jews off the land where the Russian population lived. Sometimes Jews were not permitted to live in big cities and were forced back to the countryside; at other times they were driven from the rural countryside into the towns. Mostly the Jews ended up living in medium and small towns, *shtetls* and *shtetlekh*. These towns were often mostly Jewish and sometimes completely Jewish. The non-Jewish peasants lived in the surrounding villages and countryside. They would come into town to do business with the Jews, but otherwise the Jews and gentiles lived in separate worlds. If the Russian rulers really wanted the Jews to "amalgamate," the law governing where Jews could live was a foolish way to reach that goal.

The Jews taken over by the Czar were poor, and under the Czars they became poorer. Laws were decreed that kept Jews out of many occupations. Most Jews were forced to earn their living by buying and selling. Some, especially after the 1860s, did become successful businessmen, but most were the poorest kind of peddler and stall-keeper. At some points during the 1800s, about half the Jews were living only with the help of charity from other Jews, and most of those other Jews were themselves extremely poor. In addition to not being allowed to do many kinds of work, Jews were much more heavily taxed than other Russians. These extra taxes also contributed to the Russian Jews' extreme poverty.

The Cantonists

Of all the bad things the Czars did to the Jews, none was hated and feared by the Jews as much as its military conscription system, that is, the Czarist way of forcing boys into the army. Men were taken into the Army for twenty-five years. Shortly after Nicholas I became Czar in 1825, the Jews were required to provide Jewish boys for the Army at the age of twelve, so they could have 6 years of preparatory training before starting their 25 years of Army service. This was called the cantonment system and the boys taken were called cantonists. The total of 31 years these Jews spent in the Russian Army meant that almost all of them stopped being Jews. Many simply died from the hard conditions of the Russian Army and the extra rough, anti-Semitic treatment they received. Those who didn't die were pressured to give up being Jews and certainly had no opportunity to practice Judaism in the Army. When these young boys were taken into the Army their families would mourn for them as if they were dead.

The Jewish community was responsible for giving the Army a certain number of boys. As you might expect, rich families were often able to buy their sons out of having to go to the Army. The most common way of getting the boys into the Army was by kidnapping them. The Jewish communities would employ child snatchers, called *khapers*, who would be paid to round up the needed number of boys. Boys would be hidden in a panic whenever there were rumors that *khapers* were about. Naturally such a system made everyone hate the Czarist government, and made the poor Jews resent the rich Jews.

The entire reign of Nicholas I, from 1825 to 1855, was a disaster for Jews. He was the most reactionary Czar, which is a little like being the tallest giant. Under Nicholas there was a serious attempt to destroy the Jews as a community. All official Jewish institutions were closed down. Yiddish was forbidden in any public documents. Most Jewish printing presses were shut down. Censorship was increased, so that all sorts of Jewish books were made illegal and destroyed. And the Pale of Settlement was narrowed further.

Crown Schools

The one thing done during Nicholas' reign that could have been for the benefit of Jews was really of no benefit at all. Jews had long had their own religious school system that all Jewish boys went to: *cheder*, for the youngest boys, then *talmud torah* (a sort of high school) and finally, for the best scholars, *yeshiva*. All these schools only taught Jewish religious books: the Bible, the Talmud, and books about the Bible and the Talmud. Some Jews in Russia were beginning to become interested in giving their children an education in other subjects too. In 1841 the Russian government started schools for Jews. They were called Crown Schools. It looked as though the Czarist government was finally doing something for the Jews. These schools were to teach Jews non-religious subjects, such as math and Russian. To get Jews to come to these Crown Schools, instead of going to the Jewish community schools, the Crown Schools were advertised as not just secular schools but ones where Jews would also get a Jewish education. The Russian government even got a well-respected Jew, Max Lillienthal, to head up the schools. Hebrew was supposed to be taught in the Crown Schools. But the real purpose of the schools was to draw Jews away from Judaism. Most of the teachers were gentiles, completely ignorant of Jewish knowledge and so unable to teach it. Most Jews quickly saw through the Crown Schools, so the schools never got a large attendance, even though boys who went to them were automatically excused from having to go into the Army. Lillienthal quit when he realized what the government was up to. The Crown Schools may not have been as cruel as the cantonment system, but Jews understood it was another attempt to amalgamate them into Russianness and out of Jewishness. In 1852, the Crown Schools were closed down.

Disappointed Hope

In 1855, Czar Nicholas I died and Alexander II came to the throne. Compared with Nicholas, Alexander appeared very liberal. Russia had done badly in the Crimean war and many Russians believed that the country would have to modernize to keep up with the rest of Europe. And since the rest of Europe was becoming liberal, it was thought that to become modern the country must become liberal. Alexander II seemed to think that too, and hope spread throughout the Empire that there would be a burst of freedom in Russia.

At first these hopes seemed like they were going to be fulfilled. In 1861 Alexander freed the serfs; this act alone was a great advance of freedom. Many millions of Russians who had been near slaves were now liberated. But, just like the African-American slaves who were freed a few years later in the United

States, the newly freed serfs weren't given the land or the rights to escape poverty or become equal members of society. Still, their liberation from serfdom was great progress.

Alexander also increased political freedom. Censorship was loosened up. The government still watched what was printed in the newspapers, but it allowed more things to be printed. Books that Nicholas wouldn't have allowed to be published were now permitted. There were even some very small steps toward democracy. Local councils were established, giving Russians some say in how they wished to be governed.

All of these changes affected the Jews. More directly, the end of the cantonment system in 1856 and the limiting of military service to a total of six years instead of 31 years was a great liberation for Russian Jews. The fear of the *khapers* was ended. Some Jews, ones the government called "useful," were allowed to move out of the Pale. Some Jews began to go to Russian schools, some were admitted into the professions, such as medicine and law, and some Jews even participated in the local government councils that had been set up.

But the liberalism of the Russian government did not last long. In 1863, the Poles rebelled against Czarist rule. Their rebellion was crushed. The Russian government decided that the rebellion had been caused by too much freedom. The government responded with more police repression, more censorship, more harsh laws, and more restrictions on minorities.

For Jews things became especially bad when Alexander III became Czar in 1881. Alexander himself was a Slavophile, a person who believed that Russia should stick with traditional Russian ways and reject all of the liberal, modern, and cultural influences of Western Europe. His top minister, Constantin Pobedonostsev, was an extreme reactionary. Repression was increased for all peoples throughout the Empire. The police were given almost unlimited power. Censorship was total. Minorities were not allowed to use their languages in any official places. All of these measures were applied with special force to the Jews.

The May Laws

In 1882 the "May Laws" were announced. These laws severely restricted the movement of Jews. They reduced the size of the Pale once again. Whole Jewish communities were expelled from where they lived. In 1891, all of the Jews who had managed to settle in Moscow were forced to leave the city. Jews were also expelled from St. Petersburg and Kharkov. Almost all rural areas were made off-limits to Jews.

The May Laws also put strict limits, quotas, on the number of Jews that could attend secular schools or be in the professions. The quotas were called the *numerus clausus*, and they were meant to prevent too many Jews from advancing in Russian society. Amalgamation was no longer the government policy toward Jews; the new policy was to keep them down and separate. Part of the reason for this new policy was the beginnings of a Russian middle class of businessmen and professionals. Those "useful" Jews who had been tolerated for their commercial and professional skills were now viewed as competition to Russian merchants and professionals. They were thought not to be needed any more.

Pogroms

Pobedonostsev and the government did not limit their efforts to making the Jews poor and isolated. They also encouraged and even organized violence against Jews. Russia still had plenty of medieval Christian anti-Semitism. Alexander III himself said that Jews were the killers of Christ. Pobedonostsev, like most government officials, was a Jew-hater. Under Alexander III's reign there was a great increase in violence against Jews. The government allowed, encouraged, and sometimes organized mobs to attack Jewish towns and neighborhoods. These attacks were called pogroms. Jews were beaten, tortured, raped, and murdered in the pogroms. Houses and shops were burnt and looted. The first government-inspired pogrom came in 1881, but pogroms continued right into the regime of Nicholas II. In 1903, 1500 shops were destroyed in Kishniev and 45 people were murdered.

In 1905 there were 400 Jewish victims of a pogrom in Odessa. Often these pogroms were started by a rumor that Jews had murdered a Christian child for religious purposes. This was the old blood libel we saw in medieval Western Europe. Angered by such a rumor, mobs of Russians rioted, and terrorized and killed Jews.

The blood libel was sometimes directed at an individual. In 1911 Mendel Beilis, a Jew of Kiev, was accused of murdering a boy and draining his blood in a religious ritual. For two years Beilis was tortured to make him confess. He refused. Finally, the international protest against the case forced the government to bring him to trial, and the evidence against him was so flimsy that the jury acquitted him. But the government said it was glad that the case alerted Russians to the menace of Jewish ritual murder.

The government policy of violence against Jews had many purposes. First, of course, was simple hatred and cruelty. Most Czarist officials were genuine, old-fashioned anti-Semites. But the government also wanted to use the Jews as scapegoats. There was a lot of anger at conditions in Russia. It was a poor, undemocratic, and repressive society. The government wanted to direct blame away from itself. If people thought that the Jews were the cause of the problems, they would get angry at the Jews and not at the government. Angry violence against the Jews was angry violence that wasn't directed at the government.

A third reason for Czarist anti-Jewish policies was the government belief that Jews were the cause of the government's, if not the people's, problems. There were many groups in Russia working to reduce the Czar's power or even overthrow him altogether. The government believed that Jews were the leaders and main forces in these groups. In the next chapter, we will see that there was considerable truth in this belief. While most Jews weren't active opponents of the Czar, many of the Czar's most dedicated and serious opponents were Jews. The Czarist police, who were constantly hunting, arresting, and assassinating the Czar's opponents, naturally came to see Jews as enemies of the regime.

Shtetl Life in Czarist Russia

This poor, unfree, dangerous, and Jew-hating world is where the great-grandparents of most American Jews came from. By all reports, it was a very hard place to live. Yet many memories of that world are warm. Some of this is probably just the nostalgia that usually accompanies thinking about a past that can't be returned to. However, in spite of its harshness, there was also truly satisfying parts of life in the *shtetl*.

In Chapter 9 we described Jewish life in an East European *shtetl* in the sixteenth, seventeenth and eighteenth centuries. Of course there had been changes over time. By the second half of the nineteenth century, the biggest change was that the modern western world was beginning to affect the *shtetl* way of life. We will discuss those effects in the next chapter. But in many ways East European *shtetl* life had not changed over the centuries. For most people, being Jewish remained a complete way of life, a way of life that was quite different from the life of the Christian East Europeans that the Jews lived with. It was not just a difference of religion. Although they lived next to each other and interacted every day, the Jews and Christians of Eastern Europe were like people living in different countries, with different languages, values, beliefs, holidays, dress, customs, rules, schools, and ways of earning a living.

The Jewish language of Eastern Europe remained Yiddish. It was spoken with different accents in different places, but throughout Eastern Europe it was the same language that could be easily understood by all Jews. It was the Jewish language of the family and everyday life, the *mamaloshn*, mother tongue. Men also knew at least some Hebrew, which they studied in school, and women knew at least some of the local language, whether it was Polish, Russian, Ukrainian, Hungarian, Rumanian, Serbo-Croatian, Lithuanian, Czech, or Slovakian. They used the local language in the marketplace. But for both men and women of the shtetl, Yiddish was the language they were most at home speaking.

The Jews lived a very communal life in their towns. Jews knew all the other Jews in the shtetl and usually knew all about one another's lives too. There wasn't much privacy. People cared about what others would think of them if they didn't behave like proper Jews. There were no Jewish police to enforce Jewish customs, but the question "What will people think?" and the fear of being ashamed in the community usually were enough to control people's behavior. In a very extreme case (and this almost never happened) someone could be excommunicated, put in *herem* from the Jewish community. Then no one was to have anything at all to do with the excommunicated person; it was as if he or she was dead. If someone left the Jewish people voluntarily and converted to Christianity, they were also treated as if they were dead. Their parents would mourn for them and sit *shiva*, and then never speak of them again. Having a child convert out of Judaism was the most shameful thing that could happen to a family.

Of course, *halacha*, Jewish law as interpreted by the rabbis, was supposed to be the guide to all behavior. As always, some people were much stricter in following the law than others. But almost all agreed that it would be best to follow all the laws and traditions. The picture of the ideal Jew was of a man with *peyes* (sidelocks), and an uncut beard. His head was always covered. He always wore *tsitsis*, a fringed religious undergarment. He wore a long dark overcoat. He prayed at *shul* three times a day and studied Talmud daily. He said all the proper blessings when he woke, washed, dressed, ate, made love, and went to sleep. In all of his activities he followed the detailed laws of *halacha*.

Although they tried, most men couldn't fit this picture completely. This ideal said that Torah, its study and its law, were the center of Jewish life. But *shtetl* tradition also recognized that if there is "no bread, there is no Torah." *Shtetl* Jews recognized that you have to earn a living before you can attend to your religious life. Earning a living, getting *parnoseh*, was the most common daily concern of Jewish families in Eastern Europe. Most Jews were poor and all were a minority that the government discriminated against, so making a living was a challenge. The most common Christian job was farming, but Jews were not allowed to own land, so they couldn't farm. The struggle to make ends meet, usually through some kind of small business dealings, kept men from praying and studying as much as they would have liked. You could not dress as a fully traditional Jew if it got in the way of work. Not all work allowed you to get to synagogue for the afternoon prayers. A long, uncut beard might get in the way of some tasks. So even though they would have liked to spend their days arguing and shmoozing with others about the meaning of the law and the correct understanding of Biblical stories, most Jews had to spend their days *shlepping*, sewing, buying, and selling. The ideal picture of prayer and study did not fit the poor working person.

Women and Men

The idealized picture of "the Jew" meant a Jewish man, not a woman. Men and women had very clear and different roles in *shtetl* society. Boys began their education at three years old and usually continued it till at least thirteen. Good students might go on to advanced studies. Some men remained students all their lives. All of their studies were of Jewish law and tradition, their only texts the Bible, Talmud, and commentaries on the Bible and Talmud. Their school languages were written Hebrew and spoken Yiddish. At best, girls went to a separate school for a couple of years. The girls would learn to read Yiddish and perhaps learn to write enough Yiddish to compose a letter. Sometimes, girls would also learn how to sound out Hebrew words, but they were never taught what they meant.

There were all sorts of ceremonies to mark a boy's life, starting with his *bris*, circumcision, when he is born on through to his thirteenth birthday, when he becomes a bar mitzvah (there were no bat mitvahs for girls). There were other ceremonies for boys along the way. The only ceremony in which the girl played a central role was her wedding, when she was the *kalah*, the bride. Then the whole town gathered to celebrate her and her parent's success, for the goal of every girl's life is to marry and have children (this seems to have been true in many traditional societies). Weddings sometimes lasted for days, with plenty of food, drink, music, and dancing. A *badchan*, a sort of wedding jester who would tease and make fun of everyone, was the wedding party's master of ceremonies. Parents great joy was in "*naches fun kinder*," pride and pleasure in one's children, and nothing gave parents more *naches fun kinder* than bringing them to the *khupe*, the wedding canopy.

If she didn't get married, a girl's life was a failure. All boys were supposed to get married too, and their life was also considered incomplete if they didn't. But although very important for them, marriage and children were not considered the whole point of a man's life. His ideal purpose was to study and fulfill God's law.

After marriage, a woman was supposed to give birth to and raise lots of children in a proper, Jewish, Kosher home. *Kashrut* (keeping kosher) made housekeeping complicated. Many foods were completely forbidden, *treyf*, such as animals that ate other animals, animals that didn't have a split hoof, and shellfish. Animals that could be eaten, such as cows and chicken, had to be killed in a special way. Even then they might not be kosher if they had something about them that the kosher laws forbid. Women would sometimes bring a chicken with a spot of blood on it to the rabbi to see if it was kosher. Milk, and things with milk in it, *milkhiks*, couldn't be eaten with meat, *fleyshiks*, and a kosher home even needed two sets of pots and dishes, for meat and dairy food. Thankfully, the main part of the shtetl food—potatoes, breads, noodles, onions, and fish—could be eaten with either milk or meat. This was called *parve* food.

Women also had to worry that clothing was kosher, no mixing wool with linen or silk. Women had to prepare the house for holidays, such as Passover when all *chometz*, breads and cakes made with leavenings, must be out of the house. Every week, Shabbes required a special meal and a thoroughly cleaned house. Mothers were also responsible for child care. Sons were off to school and synagogue at an early age. Daughters would stay around the house, where they were helpers and apprentices to their mothers, learning all they needed to know to run a Jewish home.

Only when it came to getting *parnoseh*, making a living, did men and women's roles overlap. The small Jewish businesses were family business and everyone pitched in with the work. In fact, because the men would try to pray and study as much as possible, often the women would spend more time earning the family living than the men did. The shtetl market would be filled with more women than men, doing most of the buying and much of the selling too.

Marrying off the children was the parents' main family responsibility. But just marrying them off wasn't enough; the children had to be married well. To understand what shtetl Jews considered marrying well, you must understand how the shtetl viewed and valued types of people.

Sheyne and Proste Yidn

First came the *sheyne yidn*, the "beautiful" (most distinguished), Jews. They were the most honored, respected and powerful people in the *shtetl*. To belong to the *sheyne yidn*, you had to be well educated or rich. These two groups overlapped, because rich men wanted their daughters to marry well educated men, and naturally, those who were well educated were eager to marry into wealthy families. These marriages were usually arranged by the families through a *shadchan*, a matchmaker. Poorer people also had marriages arranged by the *shadchan*, although sometimes poorer people just married "for love."

The *sheyne yidn* were made up of rabbis, religious officials, scholars and wealthier merchants and shopkeepers. They didn't work with their hands and they followed the traditional laws closely. If you had lots of ancestors who were like that, you had big *yiches*. "*Yiches*" was your family background and connections. When couples were being matched, the families were trying to size up the other family's *yiches*. Everyone tried to marry as big a *yiches* as they could. A big dowry, money that the bride brought to the marriage, could get big *yiches* in the groom's family. At the margin of the *sheyne yidn* group, families who were reasonably well-off but weren't educated or rich enough to be fully part of the *sheyne yidn*, were the *balabustn*, the middle class merchants. They were always trying to become *sheyne yidn*. Giving a daughter a big dowry, so that she could marry a rabbi's son, was the quickest way to get there.

The common people were called "*proste mentshn.*" The *sheyne yidn* looked down on the *proste*. Although some common people were proud to consider themselves *prost*, it was usually insulting to be called a *proste*. It meant you were ignorant and rude and would act in un-Jewish ways. The *proste* worked as porters, tailors, shoemakers, peddlers and small shopkeepers. At the bottom of society were the beggars, the *shnorers*.

The *sheyne* and the *proste* would ridicule each other. The *sheyne* looked down on the *proste's* bad manners and careless attention to Jewish laws. The *proste* thought many of the *sheyne* were hypocrites who put on airs. But they all, *sheyne* and *proste* alike, considered everyone as legitimate members of the same community. Even the *shnorers* had their place, and giving charity, *tzedukah*, to them was a religious duty.

Jewish Hearts and Jewish Heads

Even though people worried about their *yiches*, the quality the *shtetl* most often praised had nothing to do with education or wealth. It was *mentshlichkayt*, humanity. A real *mentsh*, a real human being, was mature, honest and kind. The poorest, most ignorant Jew might be a real *mentsh*, and the most outwardly pious, wealthiest Jew might not be a *mentsh* at all. Even a gentile might be a *mentsh*, although shtetl Jews clearly thought *mentshlichkayt* was most commonly a Jewish quality. If one had a *yidish harts*, a Jewish heart, that meant one had a feeling, humane heart, a heart that made one a *mentsh*. It was the *yidisher hart* that made you a *mentsh*. The *proste* would often accuse the *sheyne yidn* of being pious on the outside without having a Jewish heart. "Better a Jew without a beard than a beard without a Jew," they would say.

A *yidisher kop* (a Jewish head), meant that you were clever and used your brains. Jews were proud of this quality too. Jews considered themselves not only clever, but reasonable. They settled things with words, not violence. At least that was the *shtetl* stereotype of the Jewish character. *Shtetl* Jews looked down on their gentile neighbors as drunken, violent people who were ignorant and superstitious. In truth, the *shtetl* Jews were a fairly superstitious group themselves. This is one area, besides the marketplace, where *shtetl* and Christian peasant culture did interact, sharing each other's superstitions. Jews were always worried about the evil eye, a harmful spirit that caused misfortune and would hurt you if you boasted about good fortune or even pointed out anything good at all. *Shtetl* Jews were forever saying *kinanhora*, "no evil eye," to prevent any good thing they said from inviting bad luck.

Shul, Rabbi and Holidays

The *shul* (Yiddish for synagogue), was the center of Jewish communal life. Not only did men go there to pray every day, not only did the whole town gather there for holidays, but that is also where communal problems were discussed and decisions often made. It was often a noisy place, filled with arguments, shouting, constant interruptions, anger, and laughter (for biting humor was as much a part of the Jews' talk as *pilpul*, the sharp debates that were part of their studies). In other words, the *shul* was nothing like what many Americans today would consider a dignified house of worship. And although it was where Jews prayed, in some ways it was more like a town hall and clubhouse than a church, mosque, or temple.

A large town might have a few *shuls* and many rabbis, and a small one might not have any. But even the smallest town needed to be close to a rabbi. The rabbi was a judge, pastor, psychotherapist, and teacher rolled into one. If two Jews had a business dispute, the rabbi decided who was right and what should be done. The rabbi declared whether a particular chicken was kosher and when an abandoned wife could remarry. He comforted people in their *tsores* (troubles), gave them hope for better times, explained the meaning of the Bible, and lectured them about right and wrong. He was the most respected man in the *shtetl*.

The *nogid*, the rich man, was also a powerful figure in the *shtetl*. He had an honored seat in the synagogue along the eastern wall. He had a lot of influence on how the community funds were spent. A nogid would also often serve as the *shtadlen* of the *shtetl*, the person who spoke on behalf of the town to the government. This "speaking" usually meant bribing. If Jews had to give money to the authorities in order to protect the community, it made sense to have the rich people do it.

The busy and hard routine of chasing *parnoseh* was broken up every week by *Shabbes* (Shabbat, the Jewish Sabbath), when all work stopped, best clothes were worn, and everyone ate as well as they could afford to. Shabbes was supposed to be a little taste of heaven here on earth, a time for family, study, song, and rest. It was considered a gift God gave the Jews.

The holidays also broke up life's routine, and *shtetl* Jews thought of the year's calendar according to the holiday schedule. Late summer was *sliches*, days of prayerful preparation for the early fall Days of Awe, *Rosh Hashanah* and *Yom Kippur*, the New Year's Day and Day of Atonement, when your sins could be forgiven and your fate for the next year was decided. *Succos* and *Simches Torah* marked the middle of Fall and the start of the year's Torah reading. The winter holidays of *Chanukah* and *Purim* broke up the cold East European winters with light and lighthearted fun. *Pesach*, Passover, marked the Spring, and *Shevues*, the holiday celebrating God's giving the Jews the Torah, came at the beginning of summer. All of these holidays had special foods, prayers and customs. And just as *Shabbes* was separate from the *vokhedike* (weekday), ordinary life, so *yontevs* (holidays), were special times of the year.

Although this traditional Jewish life was still strong in the nineteenth century, it was beginning to come under attack from new ideas and forces. That is the story of our next chapter.

FIGURE 26 - Map of the Pale of Settlement, the area of the Russian Empire where Jews were required to live.

FIGURE 27 - Ceremony discharging Alfred Dreyfus from the French army,
a cover illustration of a French newspaper, 1895.

Chapter 15

New Ideas, New Troubles, New Hopes

Starting in the middle of the nineteenth century, the traditional *shtetl* way of life started to change. The *Haskalah*, the enlightenment, which had begun in Western Europe fifty years earlier, came to the *shtetl*. But because it was half a century later, and because the East European Jews were different from the West European Jews, and especially because the countries of Eastern Europe were different from the countries of Western Europe, the *Haskalah* was different in Eastern Europe than it was in the West. Lithuanian, Polish and Russian Jews entered the modern world differently than French, English and German Jews did.

As we saw in the last chapter, the Czarist Empire was not a liberal country. Unlike in the West, democracy was not growing and discrimination against Jews was not decreasing. Jews who wanted to enter modern life as free and equal citizens had two problems:

1) Russian society and the government would not accept them, and,

2) Even if they were accepted, they wouldn't be free because the whole society was not free.

Many Jews thought this second problem had to be tackled first. They thought that once society was free and fair to all, the Jews would be automatically accepted as free and equal people. So many Jews became part of the movements for freedom and equality. One such movement, the movement for socialism, played a large role in Jewish and world history.

Socialism and Capitalism

When it came to politics and society, the first Enlightenment thinkers believed that if everyone had the same legal rights and the government didn't interfere in people's lives too much, then society would be free and equal. But later thinkers thought that wasn't quite right. They thought that some of the rules of society weren't fair, so that even if everyone had to obey the same rules, the results might be an unjust society. The rules that these thinkers questioned were the rules of property, the rules that said who owned what. The property rules of nineteenth century Europe created an economic system called capitalism. We still live with pretty much the same rules, so we still live in a capitalist economic system. Under these rules, private individuals are allowed to own farmland, factories, hospitals, railroads, office buildings, newspapers, television networks—all the places people work to make things and provide services a society needs. Most people don't own any of these things and therefore have to work for the people who do.

In the nineteenth century, this resulted in a society of rich owners and poor workers. The socialist movement arose to change this system. There were many different types of socialists, but the central idea of most of them was that the wealth of a society should be produced in common and shared equally, so there would be no rich and poor, only a society of prosperous equals.

The most influential socialist ideas were those of Karl Marx, a German philosopher born in 1818. Marx's grandfather was a rabbi, but Marx's father, like many German Jews of the time, converted in order to be accepted in German society. Marx himself was against all religion, and even expressed some of the common anti-Jewish feelings of the time.

Marx believed that throughout history every society had been divided up into groups. He called these groups classes. Whichever group controlled the economy he called the ruling class. They would, he believed, also control the politics, laws, and ideas of a society. Marx said that in some societies the ruling class had been warriors—kings and knights. This "nobility" controlled the economy by owning all the land. But in capitalist society it was the owners of industry who were the ruling class. He called these owners the bourgeoisie.

Different societies had different classes, but they all had some classes that did most of the work. In some societies it was a class of slaves, or serfs or poor peasants. In capitalist society it was the industrial workers. Marx called them the proletariat, or the working class. Marx felt that because the working class created the wealth of a society, they should be able to control it; they didn't need the owners at all. Instead of creating wealth and giving most of it to the owners (which is called "profits") and only getting a small part back (called "wages"), Marx wanted the working class to do away with all private ownership of industry. Everyone should work as best they can, and the wealth created should be divided fairly to take care of everyone's needs. Workplaces and industrial machinery should be public property.

Of course Marx didn't think the owners would voluntarily agree to this new "socialist" arrangement. He expected they would use their control of the laws and culture to discourage the socialist movement, and, if necessary the police and army to stop it. But in the end, Marx was confident that the working class would win and create a socialist society. This society would not only do away with rich and poor, but Marx seemed to think it would automatically do away with all social injustices. There would be no more sexism, or racism, or national hatreds, or war, and of course, no more anti-Semitism. But before there could be such a society, there had to be a complete overturning of capitalist society. There had to be a revolution—a socialist revolution.

Marx believed the socialist revolution would come when the working classes of the world united because they understood that they had more in common with the workers of other countries, religions, and ethnic groups than they did with their own ruling class. The international working class would make the revolution and bring in the age of worldwide justice.

These ideas appealed to many Jews. Jews had long hoped and expected for justice to rule the world, but thought that it would have to wait till God sent the Messiah to the world. Now Marx was saying that poor people themselves, by joining together, without any help from Heaven, could make the world good. Marx also said that all the working classes, Jewish or Christian, Muslim, Hindu or Buddhist, Black or White, Asian, African, American or European—all of them had no real differences worth fighting each other over. Instead they had a common fight with the ruling classes of owners.

FIGURE 28 – Karl Marx

The victory of the working class was guaranteed by Marx just as the coming of the Messiah was guaranteed by the Talmud. Also like the Talmud, Marx's writings and his followers' writings were complicated. You could study and debate their meaning endlessly, especially when you were trying to figure out what those ideas told you to do. For Jews of the Czarist Empire, a movement that united them with gentiles to fight oppression and bring about a just world without discrimination, a movement that made use of their study and debating skills and was, according to Marx, definitely going to win, was a movement that many wanted to be a part of.

Marx also said that religions were false beliefs that promised poor people that things would be better after they died, or told them that God meant for them to be poor and work hard. Religion kept people from fighting for fairness and a better life. In those days, most socialists, but not all, agreed with Marx that religion confused people and held people back. Jews who had lost faith in the Jewish religion were drawn to socialism, and Jews who were drawn to socialism would usually lose faith in Judaism. Non-religious Jews are called "secular Jews," and most socialist Jews were secular.

Socialist Parties

Before long there were many different types of socialists and even many different types of Marxists. Sometimes these different socialist groups fought against each other as much as they fought against the bourgeoisie. There were anarchist socialists who were against any kind of government that used any force. There were socialists who thought that peasants would make the revolution instead of the workers. There were socialists who thought the revolution would be legal and gradual, and socialists who thought the revolution would be violent and sudden. Jews were in all these movements, and often were their leaders.

The most historically important socialists called themselves Social Democrats. In much of Western Europe there were strong Social Democratic parties by the end of the nineteenth century. The biggest one was in Germany, and its founder and leader was a Jew, Ferdinand Lassalle. He made the German Social Democratic Party one of the strongest political parties in Germany and the strongest socialist party in the whole world. A Jewish woman, Rosa Luxembourg, was a leader of the Social Democrats in Poland and Germany. In Austria, Victor Adler became a leader of Austrian socialism, and the French socialist, Leon Blum, eventually became Prime Minister of France. These were only a few of the Jews who were important in the socialist movement. They never said they were fighting for Jewish rights, but for the rights of all working people. Of course, they and their parties were strongly against anti-Semitism, just as they were against any oppression. They wanted equal rights for all. But they thought the best way to get those equal rights was to build a socialist society. In addition to believing that they shouldn't make a special fight against Jewish oppression, these Jewish socialists often had no or very limited personal interest in Jewish culture or their own Jewish heritage. But many historians think that there are reasons so many Jews became socialists and socialist leaders: Jewish history made Jews oppressed outsiders who identified with the lower classes, and the Jewish religion put a strong emphasis on justice. Justice for the oppressed is what socialism is about.

The Bund

Clearly Jews played an important role in the socialist parties of many nations. But some Jewish socialists thought that Jews needed a socialist party of their own. The main socialist parties thought that religion and nationality weren't important. Jewish workers, they thought, should join with the German, French, Polish, Lithuanian, and Russian workers and fight as non-Jewish workers for socialism. Many Jewish socialists agreed with this, but others thought this was unfair and wouldn't work. It was unfair because the Jewish workers had as much a right to speak their language, Yiddish, as Russian workers, for instance, had to speak Russian. In addition, they said that trying to make Jews part of the Russian socialist parties just wouldn't work, because Jewish workers didn't want to give up their Jewish customs to join the socialist movement.

In 1897, in Vilna, the General Jewish Worker's Union of Russia, Poland and Lithuania was formed; it was known as "the Bund." The Bund, at first under the leadership of Arkady Kremer, fought to organize Jewish factory workers to strike for better working conditions. Bund organizers spoke to the Jewish workers in Yiddish. The Bund thought its job was simply to bring Jewish workers into the worldwide fight for socialism.

But soon Bund leaders, such as the young Vladimir Medem, became influenced by the ideas of Chaim Zhitlowsky and Simon Dubnow. Both Zhitlowsky and Dubnow said that Jews were a nation like other nations, even though Jews did not live in one territory. They said that like other nations, Jews should be able to rule themselves. Zhitlowsky emphasized the Yiddish language as the glue that held Jews together, and Dubnow emphasized Jewish history as the common bond between Jews. But they agreed that even if modern Jews stopped having traditional Jewish religious beliefs, still their language, customs and culture—their whole Jewish heritage—made them a separate nation. So the Bund started to fight not only for Jewish rights as workers, but also for Jewish rights as a nation. The Bund's idea of the Jewish nation was not that Jews should have their own country, but that they did have, and should nourish, their own culture. This culture was based on the Yiddish language and a common Jewish history—it was not just a religious faith. In fact, the Bund considered itself "anti" all religion, including Judaism, but "pro" national cultures, especially Jewish culture. The Bund said Jews should protect this culture and that this culture should be given the same rights as other cultures. So besides organizing Jewish labor unions and strikes of Jewish workers, the Bund organized Jewish cultural activities. There were Yiddish schools, Yiddish choruses, Yiddish lectures, and Yiddish reading groups organized by the Bund.

Yiddish Literature and the Yiddishist Movement

The Bund's idea of a non-religious Jewish culture was supported by the growth of Yiddish literature. Sholom Abramovich, better known by his pen name, Mendele Mokher Sforim, is considered the "grandfather" of modern Yiddish literature. He was born in Pereyeslav, Ukraine, in 1835 and his first writings were in Hebrew. But Mendele wanted all Jews to be able to read what he wrote, so he began to write in Yiddish. He wrote satires of Jewish life, that is, humorous stories that pointed out the problems, foolishness, and narrow ways of Jewish society. Although these stories were critical of Jewish society, they always showed a love and concern for the Jewish people. Mendele developed the modern style of writing Yiddish.

Mendele was followed by Sholom Rabinowitz, the famous Sholom Aleichem, who was also born in Minsk, twenty-four years after Mendele was born there. Like Mendele, Sholom Aleichem wrote humorous stories about Shtetl life. But Sholom Aleichem's stories weren't as critical of the Jews as Mendele's were. Instead, his stories just tried to show all of the common, interesting, and unusual characters in Jewish society, so Jews could laugh at themselves. But it wasn't a mean or disapproving laughter; it was a loving and affectionate laughter. He wrote about poor people and the problems they had, often leading to silly situations when they tried to solve their problems. Sholom Aleichem's stories also showed the warm and human face of Jewish life. His narrators and characters chatted with the readers in a relaxed way, so that when you read a Sholom Aleichem story it was just as if you were listening to a neighbor's stories about friends you both knew. Sholom Aleichem was the most beloved of Yiddish writers, and many Jews felt that his stories were the best picture of the lives and feeling of the Yiddish-speaking Jews of Eastern Europe. Tevye the Dairyman, a poor shtetl Jew, who was always having friendly, informal talks with God and was always trying to marry off his many daughters, was the main character in some of Sholom Aleichem's stories. Teyve became known around the world when his stories were made into a musical play, "Fiddler on the Roof."

I. L. Peretz, born in Poland in 1852, was the third giant of Yiddish literature. Although Peretz was not traditionally religious, he believed that the values in the Jewish religion and traditional Jewish customs were highly moral. He believed that traditional Jewish life taught that poverty should be ended, great riches were unjust, and oppression should be fought. Peretz retold old Jewish stories to bring out these lessons. He turned Hasidic folklore into socialist fairy tales. Peretz also wrote about politics, literature and history. He, more than anyone else, helped established the idea that the Yiddish language was the key to Jewish life. He also helped tie the Yiddish language movement to the socialist movement.

Peretz died in 1915, Sholom Aleichem in 1916 and Mendele Mokher Sforim in 1917. By the end of the First World War in 1918, the golden age of Yiddish literature was past. Still, for a few more decades, Yiddish poets, novelists, essayists and journalists continued to create a rich literature. But it came to a pretty sudden end in Europe when Hitler murdered most Yiddish speakers. Stalin also helped end Yiddish literature with anti-Jewish policies, including the murder of most of the Yiddish writers in the Soviet Union. We will talk more of that later.

The Yiddish language movement, sometimes called the Yiddishist movement, got a big boost at a conference called to discuss the Yiddish language at Czernowitz, in the Romanian part of the Austrian Empire, in 1908. The Conference was a gathering of Jewish writers and thinkers. They passed a resolution declaring Yiddish a national language of the Jews. (They argued over whether to say it was THE national language of the Jews. Some thought Hebrew would be neglected if they said that.) The Conference also encouraged the support of Yiddish culture through education and standardization, that is, making the spelling and vocabulary of Yiddish the same in all regions.

The Bund was part of the socialist movement and part of the Yiddishist movement. Before World War I, Yiddish was the mother tongue of most Jews, and most Jews were also very sympathetic to socialist ideas. Naturally the Bund was very strong at that time and had a big influence on Jewish life. But things happened to the socialist movement, the Jews, and the world, all of which weakened the Bund.

Socialist Politics and the Outbreak of World War I

In the years before World War I, socialists had been arguing among themselves about the best way to end capitalism and bring about socialism. The largest socialist party, the German Social Democrats, came under the control of socialists who said that gradual and legal methods were the best way to establish socialism. They said socialists should run for election, and then, when they won control of the government, they should pass socialist laws. Eduard Bernstein, a Jew, was a leader of this group of socialists. These socialists that wanted a gradual, legal, and peaceful change to socialism were called Revisionists.

Other socialists believed that the capitalist ruling class would never give up power peacefully. They thought a revolution, probably with some violence, would be needed to start a socialist society. Throughout the European socialist movement there were Revisionists and anti-Revisionists. Often they were in the same political party.

In 1914, World War I broke out. On one side of the war were France, Britain, and Russia (eventually joined by America). On the other side were Germany, Austria, and Turkey. Historians still argue over what caused the war, because it was never clear what all the fighting was about. In part it may have been a fight to see which parts Asia and Africa each European country would control. In part it may have been caused by the idea that war was a glorious thing. It was actually set off by the assassination of a prince of Austria by a Serbian nationalist.

Some socialists said that socialists should tell the workers of all these countries to refuse to fight or make weapons. After all, these socialists argued, if workers in all nations are supposed to unite to fight the ruling class of owners, why should they fight each other?

But most of the big socialist parties, especially the Social Democratic Parties in Germany and France, supported the war. The German Social Democrats told the German workers to fight against the French workers and the French Social Democrats told the French workers to fight against the German workers. Other socialists felt this was a complete betrayal of socialism. The socialists who were against the war noticed that most of the socialist war-supporters were Revisionists. This war support gave Revisionism a bad name among socialists who took seriously the idea of international workers' unity. The socialist movement began to break in two. There were Jews on both sides of this break.

At this time there was a small Russian Social Democratic party that had many Jews and Jewish leaders, such as, Julius Martov, Paul Axelrod, and Leon Trotsky. Years before World War I this small party had itself already split in two. One part of the Russian Social Democratic Party was called the Mensheviks and the other part the Bolsheviks. The Bolsheviks believed the Russian Social Democratic party should be tightly controlled by the leaders. They said the leaders should be indirectly elected by the party members, and after the leaders were elected the leaders should say exactly what everybody in the party should do, almost like an army. The Mensheviks were against this. They thought it would lead to a party dictatorship. The Bolsheviks were led by V.I. Lenin and the Mensheviks were led by the founder of Russian Social Democracy, Georg Plenkhanov. There were Jews on both sides of this split too. Martov and Axelrod were leading Mensheviks and, after a while, Trotsky was a leading Bolshevik.

Both the Mensheviks and the Bolsheviks agreed that the war should not be supported by socialists. In fact, after the war, when looking back, most socialists, including the Revisionists, thought that the horrible war should not have been fought. Everyone agreed that the war had hurt working people and socialism. At first, both Mensheviks and Bolsheviks also agreed with the anti-Revisionists that the Revolution could not be achieved by legal methods. This made sense, because in Russia there wasn't any democracy, so there was no legal way to change society. But soon things would happen in Russia that would change the Mensheviks' minds.

World War I and the Russian Revolution

World War I lasted four years, from 1914 till 1918. Many millions of soldiers were killed. The war was mostly fought in two places: in Western Europe, where Germans fought against the French, British, and later Americans, and in Eastern Europe, where Austrians and Germans fought against Russians.

The millions of Jews of Eastern Europe suffered greatly from the war. Part of the suffering was shared by all the peoples of Europe. Jews died in the trenches and fields as soldiers. Their homes were destroyed by the passing armies. They went hungry because the war caused food shortages. But in addition to all of the "normal" horrors of war, Jews had special suffering. Usually, people become angry and afraid during war. They also forget the basic rules of decent behavior. Those are perfect conditions for anti-Jewish violence. And that is what happened during World War I; angry, frightened people massacred Jews. In addition, the Czarist government of Russia considered its own Jewish subjects enemies and expelled hundreds of thousands of Jews from their homes. Most of these Jews died of disease and starvation.

In 1917, Russia was losing the war and Russia itself was in terrible condition. Millions of soldiers were dead, villages and farmland had been destroyed, the economy had fallen apart, starvation was everywhere. Many Russians were disgusted with the war and the Czarist government. In February there was a revolution that overthrew the Czar. It was not a socialist revolution, but it was a democratic revolution. Russia was to be ruled by elected officials. Socialist parties participated in this revolution and were well represented in the Russian parliament.

In October of that year, the Bolsheviks, with the support of some workers and soldiers in St. Petersburg, overthrew the new democratic Russian government. They took power and declared that they would end the war and start to build a socialist society. The Bolshevik government did end the war with Germany, but before they could attempt to build a socialist society they were in a civil war in Russia. The Russians who wanted the Czar back or hated the idea of socialism fought against the new Bolshevik government. They were called the "Whites." The Bolsheviks and their allies were called the "Reds."

Many Russian socialists didn't think it was right and wise for the Bolsheviks to attempt an undemocratic socialist revolution. But when the Bolsheviks won power, their success convinced many socialists that the Bolsheviks understood the right way to build socialism. And in the war against the Whites, all socialists supported and fought for the Bolsheviks. The Bolsheviks now called themselves Communists, and their Bolshevik government they called Soviet. The Bund, the Mensheviks, and all other socialists were part of the Red Army on the side of the Soviet government during the Russian Civil War.

The Civil War was a catastrophe for Russian and Ukrainian Jews. The Czarist White Armies, especially in Ukraine, were very anti-Semitic. They massacred Jews throughout the war. They raped Jewish women and robbed Jewish towns. Not since the Khmelnytsky massacres of three hundred years earlier had so many Jews been murdered. In addition, there was widespread starvation throughout Russia that hit the Jews particularly hard.

Peasants could grow and keep a little food for themselves. The Soviet government fed its soldiers first and any food left-over went to city factory workers. There were Jewish soldiers and factory workers, but most Jews were small town shop-keepers, and they were the last to get food or make a living during the Civil War.

The war ended in 1921 with a Soviet victory. After World War I and the Civil War, the Jews of Russia were poor and terrorized. The new Communist government, which was unfriendly to all religion and against even small businesses, left no hope for a renewal of traditional Jewish life.

But Jewish socialists were hopeful that a free, socialist society would be built. This would be a society of equals, with full liberty for all and no tolerance for anti-Semitism or any kind of racism. Yiddishist socialist Jews expected the Soviet government to support non-religious Jewish cultural life.

At first these hopes seemed justified. The early Soviet government did fight anti-Semitism. There were many Jews in the government at the highest levels. But freedom for Jews, or anyone else in the Soviet Union, did not last long. The Communists wanted to run the whole country in the same undemocratic way Lenin said the party should be run. All political parties other than the Communist Party were outlawed. Secret police arrested all opponents of the government. The Mensheviks, the Bundists, and other socialists were not allowed to organize. Their leaders were arrested, sometimes killed. After a few years of encouragement, Yiddish culture stopped being encouraged and started to be repressed.

By ten years after the Russian Revolution, Joseph Stalin had gathered all the power in the Soviet Union to himself. He was an absolute dictator. Bolshevik "socialism" did take the factories and the land from the capitalists (and from small shopkeepers and peasants too), but it did not give control to the worker. It gave control to the Communist Party. And now Stalin controlled the Party and everything else in the Soviet Union. First Stalin had everyone who disagreed with the Communists killed. Then he had any Communist who disagreed with him executed. Then he killed anyone who he thought might disagree with him or who he thought didn't praise him enough. People lived in terror of Stalin and his police. Before he was done, Stalin and his accomplices imprisoned and intentionally starved millions.

It was a great tragedy for the socialist movement that Stalin called his terror government of murder, no freedom, and total control a "socialist" government. Except for the fact that an owning capitalist class had no power, Stalinism had little to do with the original vision of the socialists. Neither workers nor anyone else had freedom or rights. Stalin forced the people to work hard so that the Soviet Union did build some industry and drag itself out of complete poverty. The Soviet Union did have some important socialist features. There was health care for all, education for all, and no unemployment. But the most important parts of socialism, respect for all people, democratic control of the economy, and lots of personal freedom, were totally absent. Stalin created a nightmarish society. The Soviet Union was the opposite of what socialists believe a society should be.

Jews, once again, suffered what all others did, and then had some special suffering of their own. The many Jewish Mensheviks and Bundists were wiped out. The Jewish Bolsheviks, including leaders like Trotsky, were murdered. These groups Stalin killed because they were political enemies or personal rivals. But Stalin was also an anti-Semite. Officially the Soviet government was against ant-Semitism. In 1931, it even established Birobidzhan as a region for Jews and Jewish culture, in Siberia. But really, it often acted out Stalin's and traditional Russian hatred of Jews. At the end of his dictatorship, in 1952, Stalin had the last remaining Yiddish artists and writers arrested and murdered. When Stalin died in 1953, there were still descendants of Jews living in the Soviet Union and there were still Jews with the word "Jew" marked on their identity cards, but there was almost no Jewish life in the Soviet Union. And today, Birobidzhan has only a few Jewish residents and a few Yiddish symbols remaining.

Zionism

But now let's go back to well over a century before Stalin's death. Up until the nineteenth century, for almost two thousand years

Jews believed they were in exile. They believed that their true homeland was Palestine, the Land of Israel. Jews had lived in many countries over that time—Persia and Babylonia, Spain and Turkey, Germany and France, Poland and Russia—and in some of those countries, at some times, Jews were well off and happy. But even when they were, the traditional Jewish belief remained that someday all Jews would return to *Erets Yisroel*, the Land of Israel, where they would be truly at home.

Throughout the centuries, some very religious Jews went to Palestine to live a religious life. Sometimes old people went there to die and be buried. These old and religious Jews would be supported by charity collected from Jews in the Diaspora, that is, in countries outside of Palestine. But for most Jews, the end of exile was a job for God. God would send a Messiah to lead the Jewish return to Palestine. Till then the Jewish people were supposed to remain in exile.

Starting with the Haskalah at the end of the eighteenth century, many Jews began to question the idea that they were in exile or that someday they would return to Palestine. Reform Jews said they were already at home in the countries they lived in. They said "we may have a different religion than the majority of our countrymen, but we can be just as German, French, or English as they are. Our job is to get fully accepted, and it looks as though that job will soon be done."

Socialists Jews agreed. Like most Reform and some Conservative Jews, non-religious socialist Jews rejected the idea that Jews were in exile. They mocked the notion that a Messiah would bring Jews back to Palestine. What Jews needed to do, the socialists said, was become part of the local working class in every country they lived in. In a socialist world, they would be at home wherever they were.

So the wish for a return to Palestine was dying among Jews entering the modern world in the 19th century. And even the hope for return among the religious was not a practical expectation, not anything religious Jews should do something to bring about.

But at the same time the religious hope for return was being put aside by many Jews, something else was going on. A small movement began that thought there were good political and cultural reasons for Jews to establish a Jewish homeland in Palestine. This Jewish nationalist movement was surely influenced by all of the nationalist ideas that were then popular in Europe. There are many different types of nationalist ideas, but usually nationalism says "our people" (whoever "our people" happen to be) should have our own country to rule, all our people should live in it, and our culture should be kept alive there. In the 19th century, there were nationalist movements among Italians, Greeks, Germans, and Hungarians, to name just a few. Zionism was a Jewish nationalist movement (the Bund could be seen as another form of a Jewish national movement). Zion was the name of a hill in Jerusalem near where the ancient Temple stood. Zion came to stand for all of the Land of Israel. That is why the movement for Jewish return to Palestine, Jewish nationalism, came to be called Zionism.

The first Zionist sort of ideas got little attention. In the mid-1800s a German Jewish writer named Moses Hess wrote a book that imagined a Jewish nation in Palestine called "Rome and Jerusalem." Hess imagined a Jewish country in Palestine as part of a socialist world, but his book was soon forgotten. At around the same time, small groups called "Lovers of Zion" met in Eastern Europe to encourage Jews to go to Palestine. But the first book that explained the reasons for modern Zionist ideas was written in 1882. It was Leo Pinsker's *Auto-Emancipation.* The title means "freeing yourself."

Pinsker was a Russian Jew who at first thought that Jews could assimilate and become good Russians. But the pogroms changed his mind. Even though Pinsker knew that the Czarist government had encouraged the anti-Jewish riots, he saw that there was lots of deep hatred against the Jews. He wasn't sure of all of the reasons for this hatred, but he thought the reasons weren't just religious. He believed that one of the reasons people hated Jews was that the Jews were without a country of their own. People looked down on them. Pinsker believed hatred of Jews would always exist as long as Jews were a homeless nation. He decided that Jews would never be safe in non-Jewish countries. They needed their own country, where Jews would have political power.

Asher Ginzberg, better known by his Hebrew pen name, Ahad Ha'am, "one of the people," was another important early Zionist. Ahad Ha'am was more worried about the survival of Jewish culture than he was about the physical safety of the Jews. Ahad Ha'am thought that without a Jewish homeland, a place where Jews could lead fully Jewish lives, Jewish culture was going to get weaker and weaker until it faded away completely. He wanted a Jewish homeland where Jewish art, music, philosophy and literature would become strong and creative again. He did not expect all Jews to live there. He thought that many Jews would continue to live in the diaspora. But the Jewish homeland would serve as a spiritual and cultural center for all of the world's Jews. If we call Leo Pinsker's Zionism "political Zionism" we can call Ahad Ha'am's Zionism "cultural Zionism." Like the Yiddishist Bund, the cultural Zionist wanted to preserve Jewish culture. But they were convinced that Jewish culture couldn't be preserved without a territory to be a Jewish homeland. And for the cultural Zionists, only Palestine, with its place in Jewish history and memory, could serve as that territory.

There were many other types of Zionism. Some were part political and part cultural and part something else. Joseph Brenner and A.D. Gordon wanted Jews to return to Palestine to become farmers again. They thought it was unhealthy for a people not to grow their own food and work their own land. Because of anti-Jewish laws, there had not been many Jewish farmers in Europe for centuries. Brenner and Gordon wanted to bring Jews back to physical labor and the land

There were also many socialist Zionists. In fact this group, called the Labor Zionists, became by far the largest Zionist group. They believed that the Jewish working class needed its own homeland where it could build a socialist Jewish society, just as workers in Germany and France would build a German and French socialist society. The Labor Zionists didn't think that socialism would get rid of national groups, just make them equal and peaceful. But to be equal, Jews needed their own land. In fact, Labor Zionists believed that because of anti-Semitism, Jews could only join the struggle for socialism in their own country, where Jewish workers could struggle against Jewish bosses without worrying about gentile persecution of Jews. Nachman Syrkin was an early leader of Labor Zionism, and Ber Borochov a Labor Zionist who thought that Zionism had to be a part of Jewish Marxism. Most of the leaders of the Jewish settlement in Palestine and the new State of Israel were some kind of Labor Zionist.

The Dreyfus Affair

In 1894, Captain Alfred Dreyfus of the French Army was arrested. He was accused of being a traitor to France. It was said that he had sold French military secrets to the German Army. There was little evidence against Dreyfus, but he was quickly tried in a military court, thrown out of the French Army, and sent to prison on Devil's Island.

Dreyfus was Jewish. The evidence against him was faked. The real spying was done by someone else. Dreyfus was completely innocent. But because he was Jewish, many people in France thought he must be guilty or thought that even if he wasn't guilty, it would be bad for France and the French army to admit that Dreyfus' trial wasn't fair and that he was really innocent.

When Dreyfus was first accused, many French people let their fear and hatred of Jews come out. There were people in the streets who shouted "Death to the Jews!" Newspapers wrote about the need to stop Jews from trying to take over France and the world. Others said that Jews weren't really French and didn't belong in France.

Some French liberals came to Dreyfus' defense and fought French anti-Semitism. The popular novelist Emile Zola wrote a famous article "*J'accuse*," ("I Accuse") In that article, Zola angrily condemned all those who unfairly put Dreyfus in prison because they hated Jews.

The Dreyfus Affair, as the case was known, divided all of France into two camps, those for Dreyfus and those against him. Against Dreyfus were the Army, the Church, and most other conservative parts of French society. For him were liberals, socialists and most other progressive parts of French society. Even after Dreyfus was proved innocent and let out of jail four years later, the controversy didn't go away. The Dreyfus Affair brought out strong feelings in France for the next forty years. You could usually tell a lot about a French person's politics by finding out their opinion on the Dreyfus Affair, especially his or her attitude toward Jews.

Theodor Herzl

Theodor Herzl was an Austrian Jewish journalist. He had only a slight Jewish education and was quite ignorant of Jewish history. He did not, in any way, lead a Jewish life. In 1895 he was in Paris reporting on the Dreyfus Affair for his newspaper. For a few years he had been thinking about the situation of Jews in Europe and he was concerned about the growing anti-Semitism he saw in France, Austria and Germany. As a reporter, Herzl was at the public ceremony where Captain Dreyfus was humiliated and kicked out of the Army. He saw the crowd act wildly, full of Jew-hatred. That helped him decide that Jews must have a land of their own. He felt that since Jews would never want to give up their Jewish identity, and others would always hate Jews, Jews would never live safely, in peace, in non-Jewish countries. The only solution was to leave the non-Jewish countries and live in a land of their own. In 1895 he presented these ideas in his book, *Der Judenstaat* (*The Jewish State*). Herzl had never read Pinsker, but he had come to the same conclusion.

Although he preferred Palestine, Herzl did not much care where the Jewish state was set up. He thought Argentina might do, and at one point wanted to try Uganda. But he came to realize that only the ancient Jewish homeland of the Land of Israel had a chance of drawing Jews to it. So he became a Zionist. He wrote another book, *Altneuland* (*Old-New Land*), where he described Jewish yearnings for a return to Zion and his own vision of a future Jewish state in Palestine.

But Herzl didn't just write about his beliefs. He organized and worked politically to make them happen. He met with rich Jews to get them to give money to settle Jews in Palestine (an activity some rich Jews had already been doing). He met with Jewish community leaders to get their support. He also met with political leaders in Europe to see if they would help. The Ottoman Turkish government controlled Palestine at that time, so Herzl tried to get the help of its ruler, the Sultan of the Ottoman Empire. None of these people helped as much as Herzl had hoped.

Herzl finally decided he needed to organize other Zionists so that they could work together. In 1897 Herzl arranged the first international Zionist Congress in Basel, Switzerland. Zionists from all over Europe attended, and the movement of political Zionism got underway. It might have seemed very unrealistic at the time. Turkey had no interest in creating a Jewish homeland in Palestine. In Western Europe and America, liberal Jews weren't interested. Zionism was slightly more popular in Eastern Europe, but even there most Jews were Bundists, or Social Democrats, or religious, and all of those types weren't interested. Herzl's idea seemed like a hopeless dream. But in *Old-New Land* Herzl wrote "If you will it, it is no dream," that is, if you work hard enough, it could really happen.

FIGURE 29 – Theodor Herzl at the First Zionist Congress in Basel, Switzerland, 1897.

The Zionists did work hard. And something close to their dream did happen. How it happened, the story of Jewish settlement in Palestine and the establishment of the State of

Israel, we will discuss in Chapters 18 and 19, but the story we will tell there was greatly shaped by the Zionist ideas we describe in this chapter. So it pays to notice that these early Zionist ideas did not pay much attention to the Arab people who were already living in Palestine. A few Zionists, such as Judah Magnes and Martin Buber, did. They wanted Palestine to be the official homeland of two peoples, Jews and Arab Palestinians. But most Zionists didn't give it much thought. Some Zionists didn't seem to realize there already were people living in Palestine. Others thought, like most Europeans of the time, that non-European peoples, were unimportant or inferior and didn't have to be taken into account. Many Zionists were socialists, and they just assumed that the arrival of a modern, socialist Jewish working class would somehow be good for the Arab peasants of Palestine. One way or another, the early Zionists gave little thought to the Arab Palestinians.

All of these ideas—Zionism, Socialism, and Yiddishism, combined with all of the poverty, destruction and anti-Semitic violence caused by wars, pogroms, and revolutions—shook and changed the world's greatest Jewish population, the Yiddish speaking Jews of Eastern Europe. The most common Jewish reaction to all the turmoil was to leave their shtetls and cities throughout Eastern Europe. A few Zionists went to Palestine. Others went to South Africa, South America, Mexico, and Canada. Some settled in Western Europe. But of the millions that left Eastern Europe between 1881 and 1924, most went to the United States. It is to their story that we now turn.

FIGURE 30 – "Welcome to the Land of Freedom," a newspaper illustration from 1887 showing immigrants, including Jews, on the steerage deck of a ship looking at the Statue of Liberty.

Chapter 16

From Old Country
to *Goldene Medina*

Between 1881 and 1924, the population of American Jews went from tens of thousands to millions. In those forty-three years, Jews streamed out of Eastern Europe, fleeing the oppression and poverty they suffered there. At first they came mostly from the small *shtetl*s. Later they came from big cities too, such as Warsaw, Minsk, Vilna, and Lodz.

Leaving the *shtetl* meant leaving friends, family, and a way of life that the emigrants knew well. Most of the people left behind, such as father and mother, would probably never be seen again. Parents hated to see their children leave. Often a married man would come to America without his family. He hoped that he could save enough money in America to bring over his wife and children. Many men did this. But some abandoned their old European families and started new families in America.

At first the poorest and least educated Jews came. They were the ones with little to lose. Rabbis, and other *sheyne yidn,* were not so quick to give up their power, property, and position. In addition, the *sheyne yidn* worried that it would be difficult to maintain a traditional Jewish life in America. They understood that the freedom and choices available in America would allow many Jews to give up the old ways. The rabbis thought of America as an impious, un-kosher land.

Eventually all kinds of East European Jews became part of the great migration to America, educated and uneducated, very religious and not religious, villagers and city people—but almost all of them came poor. Some fled persecution, but it was economic opportunity that most were seeking.

The Journey

Many Jewish emigrants began their journey on foot. They may have gotten enough money together to buy a ticket on a boat to America, but first they had to get to the boat. These *fusgeyers* might walk hundreds of miles to get to a port, or at least dozens of miles to get to a train that would take them to a port. Lucky ones may have begun their journey in a horse drawn wagon. But no matter how they traveled, just getting to the boat was often an adventure of many weeks or even months. There were robbers and thieves to avoid. All kinds of people would try to cheat the simple *shtetl* Jew out of the little money he or she had. Many emigrants didn't have the proper papers allowing them to travel legally, so they had to be smuggled across borders or bribe officials. Just getting to the boat required strength and courage.

Things did not get easier on the boat. Most Jews came over on the cheapest ticket—steerage. Steerage was always terribly crowded. The food given steerage passengers was mostly slop and soggy bread. Jews who wanted to keep kosher couldn't even eat all of that. They had to survive for weeks on whatever food they managed to take on board. People were sea sick much of the time, throwing up everywhere. The washrooms were dirty. And the noise of the steam engines could be heard in steerage all the time. There was no fresh air down in steerage, so people spent lots of time exposed to the weather on deck. After weeks of such conditions, the immigrants arrived in America, tired, sick, and frightened.

But in some ways the worst, most frightening part of the whole trip to America was the final part. That was when American officials decided whether they were going to let an immigrant into America. After 1892, the place where this decision was made was Ellis Island, an island in the port of New York.

On Ellis Island every immigrant was examined to see if he or she should be allowed into the country. Immigrants were examined for contagious diseases. Their lungs were listened to for tuberculosis. Their eyes were examined for infections. In a few cases, people would be sent back to Europe. The possibility of that happening is what made passing through Ellis Island so terrifying. More often a sick person was quarantined, that is, forced to stay in a hospital on Ellis Island for a few weeks before being allowed into the country.

If you were not held up by the medical examiners, it took a little over a day to pass through Ellis Island. Then you were out on the streets of New York, where perhaps a relative or friend would meet you and take you in. Most Jews stayed in New York or went to other big cities. This chapter will describe what New York was like for the Jewish immigrants of the time. But conditions were pretty similar in the other cities Jews went to, such as Cleveland, Boston, Baltimore, Philadelphia, and Montreal.

The Lower East Side

New York was very different from a *shtetl*. The *shtetl* Jew went from a small, old fashioned town to the most modern big city in the world. In the *shtetl* you knew everyone; New York was filled with millions of strangers. In the *shtetl*, everyone understood everyone else's role and position; In New York, no one seemed to have a fixed role or position. People changed jobs, earned money, lost money, moved away, stopped being religious, gained status, and lost status. The *shtetl* was a poor and strict place, but it was familiar, and everyone knew who they were and what they were supposed to be doing. New York, and the other big American cities that the East European Jews came to, was surely exciting for many immigrants, but for most it was a confusing, strange place— a place where nothing was certain.

The first generation of East European Jewish immigrants mostly settled on the Lower East Side of Manhattan. They shared it with other immigrants of the time, Italian, Irish and Slavic. The Lower East Side became the most crowded neighborhood in the world. People lived in "tenement" buildings. These were narrow buildings, four or five or six stories high, jammed up against one another. Each floor of the building contained a few apartments. The apartments had small, dark rooms. Only a few rooms at the front and back of the building had much daylight from windows. Of course, there were no elevators in the buildings. If the building had running water, there might have been a shared bathroom in the hallway. Otherwise, there was an outhouse in the small yard behind the building.

These apartments were very crowded. Sometime a number of families would share one apartment and almost always there were many people living in each room. People shared beds with brothers, sisters, parents, and grandparents. Beds were being used by someone or other day and night. There was little chance for privacy in a tenement apartment.

The streets of the Lower East Side were no less crowded than the apartments. They were always filled with people, wagons, and horses. Peddlers and shopkeepers selling their wares, housewives buying food, children playing, workers heading to work, students going to school—the streets of the Lower East Side—Delancey, Rivington, Hester, Grand, Essex, Orchard, Ludlow—were always noisy and bustling. On some streets you heard more Yiddish, on other streets more Italian, but throughout the neighborhood you found evidence of the great mixture of peoples. Italian bakeries were on the same streets as kosher butchers. Yiddish signs hung next to Polish signs. A traditional Jewish synagogue (*shul*) was close to a Ukrainian Orthodox church. The immigrants from each nation mostly socialized and worked with their old countrymen, but they lived next to and had many dealings with all the other groups.

Work

After finding a place to live, the immigrant next had to find work. The chance to get out of poverty was the main reason most Jews had come to America. Some became peddlers or small shopkeepers, as they had been in the old country, but most found jobs in the small factories that were starting to spring up in New York City. There were factories of many different kinds, but the biggest industry and the one that employed the most Jews were the "needle trades," that is, the various kinds of clothing manufacturers. Throughout New York, in warehouses, lofts and even small tenement apartments, hats were stitched, coats were cut, pants, blouses, dresses, skirts, shirts, suits, and gloves were sewn—all designed, cut, and assembled by the immigrants of the city.

For many Jews these were their first jobs in America. Pay was low and conditions were bad. These factories were called "sweatshops," perhaps because they were hot and stuffy in summer or because workers had to work so hard that they were always sweating. But mostly because the bosses "sweated" as much work out of the workers as they could. The days were long, 12 or more hours, six days a week at least. The workrooms were crowded, with one worker sitting at her or his sewing machine right next to the other. There was seldom fresh air and nothing softened the noise of the machines. There was no job security and the boss could fire you at any time. Conditions were not healthy or safe. Fire was a constant danger.

FIGURE 31 – Sweatshop on Ludlow Street.

One horrible fire took place in 1911 at the Triangle Shirtwaist Company. It was a large company that employed hundreds of teenage girls and young women at its sewing machines. There were workers of all nationalities, but the majority were Jewish immigrants. They worked on the top floors of a ten-story building. In their crowded sweatshop, they were surrounded by piles of scraps and cloth that could easily catch fire. Because the bosses didn't want the workers to take work-breaks, they locked many of the factory doors from the outside. When the fire broke out, hundreds of young women were trapped in the building. Some were burnt to death in the factory. Others died when they jumped out the windows of the eighth floor. One hundred and forty six people died in the fire. There was much anger after the fire. People organized to get the government to pass work-safety laws and the workers' union movement got stronger.

Labor Unions

Two years before the Triangle Fire, a small union with just a couple of hundred members, called the International Ladies Garment Workers Union (ILGWU), went on strike to force the bosses of the shirtwaist (blouse) factories to give better pay and work conditions. The strike wasn't going well, so a meeting was called to decide what to do. Leaders of the union movement, such as Samuel Gompers, spoke at the meeting. So did the Jewish socialist politicians, such as the congressman Meyer London. They were trying to figure out whether to make their strike into a "general strike," that is, instead of stopping work at just a few shops until the workers' demands were met, they would ask workers at all of the city's blouse manufacturers to go out on strike. They couldn't decide what to do. Then a young woman got up and said in Yiddish, with strong feeling, that there had been enough talking and that it was time to go on a general strike. Her name was Clara Lemlich and her short speech started the great general shirtwaist-makers strike of 1909-1910. Tens of thousands of women across the city left their jobs for months. The strike did not end in a full victory for the strikers, but by the time it was over, ILGWU had become a strong union with thousands of members.

ILGWU was one of the main unions of the immigrants, but it was not the only one. There were the United Garment Workers, the Amalgamated Clothing Workers, unions in the United Hebrew Trades, and many others. Rose Schneiderman, an immigrant Jew, spent a lifetime organizing workers in one industry after another. She was head of the Women's Trade Union League for thirty years. The leaders of the many needle-trade unions were usually socialists and often members of socialist parties. Some of the most important leaders, such as Sidney Hillman and David Dubinsky, had been Bundists in Europe. These leaders brought the political disagreements of the socialist movement to the union movement. There were lots of angry arguments and fighting between the Communist socialists and the non-Communist socialists. Sometimes they could not even cooperate with each other in their fight against the bosses.

Most of the Jewish immigrants' bosses were themselves Jews, many of them immigrants who had saved enough money to go into business for themselves. On the one hand, it was good for Jewish immigrants to work for a Jewish boss because there was at least a chance that you would get Shabbes off and at least you and the boss spoke the same language and maybe had some understanding of each other. But Jewish bosses were under the same pressure to make as much money as possible as were the other business owners, and were just as willing to treat their workers badly to increase profits.

The bosses fought the unions in many ways. When the workers went on strike, the bosses tried to fire them and hire other workers—strikebreakers, whom union workers called "scabs." The bosses hired criminals, "goons," to beat up union organizers and striking workers. It took decades to organize New York's workers into unions that were strong enough to win basic workers' rights, but by the 1950s, the fight had pretty much been won. Sweatshops had been eliminated and workers had decent pay. But it was not a permanent victory. New groups of non-Jewish immigrants, Chinese, Koreans, Central Americans, came to New York in the 1970's, 1980s, and 1990s and once more there were sweatshops in New York.

Political Life

The first East European immigrants who came from *shtetls* in the Czarist Empire did not bring well developed political opinions with them. After 1905, more Bundists and Zionists came, bringing European political ideas to the Yiddish speaking immigrants. Because most immigrants were poor workers, and many were in unions or wanted to be in a union, socialist ideas had a big following among East European immigrants. Every kind of socialist group had its followers. Each group had its own newspapers. They debated with other groups in cafes. They held lectures. The Zionists, most of whom were also socialists, had their followers too. Jewish New York was very alive with political talk, and many of the talkers believed that they were part of a movement to change the world.

Before long, Jews became the backbone of American socialism. An immigrant Jew, Morris Hillquit, helped Eugene V. Debs found the Socialist Party. Hillquit became the Socialist Party's leading speaker and writer. Meyer London was elected to Congress as a Socialist. He too was an immigrant, and he gave his speeches in Congress with a Yiddish accent.

American socialists, unlike European socialists, all agreed that the First World War was bad for all working people and shouldn't be supported by socialists. But just like the European socialists, American socialists had big, angry disagreements about the Soviet Union. Some American socialists thought the Soviet Union was a real socialist government that was good for the world's working people. These socialists became Communists. Other socialists thought the Soviet Union was a terrible dictatorship that didn't give workers, or anyone else, freedom. They continued to call themselves Socialists. Over time, both the Communists and the Socialists broke into even smaller quarreling groups. By the 1930's, the immigrants' children were filling up City College in New York, and each little socialist group had its own table in the cafeteria. The communists who followed Trotsky were at one table and Communists who supported Stalin at another. There were Bundist tables and Socialist Party tables, and different kinds of Zionists tables too.

FIGURE 32 – Women surrounded by posters in English and Yiddish supporting Franklin D. Roosevelt, teach other women how to vote, 1935.

Roosevelt Democrats

By the 1930s, however, most American Jews, had become prosperous enough and American enough to behave politically like other Americans. A very high percentage of American Jews became strong supporters of Franklin Roosevelt's New Deal and the Democratic Party. President Roosevelt was trying to make the government give to the whole country the same sorts of benefits that the Jewish immigrants sought in their own fraternal organizations (*landsmanshaftn*, which we will read about in the next section). These benefits included retirement money, unemployment insurance, and funds to prevent starvation for the poor. Jews mostly left their socialism behind and became Roosevelt Democrats. Politically, from the 1930s till the 1960s, Jews resembled other working class Americans. But they didn't leave behind all socialist feelings and hopes for a better world. American Jewish socialists remained loyal members and strong fighters in the union movement. Jews, more than any other "white" group, became allies of African-Americans fighting for civil rights. Even three generations later, in the anti-Vietnam war movement, there was a very large number of Jews among the student leaders.

Fraternal Organizations

The immigrants couldn't bring all of the *shtetl* ways to the new country, but they did create many organizations that made them feel more at home in America. In fact, in the first half of the 20th century New York became the center of Jewish life and Yiddish culture.

The first important organization that helped the immigrants was the Hebrew Immigrant Aid Society (HIAS). HIAS was organized and run by the German Jews who had come to America two generations before the East European Jews. These German Jews were now better established in America. They were prosperous Reform Jews who were fitting into American society very well. Many of them looked down on the East European Jews. They thought the East Europeans were old fashioned and superstitious in religion, and uneducated in modern ways, and behaved like peasants. The German Jews didn't want to socialize with the new immigrants. They looked down on the Yiddish language. But still, they did feel responsible for their fellow Jews. They founded HIAS. HIAS met immigrants as they came off the boat, answered their questions, translated for them, tried to find them jobs, and tried to help in various ways. Besides comforting and assisting the new immigrants, HIAS and the established German-American Jewish community fought for immigrants' rights. Jacob Schiff, the most prominent American Jew from 1889 to 1920, worked for open immigration, so East Europeans could continue to come to America, and he worked for better conditions once they were here. A German Jew, Lillian Wald, founded the Visiting Nurse Association to improve the terrible health conditions the new immigrants lived with.

The help of the German Jews was important to the early immigrants, but it was the organizations they made for themselves that made New York into a great Jewish city.

Landsmanshaftn were clubs of people who came from the same *shtetl* or district in Europe. They tried to do for Jews in the big city what the *shtetl* community had done in the old country. For small monthly dues, a *Landsmanshaft* would give benefits to its members: money if they were sick and couldn't work, a burial plot when they died, and a place to go to see familiar faces.

Larger organizations were also formed. The *Arbeter Ring*, the Workmen's Circle, which was originally formed by working-class German Jews to help immigrants adjust to America. But it soon became a large organization of East European Jews that did many things for the new immigrants. Like the *landsmanshaftn*, the Workmen's Circle provided members with benefits: there was Workmen's Circle life insurance, health insurance, unemployment benefits and burial plots. (This was before the New Deal, before the American government provided any of these things to people in time of need.) The Workmen's Circle also became a center of social and cultural life. Under the influence of immigrants from Europe who brought Bundist ideas, the Workmen's Circle became an organization devoted to non-religious (called "secular") Yiddish culture and to socialism and labor unions. It sponsored lectures and adult education classes. There were Workmen's Circle schools ("*Shuln*") to teach Yiddish and socialism to the immigrants children. There were choruses and children's summer camps. There were secular holiday celebrations and Yiddish poetry readings. By the 1930s the Workmen's Circle had over 80,000 members in big cities throughout the United States. It was the largest Jewish organization in America.

There were other organizations similar to the Workmen's Circle. Socialists who supported the Soviet Union quit the Workmen's Circle. These Jews, mostly Communists, started their own housing co-ops, Yiddish choruses, social clubs, Yiddish schools, and summer camps under the umbrella of the Jewish People's Fraternal Order. Jews who weren't socialists also began their own Yiddish school organizations, such as the Sholem Aleichem Institute, and summer camps. By the 1930s many thousands of immigrant children were studying in these *Shuln* and going to these camps.

Yiddish culture also grew outside of organizations devoted to it. The majority of immigrants didn't think about keeping Yiddish alive. While many immigrants were followers of Chaim Zhitlowsky, a man who said that Jews must keep their Yiddish language culture alive, most did not think or worry about Yiddish at all, but Yiddish was their *mamaloshn*, mother tongue, and so, even though they didn't have a philosophy about the Yiddish language, they still created a world of Yiddish to get their information and entertainment.

The Yiddish Press

Jews in the *shtetls* had not been newspaper readers. It took some time for them to develop the habit after coming to America. But when they did develop the habit, they became great newspaper fans and built a strong and lively Yiddish press. By the 1920s, almost every immigrant family read at least one daily newspaper.

A few Yiddish weekly newspapers were started in the 1870s and 1880s, but the greatest Yiddish newspaper, the Forward (*Forverts*) began in 1897. One of its founders, and the man who ran and controlled the paper was Abraham Cahan. Cahan was a socialist and he wanted the Forward to be the voice of socialism in the Jewish world. But Cahan wanted the Forward to be independent, not controlled by any one socialist party or group. He turned the Forward into a paper that represented many sides of the life of the Yiddish-speaking immigrants and many styles of writing Yiddish. The Forward published news, of course, but it also published short stories, poetry and political essays and arguments. It gave the immigrants information they needed to adjust to American life, and it also gave them personal advice. One of its most popular sections, a *Bintl Briv*, a Bundle of Letters, would answer readers' questions on almost anything, from how to solve a family problem to how to deal with a legal problem. When you read a collection of letters from *Bintl Briv*, you get a good idea of the many type of problems the immigrants worried about.

There were other important Yiddish newspapers. *Der Tog* (*The Day*) was a liberal paper that tried to maintain a higher cultural tone than the Forward; it became the second largest

Yiddish newspaper. Every Jewish political and religious group among the immigrants had its own paper. There were Zionist papers and orthodox papers. The *Freiheit* (*Freedom*) was a Communist Yiddish paper, begun in 1922, which in its early years published some of the best Yiddish literature.

These Yiddish newspapers and magazines began to close down in the 1950s, as the number of Yiddish readers began to decrease. Today, besides the Yiddish press for the ultra-orthodox religious, only the *Forward* still publishes, but just once a week. But at its peak, in the 1920s and 1930s, the Yiddish press was the voice, mirror, and town hall of the Yiddish speaking American Jews.

Cultural Life

Yiddish literature in America at first had little to compare to the great Yiddish writers in Europe of the time. When Mendele, Peretz, and Sholom Aleichem were producing masterpieces, American Yiddish literature was just beginning. It started with popular novels and stories, but its first artistic writing came from immigrant workers, the so called sweatshop poets. These were people who actually worked in the sweatshops and wrote about their experiences and feelings in poems. The most important sweatshop poets, Morris Winchevsky, Dovid Edelstadt, Joseph Bovshover and especially Morris Rosenfeld, wrote about their suffering as workers and their desire to see a better world. These are only some of the fine early American Yiddish poets. A later generation of Yiddish poets became known as *Di Yunge*, the Young Ones. *Di Yunge* included poets such as Mani Lieb and Moshe Halpern. They introduced the style and ideas of modern world literature into Yiddish writing. They were also story writers, such as Joseph Opatoshu and Dovid Ignatow. All of *Di Yunge* tried to make the Yiddish into a language that would serve as the basis for a high artistic literature.

The early American Yiddish writers concentrated on Jewish immigrant life and the writers' hopes for a socialist future. Later on, Yiddish writers took up other subjects. Sholom Asch, the most popular Yiddish novelist of the 1930s wrote, among other themes, about Christian stories. Isaac Bashevis Singer, an American Yiddish writer who became popular in translation and eventually won a Nobel Prize in literature, wrote about mystical and folk tales more than he did about the lives of immigrants.

Yiddish poems, stories, and novels had a wide audience among the immigrant Jews because they were published in popular newspapers. You didn't have to buy a poetry collection to read Morris Rosenfeld; his poem would appear in your newspaper, as would a story of Singer's. Even novels would appear one chapter at a time, in the newspapers and magazines. Yiddish literature was followed closely by the majority of Yiddish speakers, not just by a very educated minority. For a time at least, this kept Yiddish literature close to the people.

Like other forms of Yiddish literature, Yiddish drama and Yiddish theater started with popular, not very artistic work, but quickly developed an artistic tradition. Second Avenue, on the Lower East Side, became the Yiddish Broadway. There were Yiddish actors who became stars to the immigrants, such as Jacob Adler, Boris Thomashefsky, and Molly Picon. Some of the plays, were popular, soap opera type of stories and were referred to by by many as *shund* ("trash"), but there were also plays of high quality. The Yiddish Arts Theater did all kinds of plays in Yiddish: popular melodramas, such as *Mayn Yidishe Mama*, serious Yiddish dramas, such as the *Dybbuk* and *Yoshe Kalb*, classics from world drama in translation, such as Shakespeare and Moliere, and adaptations from Yiddish literature, such as Sholom Aleichem stories. The *Artef* was a socialist theater company that put on dramatic productions with a political message, using the most advanced theater techniques.

Jewish musical life also developed in America. The *shtetl* musicians, who used to play at village weddings, were among the immigrants to America. These *klezmorim* helped create music as part of Yiddish theater. They also mixed traditional *shtetl* music with the popular music and jazz that they heard in America. This blend, *klezmer*, was heard at American Jewish weddings, bar mitzvahs, holiday resorts, and on recordings. After almost dying out, klezmer music has been revived and is once again a popular music.

Immigrant Jews were also fans of cantorial music. Cantors, *chazans*, led a Jewish congregation in singing and chanting during the synagogue services. They also had solo parts. Some cantors became stars among the immigrant Jews of America. People paid high ticket prices in the 1920s to hear Yosele Rosenblatt sing. Although the immigrants were quickly losing their traditional religious ways, religion still played a large role in their lives.

Religious Life

The movements of Reform Judaism, Conservative Judaism and Modern Orthodox Judaism had changed Judaism in America and Western Europe, but they had no influence in Eastern Europe. The religion that the immigrants from Eastern Europe brought to America was Traditional Judaism. True, many of them weren't very religious when they came. In America most became even less religious. But whether they stayed very religious or became less religious, the religion that they remained connected to was the traditional, pious Judaism they had known in Eastern Europe. Even the completely non-religious, secular Jews, thought that traditional East European Judaism was the only "real" Judaism.

There were *shul*s all over the Lower East Side, in little synagogues, in tenement basements and apartments, as well as in some larger buildings. Like *landsmanshaftn*, some *shul*s were organized around people who came from the same town. The smallest ones, *shtibels*, might barely have enough members to make a regular *minyan*. The *shul*s of the Lower East Side at first tried to be the center of their members' lives, as they had been in the old country. But that was difficult in America, where the rabbi had no influence beyond the synagogue and the members had so many other places to go and things to do. Still, some immigrants went to their *shul* to pray every day, many went on Shabbes, and most went on holidays. Even if they stopped being kosher, stopped observing Shabbes and stopped believing in God, most Jews still went to *shul* on the High Holidays. Only socialist or Zionist secularists who wanted to make a point of giving up religion would not be in *shul* on Yom Kippur. In addition, the immigrant Jews used the *shul*s for weddings and bar mitzvahs. They went to *shul* to say kaddish for their dead. They would send their children to *cheder*, Hebrew school, in the *shul*, just as they did in Europe.

The immigrants' *shul*s at first had the style and feel of the old *shtetl shul*s. Crowded, filled with activity, mumbled payers, stray conversation, people chanting at different rhythms and rates—it would look completely disorganized and undignified to someone familiar with most Christian or Reform services. But this had been the synagogue atmosphere for *shtetl* Jews for centuries and it was what the immigrant felt most at home in.

The children of the immigrants became less religious and had less patience for the strictness of their parents traditional Judaism. A few became attracted to the Reform Judaism of the German Jews, but to most children of East Europeans immigrants, Reform Judaism felt almost like a completely different religion. While some children of immigrants became totally disconnected to Judaism, the majority of immigrant children became Conservative Jews.

Conservative Judaism was based on the ideas of the Historical School we read about in Chapter 12. These ideas, like Reform Judaism's ideas, said Judaism could change. But Conservative Judaism wanted the change to come slowly, and it wanted to stick to traditional ways as much as possible. In practice it meant that the rabbis led pretty traditional Jewish lives, but they didn't really expect their congregation members to follow the traditional Jewish laws. For the immigrant children, this was a comfortable solution. They didn't want anyone making them feel bad for not being traditionally religious, but when they did go to synagogue, they wanted to experience sights and sounds that reminded them of their parents' traditional *shul*. Conservatism became the most popular type of religion among American Jews.

But it didn't happen all at once. A big step on the road to Conservatism's popularity in America was the appointment of Solomon Schechter to be head of the Jewish Theological Seminary (JTS) in 1902. The JTS was the college where Conservative rabbis were trained. Before Schechter came, the JTS was not an outstanding school. But Schechter turned it into a center of traditional and modern Jewish learning. Schechter was a pious European rabbi and a great scholar of modern Jewish thought. After he was brought from Europe to America to head the JTS, he filled it with other great teachers who were like him: very religious but also serious scholars using all the modern research methods to understand Judaism. The JTS trained the Conservative rabbis for the immigrants' children's synagogues. But unlike Europe, the rabbis didn't run the synagogues—they were run by the members themselves, who hired and fired rabbis and made decisions about synagogue policy. There were no chief rabbis in America.

There were other, small but significant, Jewish religious movements that began in 20th century America. Reconstructionism, based on the ideas of Mordecai Kaplan, was similar to Conservative Judaism but had a less traditional, more open-ended idea of Jewish culture and God. Humanistic Judaism, based on Sherwin Wine's ideas, completely did away with belief in God. The Jewish Renewal movement, combined kabalistic thought with "hippie" cultural attitudes. These movements created even more religious options for American Jews.

Some immigrant children did remain as pious as their parents. They joined the Modern Orthodox movement that had a small following among America's German Jews. They followed all of the traditional laws of Judaism, but their customs, such as how they dressed, became modern. Modern Orthodox also got modern secular education as well as traditional Talmudic education.

At Home in America

In 1924, The United States Congress passed the Johnson Act. This law put strict limits on the number of people that could come to America. The purpose of the law was to keep out Italians, Jews, Poles, and other nationalities from Eastern and Southern Europe that white, Protestant Americans were often prejudiced against. A few immigrants managed to continue to come, but until the law was changed 40 years later, not very many. It was the end of the great East European Jewish immigration to America.

In the early 1920s there were still brand new Jewish immigrants, "right off the boat," (they were called "greenhorns") and plenty of immigrants had only been in America a short time. But by then there were also East European Jews who had been born, raised, and educated in America. The immigration had been going on for forty years. The East European Jewish community began to leave its closed immigrant world and move into American society.

One part of the move was physical. In all the cities in which Jews had settled, such as Boston, Philadelphia, Chicago, and Cleveland, they began to move out of the crowded immigrant neighborhoods in the old parts of town to newer neighborhoods. In New York, Jews were leaving the Lower East Side and creating Jewish neighborhoods in the Bronx and Brooklyn. The Grand Concourse in the Bronx and Ocean Parkway in Brooklyn became Jewish streets, just as Delancey and Rivington had been on the Lower East Side.

By the 1950s and 60s, Jews were leaving these Bronx and Brooklyn neighborhoods for even newer ones in the suburbs outside the city. As Jews made more money, they wanted bigger homes. Now that they had the same American habits and ways of doing things as most Americans, they felt comfortable being with other, non-Jewish Americans. In addition, African-Americans began to move into many of the old Jewish neighborhoods. There was tension between the Blacks and Jews. The Jews were wealthier and owned the stores; they bought buildings and were often the landlords of Black renters. The Jews, by then, were treated as "whites" in America. Blacks were kept out of opportunities for jobs, education, political power, and were violently mistreated throughout the country. The African-Americans had been in America hundreds of years, but were still treated worse than the newest immigrants. There was growing crime in the poor Black city communities. Some Jews picked up the traditional American racist attitudes. Jews and Blacks struggled over control of the local schools. The fear of African-Americans "taking over" the neighborhood became another reason Jews left the cities and moved to the suburbs.

Jewish success in America was achieved by using three major tools. One was business. Immigrant peddlers became shopkeepers. Tailors became manufacturers, tenement dwellers became landlords and even real estate developers. America had lots of business opportunities, and Jews, many of whom had been businessmen without opportunities in Europe, made good use of the business freedom of America. Some new industries, such as making movies, became Jewish strongholds. By the 1930s, almost all of the big Hollywood studios were owned and run by Jews. Jews were also successful in other show business industries. In Tin Pan Alley, where American popular music was composed and published, some of the most important people were Jews, such as George and Ira Gershwin and Irving Berlin. Jews were also important in the radio industry, and a little later the television industry. Jews became important in real estate, jewelry, and, of course, the fashion business. These were only a few of the businesses that Jews were in. Jewish business success helped spread wealth throughout the Jewish community, even if the majority of Jews were not themselves business owners.

A second tool of American Jewish success was organization. Jews continued to organize themselves even after they had built organizations that were meant to help the immigrants to adjust. HIAS, the Workmen's Circle, the *landsmanshaftn*, the Joint Distribution Committee all were joined or replaced by other organizations. B'nai B'rith, the American Jewish Congress, the American Jewish Committee, Hadassah, the Anti-Defamation League, and many, many others became part of Jewish American life. These organizations did many things for the Jews. Like the early immigrant organizations, some provided member benefits. Others promoted cultural life. Some were charitable or devoted to helping Jews overseas. Almost all of them, no matter what else they were trying to do, also tried to protect the Jews politically from laws and government action that they didn't like.

But Jews didn't only stay in their own organizations. As we have seen, they became very active in labor unions. It was the power and success of these unions that lifted many Jewish working families into decent living conditions, conditions that gave them a chance for prosperity in America. Jews also became active in the Democratic Party. Some of President Franklin Roosevelt's closest advisers were Jews. Jews became mayors and governors, senators and judges. Political power helped make sure that Jews were treated fairly in America, even though they were a small minority.

Finally, education contributed very significantly to the East European Jews' success in America. Maybe the tradition of studying the Torah and Talmud helped Jews become good students in America. Jews took advantage of America's free public education system. The City College of New York, a free university, was filled with Jews by the 1930s. These Jews, the children of poor immigrants, were able to become doctors, lawyers, teachers, professors, and other professionals through their City College education.

All of this success was not because there was no discrimination against Jews in America. In fact, in universities, which eventually were the main way most Jews rose in America, at first there was serious discrimination. The old elite colleges, like Harvard and Yale, would only let a certain number of Jews in, no matter how many excellent Jewish students applied. These "quotas" were like the *numerus clausus* policies of Czarist Russia. They were meant to keep Jews out. Many banks, corporations, and law firms wouldn't hire Jews or wouldn't give them the top jobs. And many Americans wouldn't socialize with Jews. They wouldn't let Jews into their clubs and they tried to prevent Jews from moving into their neighborhoods.

At first the immigrants didn't worry about this discrimination. They had more immediate problems to deal with, and compared with Europe the discrimination in America was mild. Jews had full citizenship rights in America and good opportunities to earn a living. There was some serious anti-Semitic violence: in 1913 the Ku Klux Klan, which specialized in persecuting Blacks but also hated Jews, lynched Leo Frank, a Jew who was falsely accused of attacking a Christian girl. But such serious anti-Semitic violence was rare. Most discrimination just tried to keep Jews out of Christian society. But, the immigrant Jews were not looking to rub shoulders with the rich "*goyim*" (Yiddish for non-Jews), and at first, Jews didn't expect to be part of the most powerful American groups, so they didn't resent being kept out. But by the 1930s, Jews did begin to fight anti-Semitism in America. Within one generation, that fight had become pretty successful. By the

1960s, although there might have been individual Americans who discriminated against and hated Jews, there was almost no *system* of discrimination. Every American job, school and neighborhood was open to Jews. Jews had to fight people's anti-Semitic beliefs, but they had won the fight against anti-Semitic public policies.

Jews had become very successful and very American. Jewish children were as interested in baseball as other American children. Jews listened to the same radio programs as other Americans, went to the same schools, saw the same movies, plays, and concerts, and worked at the same jobs. As the social discrimination ended, Jews also played with non-Jewish Americans. For a while, Jews had their own places to play. The Catskill Mountains, in upstate New York, was a Jewish vacation area, filled with Jewish hotels and bungalow colonies. At colleges, Jews had their own fraternities and sororities. But by the 1960s Jews were vacationing with other Americans and joining non-Jewish social organizations. In fact, Jews had become so at home, accepted and prosperous in America that some Jews worried that Jews would disappear in America. They thought Jews would just mix in with the non-Jewish majority. Many of the main American novelists were Jews, but Saul Bellow, Norman Mailer, and Philip Roth, although Jewish, were American writers. They wrote in English, not Yiddish. By the 1960s, fewer and fewer American Jews even understood Yiddish. Because Jews were successful, comfortable, and accepted in every area of American life, there was a concern that Jews would not feel a need to keep a separate Jewish life going. Some Jews were especially worried that Jews were beginning to marry non-Jews; they feared that the children of these "mixed" marriages wouldn't consider themselves Jewish.

All of this Jewish-American success, and the worries about disappearing from too much acceptance, began in the 1930s and really took off after the depression and World War II. It was at the same time that the Jews who remained in Europe experienced the Jewish people's greatest catastrophe. European Jews were in danger of disappearing, but not from too much acceptance. Their danger and disaster came from the most vicious Jew-hatred ever. The result was the Holocaust, the murder of Europe's Jews.

FIGURE 33 – Front page illustration from a 1936 issue of *Der Stürmer*, an anti-Semitic German newspaper. The bottom headline says "Jews are our misfortune."

Chapter 17

The Murder of European Jews

An Old Hatred in New Clothes

Jew-hatred has a long history in the Christian world, but in the nineteenth century it added some new ideas. For almost two thousand years Christians hated Jews because the Jews were not Christian. If any Jews changed their religion, that is, converted to Christianity, they stopped being hated. Some historians say this wasn't always exactly the case; for instance, New Christians in Spain were discriminated against because their ancestors had been Jewish. Also, at times some Jew-haters considered Jews to be devils, with inhuman souls, not just people with the "wrong" religious ideas. But mostly, Jew-hatred was based on the religious differences.

As the Enlightenment ideas of science, equality, tolerance, and freedom spread in the 1800s, many people expected Jew-hatred to fade away. People were less concerned with religious differences. But a new kind of Jew-hatred developed. It was not based on religion, it was based on ancestry, or what the new Jew haters called "race." The new Jew haters said their hatred wasn't a religious prejudice. They said it was a scientific belief because science that showed that the Jews were evil. These new Jew haters even coined the term "anti-Semitism" to make their hatred of Jews sound scientific and modern.

Anti-Semitic writers, such as the Frenchman Comte Joseph-Arthur de Gobineau and the Englishman Houston Stewart Chamberlain, shared the same basic ideas. The peoples of the world, they said, were divided into races, and race was the most important thing in human history and individuals' lives. Race was a matter of "blood": your race was the race of your biological parents, and that, of course, was unaffected by your upbringing, education, or religious beliefs. Some races were said to be superior to other races. The anti-Semites thought the "Aryans" were the best race. They identified the Aryans with northern Europeans. Lesser races were Eastern and Southern Europeans, Asians, Africans, and especially Jews. For the anti-Semites, the Aryans were responsible for everything good in the world and the Jews were responsible for everything bad.

This modern anti-Semitism was found throughout Europe, and became very influential in Germany. Of course, there is no real scientific basis for these ideas, so we must ask: Why did many Europeans, especially Germans, come to believe them? One answer was that people were afraid of all of the new changes brought about by modern life. Peasants farmers were being changed into factory workers, old religious faiths were challenged by science, old leaders and bosses challenged by democracy. The Jews were a good symbol of these changes; they were very active in modern life, as labor leaders, as businessmen, as scientists, and as politicians in democratic parties, such as the liberals or socialists. The fact that Jews were out of the ghettos was itself a reminder that the old days were gone. Germany moved very quickly into modern life, with little time for adjustment. Germany had a fairly large and fairly successful Jewish population that served as a good symbol of modern times for those most upset by modern times.

The Nazi Rise to Power

The Nazi Party was founded in Germany shortly after the First World War. It soon came to be led by Adolf Hitler, an Austrian born war veteran. Hitler was called the *Führer* (*Leader* or *Guide*); he was the leader of the Nazi Party and Party members were to obey him without question. The central program of Hitler and the Nazi Party was anti-Semitism. According to the Nazi version of anti-Semitism, Aryans were the only truly good, smart and artistic people. They were the master race and deserved to rule the world. Other races, like Slavs and Africans, should be servants and slaves. Jews were the worst race. Not only did Jews do nothing good, they were actually dangerous.

According to the Nazis, the Jews were not intelligent but they were clever in tricky and deceitful ways. They compared Jews to parasites, animals that live on other animals and make the animals they live on sick—such as tapeworms or lice—saying that Jews sneakily took over societies and made them sick, and that Germany was sick because of the Jews. The Jews were Germany's misfortune, the Nazis said. They were the eternal, unchanging enemy of the Aryan race. Jews used capitalism, or its opponent, communism, to take over Germany. Jews ruined German music, art, literature, and scholarship according to the Nazis. Jews were pure evil—sub-humans the Nazis called them. To prosper, or even survive, the Nazis said, Germany must be rid of any Jewish influence.

At first the Nazis were a small, not very important political party. But Germany was a new, shaky democracy after the First World War. For a party based on fear and anger there were many issues to use. The Germans did not expect to lose the First World War. When they did lose, the countries that won, France, Britain and America, imposed a harsh peace treaty that made Germany pay those countries lots of money. Some Germans thought that there must have been traitors in Germany who brought about the sudden defeat and the harsh peace treaty. There were also many economic problems in the decade after the war. At one point inflation was so bad that money lost all its value. Unemployment was very high. Many Germans were also uncomfortable with democracy. They were used to rulers who gave orders. There was a yearning for "strong" leadership. Big business in Germany also didn't like the power of the socialists in the government and were especially afraid that communists, perhaps with the help of the Soviet Union, would come to power in Germany.

Although it didn't make any sense, the Nazis blamed the Jews for all of these problems. They said Jewish Communists threatened business, but they also said that Jewish bankers and businessmen harmed workers. Nazis claimed that the Jews wanted democracy to keep Germany weak. Jews betrayed

Germany, stabbing it in the back, in World War I. The Jews did all of this so that they could control, and then enslave, Germany.

The Nazis praised war, the German people, and discipline. They were against democracy and equality. That combination of militarism, nationalism, populism, and authoritarianism is called fascism. But Nazism was different than the fascist movements in other countries because it made its most important belief a racist hatred of Jews. Other fascisms, following the example of the Nazis, became anti-Semitic, but only the Nazis were first and last a party of Jew-hatred.

In January 1933, less than fifteen years after the First World War ended, the Nazis came to power in Germany. In part they came to power because they became popular, winning many German votes. But they never won the majority of votes in a free election. Hitler became ruler when some conservative politicians invited him into the government. They thought they could control him. Their friends in big business thought Hitler would be useful in fighting the socialists. But once in power, Hitler quickly moved to get rid of democracy and become the dictator of Germany.

Nazi Persecution of German Jews

Over a half million Jews lived in Germany when Hitler came to power. They felt very at home there—they were prosperous, loyal Germans. Many were veterans who had fought in the German army in World War I. They spoke German and had the same customs and tastes as other Germans. They loved German culture and were major contributors to it. There were German Jewish writers, artists, musicians, and critics. There were Jewish doctors, lawyers, professors, scientists, journalists, and businessmen. If German Jews were at all religious, they were usually Reform Jews, the German-grown form of modern Judaism. By 1933, many Jews and Christians were marrying each other.

In January 1933, even before the Nazis came to power, that all began to change. Nazi thugs, who wore Brown shirt uniforms and were called Stormtroopers, had been picking on Jews and others who the Nazis considered enemies. Now that no police were going to stop them, their bullying of Jews increased. They, along with special Nazi police, the SS and the Gestapo, arrested political opponents of the Nazis. In April 1933, the Nazis called for a boycott of Jewish stores. That same month all Jewish government workers, including teachers, were fired. Two years later, the Nazis passed harsher laws: the Nuremburg Laws. Jews weren't allowed to use parks and museums. Jews were forced to sell their businesses cheaply to "Aryans." These laws defined Jews racially and made it illegal for a Jew to marry a Christian. German citizenship was taken away from Jews. Jewish men had to take on the middle name "Israel" and women had to adopt "Sarah" so they could be easily identified as Jews. Non-German Jews were expelled from the country. Altogether, there was a steady elimination of Jews from public life in Germany, and a harsh, cruel, daily existence imposed on German Jews.

FIGURE 34 – A synagogue burning during Kristallnacht, 1938.

Kristallnacht

In 1938, the Nazis organized a nation-wide pogrom against the Jews. On November 9, Jewish businesses, synagogues, hospitals, and community centers were looted by mobs and burnt. So many windows were shattered that it was called *"Kristallnacht,"* Night of the Broken Glass. Jews were beaten that night and dozens were murdered. In the following days, hundreds of Jews were arrested, as though they were the criminals in the riots instead of the victims. The arrested Jews were sent to the new prisons the Nazis had created, called concentration camps. The camps, starting with Dachau in 1933, had held Nazi opponents. These were not yet camps where everyone got killed, but conditions were bad and the guards were cruel. Many of the Jews sent to camps after *Kristallnacht* never came out alive.

After *Kristallnacht* conditions for German Jews became even more terrible. They weren't permitted out of their homes more than a few hours a day. Children were kicked out of school. Jews were often beaten or humiliated when they were out on the streets. Some Jews were forced to wash the sidewalks with toothbrushes. Because there was almost no legal way they could earn a living, German Jews became very poor.

Seeking Asylum

Jews had been leaving Germany since 1933, the moment Hitler came to power. By 1939, poor and terrorized, all the remaining Jews were desperate to get out of Germany. But throughout the Nazi persecution, and certainly by 1939, it was not easy to leave Germany. This was not so much because the Nazis wouldn't let Jews out—the Nazis didn't let Jews take their money with them, but up until 1939 the Nazis usually let Jews leave Germany. The problem for Jews was getting other countries to let them in.

The United States had ended open immigration of Jews in 1924. Although a few extra German Jews were let in because of the Nazi persecution, it was a drop in the bucket compared to the need. England, France, and other West European democracies also let in very few refugees from Germany. One reason for not admitting the refugees was worry over foreigners taking jobs. The 1930s were a time of world depression. Jobs were in short supply. Anti-Semitism was another reason. Some powerful people in the United States and Western Europe were either themselves anti-Semitic or were afraid that accepting Jewish refugees would offend anti-Semites. Even President Franklin Roosevelt, who was not an anti-Semite personally, seemed to fear the political effects of giving safe haven to too many German Jews.

German Jews were frantic to gain permission to enter a country outside Germany. A few got visas, entry permissions, to the United States or West European countries. Most tried to get visas to anywhere that would take them. Some went to Turkey, some to South America, some even ended up in Shanghai, China. Small groups of German Jewish refugees wound up in places all over the world. Of course, with the rise of the Nazis, Zionism made many converts. The need for their own country now seemed quite obvious to German Jews. But Palestine was controlled by Britain, and Britain strictly limited the number of refugee Jews it would permit into Palestine. Most German Jews found nowhere at all to go and remained trapped in Germany.

The voyage of the St. Louis is an example of the refugees' plight. In 1939, the Germans permitted over 900 German Jews to board the St. Louis. The Jews had visas to enter Cuba. But when the ship arrived in Cuba, the refugees weren't allowed to enter. They were also refused permission to enter the United States, which the boat came very close to. In the end, the ship had to return to Europe, and except for the passengers that were permitted into England, most were eventually killed by the Nazis within the following six years.

Less than half of Germany's Jews were able to find a safe haven during the six years when Nazis were trying to drive Jews out of Germany. In the next six years the German government stopped trying to expel Jews. Instead it concentrated on torturing and murdering them.

The War Begins

In September 1939, Germany invaded Poland starting World War II. Why did Germany go to war? In part to revenge its defeat in the First World War, in part to get more *lebensraum*, "living space," by conquering countries in Eastern Europe, in part because it needed outside enemies to stay popular, in part to pursue the long-term Nazi goal of destroying "Jewish Bolshevism" in the Soviet Union, and in large part because the fascist love of war leads fascist governments naturally into wars. It *may* not have been one of its original goals, but once the war started, a major, perhaps *the* major, goal of the Nazi government was the destruction of European Jewry. The Nazis wanted to make Europe *judenrein*, that is, free of any Jewish "contamination."

The Nazi armies quickly conquered half of Poland and millions of Jews. During the conquest, many Jews were immediately murdered. Synagogues were burned with their congregations inside. People were shot or hanged in the streets. But at first not every Jew was being automatically killed by the Nazis.

Between 1939 and 1941, Hitler and Stalin, the dictator of the Soviet Union, cooperated. But in 1941 Hitler attacked the Soviet Union and conquered all of Eastern Europe and millions more Jews. Along with the conquering German armies came specially trained troops called *Einsatzgruppen*, "Action Groups." It was their job to massacre Jews. They worked a little differently in each town, but usually they came into town, gathered the Jews together, and marched them into the countryside. There the Jews were forced to dig a big ditch. Then they were made to remove their clothes and stand by the edge of the ditch. Then they were all shot. They fell into the ditch, which became a mass grave. Their clothing and valuables were all looted. Something like this happened at Ponar forest, right outside Vilna. At Babi Yar, in the outskirts of Kiev, over seventy thousand people were shot in a few days. The same thing happened in countless towns and villages of Eastern Europe.

Where Jews weren't immediately murdered, they were herded into ghettos. By the end of 1941, there were ghettos in most of the major Jewish cities of Eastern Europe, including Bialystock, Vilna, Lodz, and Warsaw. These were not like the old European ghettos. Jews were forced to live in these new ghettos and to wear patches in the form of yellow stars on their clothing identifying them as Jews, (as had been the case in the earlier ghettos,) but, unlike in the old ghettos, in these Nazi ghettos Jews weren't allowed out at all. Moreover, very little food and no medicine was allowed in. The Nazi ghettos were more crowded than the most crowded of the earlier ghettos. Added to these horrible conditions of disease, poverty, and starvation was the terror caused by the Nazis coming in to force people into slave labor or kill them.

As horrible as conditions were in the ghettos, Jews tried to live normal human lives there. Against the Nazi laws, Jews organized secret schools. Ghetto Jews had theater performances and music concerts. Without medicine or medical equipment, Jews maintained hospitals, and with almost no spare money, food, or clothing, the tradition of *tsedakah*, charity, was continued. Everything was done to keep their spirits up, even though people were dying in the streets of starvation every day. Although the Nazis executed anyone who broke any rules, Jewish children smuggled food into the ghetto, and Jewish political organizations of communists, socialists, and Zionists continued to meet secretly.

The Nazis appointed Jewish Councils (*Judenrate*) and Jewish Police to carry out Nazi orders in the ghettos. Some of these officials tried to use their positions to protect Jews. Many thought cooperating with the Nazis would save their own or their families' lives, even if it meant hurting fellow Jews. As we shall see, it didn't save them in the end.

The Final Solution

Historians still argue over exactly when and how the Nazis decided to murder all the Jews, but we know that this decision had already been made by January 1942. That is when Nazi officials met near Berlin, in Wannsee, in order to figure out the best way to kill the millions of Jews in Europe who were in their power. What the Nazis called "the Jewish problem" needed a solution, and murdering every Jewish man, women and child was, for them, the "final" solution of the Jewish problem. If the Jews were like lice, as the Nazis said they were, the best thing to do was to exterminate all of them.

The *Einsatzgruppen* shootings and death through starvation and disease in the ghettos were going too slowly for the Nazis. It was decided that death factories, extermination camps, would be set up. Jews would be shipped to these death camps by train. There, all who weren't selected to work for a short time, would be taken straight from the train to a phony shower, which was really a gas chamber. After they were killed in the gas chamber, their bodies would be burned in ovens and go up in smoke through the chimneys.

The Nazis tried many methods to get the Jews out of the ghettos and into the trains to the death camps. They told Jews that they were being sent to the East to be resettled. They offered the starving ghetto Jews a loaf of bread and some jam to get on the train. They threatened the Jewish Council and Jewish police if they didn't deliver enough Jews to the trains. And sometimes they just sent in soldiers to drag Jews out of their homes and throw them on the trains.

The train rides were miserable. People were packed standing into freight cars, with no food, water, toilets, or room to even sit. It was stuffy, with little air to breathe. It was freezing in winter and horribly hot in summers. The train cars stank terribly. The trip took days, and many people who died on the trip were kept standing, held up by the tightly packed bodies. When they arrived at the death camps, the passengers were exhausted, starved, weak, and half-crazy from fear. This made it easier to force them into the gas chambers.

Millions were murdered in the death camps of Treblinka, Maidanek, Chelmno, Belzec, Sobibor, and Auschwitz-Birkenau. There were also concentration camps, such as Buchenwald, Sachsenhausen, and Dachau, that were slave labor camps, not extermination camps. But even in those camps most people died. They were worked to death or starved to death, or killed as punishment for breaking a rule, or simply killed by the Nazis for fun. All of the Nazi concentration camps, the slave labor ones and the immediate death ones, were among the most horrible places that ever existed. And no matter where the Nazis sent a person they considered a Jew, in the end, the Nazis were going to kill that person. Man, woman, child; religious, atheist, convert to Christianity; rich, poor; cooperator, resister—it didn't matter. The Nazis tried to kill them all.

By the end of the war, in 1945, the Nazis had murdered about six million Jews from all over Europe. That was more than two out of three who had lived there before the war. Jews from Holland, France, Italy, Germany, Norway, Belgium, Greece, Yugoslavia, Hungary, Czechoslovakia, Austria, Estonia, Ukraine, and Russia were murdered. The great Jewish community of Poland by itself lost almost three million Jews. Altogether, almost two million Jewish children were murdered.

Jewish Resistance

After the war some people asked "Why did Jews go like sheep to the slaughter?" They thought that Jews acted like foolish, timid animals that cooperated with their own butchers. It is true that the majority of Jews were too shocked, confused, and afraid to fight the Nazi attack. It was hard to believe that the Nazis really wanted to kill all Jews. The word "genocide," meaning the crime of killing a whole people, didn't even exist. The Nazis never openly said what they were doing. They were always lying to the Jews and keeping other sources of information from them. Even among themselves the Nazis used indirect words to cover up their crimes. They would talk about "solving the Jewish problem," instead of murdering Jews, or "special actions" instead of mass executions. If the murderers couldn't face what they were doing, imagine how hard it was for the murder victims to believe what was happening.

FIGURE 35 – Jews driven by Germans from the Warsaw ghetto.

Fighting back also seemed hopeless, and almost always was. Jews had no weapons, military training, or military organization, and practically no outside help. They were faced by the most modern, powerful army on earth. The smallest attempt to fight back and you would be killed right on the spot. So, even if you knew that the Nazis eventually planned on killing you, by not fighting you could hope that something would turn up before they got around to killing you. Maybe there would be a chance to escape or a quick Nazi defeat in the war.

Even if you were willing to die on the spot to fight the Nazis, you had to worry about what the Nazis would do to your friends and family after they killed you. When a Nazi official, Reinhard Heydrich, was killed in Czechoslovakia by an anti-Nazi fighter, the Nazis took revenge by murdering everyone in the Czech town of Lidice, even though the town had had nothing to do with the assassination. This kind of revenge was used in the camps and ghettos to discourage any resistance. If one person escaped, many left behind would be immediately killed. If one person hit a Nazi, many would be tortured as punishment. So fighting the Nazis would harm innocent others. Many brave people refused to do that.

By the time Jews realized how far the Nazis would go in persecuting Jews, the Jews were usually too weak from hunger and too depressed with grief to fight back. This was part of the Nazi plan. The people who got off the trains to enter the concentration camps were half-dead already.

In spite of all this, there was Jewish resistance. The most common kind of fighting back was the refusal to act like "subhumans" even though the Nazis treated Jews as if they were devils. We have already seen how in the ghettos Jews formed schools, performed plays, and played music. That was a way of fighting the Nazis. The Nazis tried to turn Jews into selfish animals, but many (of course not all) somehow continued to worry about each other and care for each other. Janusz Korczak was a doctor who wrote famous children's stories and was the head of an orphanage in the Warsaw Ghetto. When the Nazis sent for the orphans to be put on the trains for the camps, Korczak went with them. Korczak had enough connections to hope that he could save himself, but he would not abandon the children.

Emanuel Ringelblum was a historian, who, like Korczak, had opportunities to escape the Warsaw Ghetto. But Ringelblum thought it was important that a trained historian witness and write down the story of the ghetto. He organized people in the ghetto to bring to him all of the information about ghetto life that they could find. With this information he wrote diaries. Ringelbum was eventually killed by the Gestapo. His diaries were found after the war, buried in tin cans under the rubble of Warsaw. Much of what we know about the Warsaw Ghetto comes from Ringelblum's diaries. The Nazis wanted to hide their crimes from history. Ringelblum fought them by giving his life to record the story of the ghetto, even though he couldn't be sure that the Nazis would lose the war or that anyone would find the diaries.

Throughout the ghettos and camps there was the Korczak and Ringelblum kind of resistance—Jews who stayed humane and spiritually alive when everything possible was done to make them into unfeeling animals. There were secret Passover seders in the ghettos and Chanukah celebrations in the camps. Parents gave their lives for children and children for parents. Although very rare, even starving people would sometimes share food with strangers.

As difficult as it was, there was also Jewish physical resistance to the Nazis. The most famous instance was the Warsaw Ghetto uprising. In April 1943, after the Nazis had already sent hundreds of thousands of Jews in the Warsaw Ghetto to the Treblinka death camp, the seventy thousand Jews left fought back. They only had a few old guns and rifles smuggled into the Ghetto and some homemade bombs. The Nazis had tanks, machine guns, flame throwers, and well fed, trained, professional soldiers with plenty of ammunition. But the seven hundred fighters of the Jewish Fighting Organization (the JFO) held out for almost a month.

The JFO was led by Mordecai Anielewicz, a 23-year-old labor Zionist. Many of the Jewish political groups—socialists, communists, and Zionists were part of the JFO. Some others, not in the JFO, also fought. They all knew they had no chance of beating the Nazis, but they wanted to kill as many Nazis as they could before they died. The non-fighting Jews tried to find hiding places in cellars and bunkers. The fighters moved around the Ghetto through the sewers in order to attack the Nazis from different places. By the end of the fighting, the Nazis had destroyed the entire ghetto. Seven thousand Jews were executed, and most of the rest were sent to camps where they were killed. But a few people, including some fighters, escaped the ghetto and survived the war.

There were Jewish revolts in other ghettos. In Vilna, the Jewish communist Itzik Wittenberg led the Jewish fighters. There were uprisings in Bialystok and Kovno. Even in small towns, Jews sometimes fought the Nazis. In a few instances, a revolt in a small town led to a mass escape into the forests. Jews who did escape into the forests, in groups or as individuals, sometimes joined groups of anti-Nazi fighters, called partisans. Some partisan groups were made up entirely of Jews. They lived in the forests, had to keep moving, and got food and weapons where they could. The local population was seldom friendly to Jews. Hunger and danger were always with these Jews in the forests. But still these Jewish partisans, such as the group led by Yekhezkel Atlas in Lithuania, or the group led by the Belski brothers in Belarus, found ways of attacking the Nazis.

Even in the death camps there was physical resistance to the Nazis. In Auschwitz-Berkenau, Treblinka, and Sobibor, prisoners rose up to try and escape. Some German guards were killed in each of these uprisings, and the one at Sobibor, led by Alexander Pecherski, was fully successful: many guards were killed and many prisoners escaped. At Auschwitz, Rosa Robota, a young Jewish prisoner, helped smuggle some explosives out of where she worked to blow up the ovens. When the Nazis captured her, she did not tell the names of her comrades, even under torture. She was executed without revealing any names.

In a way, just surviving the Nazi persecution was resistance. The Nazis wanted to wipe out the Jewish people. Every European Jew who outlived the war was a defeat for Hitler. Every victim wanted the world and history to know what happened to them, so each survivor who lived to tell the tale of the camps, ghettos, and forests is a victory for the victims. Survival usually required boldness and luck, but it also required help from others. Most survivors survived in part because of the help they received from someone who didn't survive. So not only were the survivors resisters, but so were all the ones who helped others survive, even if they themselves didn't make it.

Murderers, Accomplices, Bystanders, and Rescuers

What were other people doing while the Jews of Europe were being murdered? The Nazi leaders themselves were busy planning and carrying out the crime. Joseph Goebbels was the Nazi leader in charge of getting people to hate Jews; he was responsible for what is called propaganda. Heinrich Himmler led the SS troops who did the shootings and ran the camps. Adolph Eichmann organized all the details of the genocide. Of course, Hitler himself was in charge of all of the murderers.

But a handful of Nazi leaders could not by themselves kill millions of people. They needed hundreds of thousands of others to join them in murder. And Germans from all walks of life did join them. Many did hate Jews and were glad of the chance to murder and torture Jews. Germany had a long history of Jew-hatred, and the Nazi anti-Semitic propaganda convinced many Germans that Jews weren't really human beings. Many others seem to have gone along because they thought they should always follow orders, no matter how terrible the orders were. Some people helped kill Jews as a way of making money. German construction companies built the camps and German chemical companies sold the poison gas used to murder Jews. Museums stole Jewish-owned art, banks took their money, and many companies worked Jewish slaves to death in their factories.

Even those who did not agree with the anti-Jewish actions of the government mostly didn't say anything. Hitler's government was a dictatorship, and anyone who tried to help Jews risked imprisonment and death him or herself. Most Germans, like most people everywhere, were not murderers or heroes. They tried to mind their own business and just keep themselves safe. The large majority of Germans did not actually participate in the murders, and after the war many said that they did not know what was going on. It is probably true that they didn't know exactly what was happening, but they must have had a good idea. They saw their Jewish neighbors pulled from their homes and sent away. Some received letters from soldiers that described the murders. The Nazis may have tried to keep the murders secret, but everyone in Germany knew, or should have known, that something terrible was happening to the Jews.

But there were German heroes. A very few Germans did resist the Nazis. Some Protestant ministers, like Pastor Niemoeller, publicly spoke out against the Nazis. When the Nazis arrested socialists and communists, and when they murdered the disabled and mentally ill—this was before they had even begun the massive murder of Jews—Niemoeller protested. He, and other pastors, such as Dietrich Bonhoeffer, also spoke out against the persecution of Jews. These pastors were usually arrested and sent to concentration camps, where they died. There were even a few German soldiers who tried to help Jews. Sergeant Anton Schmid was horrified by what he saw in Vilna. He decided to help hide Jews. He also gave them supplies and forged papers. In February 1943, he was executed by the Nazis. During the war, some German university students, called the White Rose group, led by Hans and Sophie Scholl, handed out leaflets protesting the murder of the Jews. They were caught and executed by the Nazis. Very few Germans followed the Scholls' example.

In other countries controlled by the Nazis, the majority of people just tried to keep themselves safe. The war was dangerous for everybody. In some countries, especially Poland, the Nazis treated the population very harshly. People felt they had to watch out for themselves and could not help others, especially Jews, whom many didn't like in the first place. So the answer to the question "What were most people doing while the Nazis were murdering Jews?" is that they were trying to ignore it.

But some people enthusiastically joined the anti-Semitic killings. This was especially true in countries with strong traditions of Jew-hatred, such as Lithuania and Ukraine. There were Lithuanians and Ukrainians who worked for the SS as camp guards, as Jew hunters, and as torturers and murderers of Jews. In some cases, Lithuanians and Ukrainians went out on their own to kill Jews. In almost every country the Nazis controlled, there were people who worked with them to kill Jews. In France, the Nazi-controlled French government, called the Vichy government, sent French police to arrest Jews and sent them to death camps. There were Norwegian and Dutch Nazis. Anne Frank, a Jewish girl who wrote a famous diary while she hid from the Nazis, had to worry about being found by both German and Dutch Nazis. She was eventually murdered in Auschwitz. In Hungary there was a whole organization that was modeled after the SS and killed Jews. Even some people who fought the Nazis, such as Polish or Russian partisans, would sometimes kill Jews they came across in the forests of Eastern Europe.

Although most did nothing, and many actually joined in with or helped the murderers, in each country there were people who risked their lives to save Jews. Jewish tradition has come to call them Righteous Gentiles. Many Jews survived the Holocaust because a non-Jew risked her or his life to save Jews.

Ona Simaite was a gentile Lithuanian woman. She was a librarian. She told the Nazis she had to go into the Vilna ghetto to get back some valuable books, but this was only an excuse for her to smuggle things into the ghetto and help the Jews. Time after time she went into the ghetto, bringing false papers to help people escape, guns for the ghetto fighters, messages from the outside, food, medicine, and whatever she could find that might help. Each trip, and there were many, she risked her life. Even after she was warned that the Gestapo was getting suspicious of her, she continued to help Jews. She was finally caught, tortured, and sent to a concentration camp.

Throughout Eastern Europe, in Lithuania, Poland and Ukraine, while some of their countrymen were helping the Nazis kill Jews, there were farmers who hid Jews in their barns, in their hay-lofts, and even in holes in the ground. They would bring the hidden Jews food and water at night. Jozefek, a Polish cattle dealer in Lvov, was publicly hanged by the Nazis for hiding 35 Jews. Some gentiles pretended that Jewish orphans were their own children to protect the children from the Nazis. In cities, there were people who hid Jews in attics and closets, protecting them for years. All these people knew that if the Nazis found them helping Jews they would be punished with death. They knew that many of their neighbors would turn them in if they knew that they were hiding Jews. Many of these gentile rescuers were caught and killed. Usually they were executed on the spot. Sometimes their whole families would also be killed. Jozef Bas, a Polish farmer, hid Jews in his barn. When they were discovered, Jozef and his entire family were executed by the Nazis.

Throughout Europe, some religious Christians protected Jews. Jewish children were hidden by nuns in convents—the Marcel Network was able to find shelter for 527 French Jewish children in convents, Catholic boarding schools, convents and the homes of Protestant families. In Ukraine, Lithuania and Poland the Nazis murdered many priests for helping Jews. These rescuers, although there were many of them, were still a tiny minority in every country. But without them, far fewer Jews would have survived the war.

Occasionally a person in power would work to rescue Jews. Raoul Wallenberg was a Swedish diplomat in Hungary. He gave tens of thousands of Budapest Jews Swedish passports. The Nazis didn't want to anger neutral Sweden. Wallenberg saved thousands in this way. He disappeared after the war and was probably killed by the Soviets because they thought he might be a spy. Chiune Sugihara was a Japanese diplomat in Lithuania. Even though Japan was an ally of the Germans, Sugihara gave exit visas for Japan to all the Jews who applied and saved thousands of them that way. All of the students of the Mir Yeshiva went to Japan on Sugihara visas. Osker Schindler was a German businessman who came to occupied Poland to make money using Jewish slaves. But when Schindler saw what was going on, he used his factories to protect Jews instead of making money off of them. Schindler saved hundreds of Jews. He even managed to get some of his workers returned from Auschwitz. These are only a few examples of the hundreds of gentiles who risked all they had, including their own and their families' lives, to save Jews.

Jews were saved best when a whole community worked together to save them. That hardly ever happened, but it did sometimes. In France, in the town of Le Chambon sur Lignon, a Protestant Minister, Pastor Andre Trocme, organized all of the townspeople to hide Jews. The town then helped the Jews travel secretly to a neutral, safe country. The town saved 5,000 Jews. Not a single Jew who came to Le Chambon was lost to the Nazis.

The most remarkable whole community rescue of Jews happened in Denmark. The Nazi occupation of Denmark was less harsh than in other countries because the Germans considered the Danes fellow Aryans, but the Danes did not cooperate with the Nazi persecution of the Jews. There is a story that the King of Denmark threatened to wear a yellow star if Danish Jews were forced to wear a yellow star. In 1943, the Nazis lost patience with the Danes and decided to round up all of the Danish Jews on Rosh Hashanah. But the Danes found out about the plans. The night before the Nazis were to strike, the Danes got hold of every little boat they could find and secretly ferried all of the Danish Jews across the sea to Sweden, where they were safely out of the reach of the Nazis. Over 7,000 Jews were saved that night. They were not saved by one or two brave people—they were saved by an entire nation working together to keep their fellow countrymen from being murdered.

Different governments, some under Nazi occupation, some neutral, some in exile, some fighting with the Nazis, and some fighting against them, did different things about the Nazi murder of Jews. There were governments that were accomplices, that is, helpers, in the murder. Vichy France is an example. There were German allies, such as Bulgaria, that didn't cooperate with the murders, and countries that half cooperated, such as Italy. There were allies of Germany, such as Hungary, that stalled a little while and then went right along with the Nazi murder of Hungarian Jews. In general, we can say that most governments, even those fighting the Nazis, didn't do much to rescue Jews. The United States government would not bomb and destroy the death camps. Perhaps it would not have helped, and perhaps nothing the United States could have done during the war would have saved Jews, but it certainly did not try very hard. The United States, Great Britain, and the Soviet Union eventually defeated Nazi Germany, and saved Jews by ending Nazi power. But they didn't fight the Nazis to stop the murders, and during the war these nations did little or nothing for the Jews trapped in Europe.

There were many reasons the world and its people did little to stop the Nazi crimes against Jews. Everyone was worried about his or her own problems and didn't want to be concerned with others. Anti-Semitism was widespread throughout Europe and America, which made some people not care about what was happening to the Jews. In addition, it was hard to believe reports of what the Nazis were doing until the evidence was impossible to deny.

Even Jews living in Palestine (there was no Israel yet) and Jews in America had trouble understanding what was really happening to the Jews of Europe. These free Jews did not do all they could have done to save their fellow Jews. Jews in America pushed the United States government to help the Nazi victims, but they did not want to push too hard. They were afraid it would cause anti-Semitism to increase in America. Some Jews in Palestine volunteered to fight the Nazis. One, Hannah Senesh, parachuted into Europe to fight against the Nazis. She was caught and executed. There were others like her, but much of the Jewish leadership in Palestine worried more about creating Israel than about what was happening to Europe's Jews. Jews in Palestine and America were very upset at what was happening, and they did try to save Europe's Jews, but out of ignorance, confusion and selfishness, even these free Jews did not do all that they could.

The Nuremberg Trials

The Second World War ended in May 1945. The Nazis were completely defeated and the victorious allies occupied, that is, took control of, Germany. The allies decided to put the Nazis on trial for the crimes they had committed. The Nazis were charged with starting the war and fighting the war in ways that were illegal according to international law. They were also charged with a new crime: crimes against humanity. This new charge was not only about the Nazi murder of Jews. The Nazis killed and imprisoned their political opponents, forced mentally retarded people to have surgery so that they could never have babies, and murdered disabled people and people with mental illnesses; gay people were put in concentration camps, where they often died; the Nazis enslaved people from all over Europe. They murdered many Polish politicians, scientists, teachers, and scholars; Christian ministers and priests who didn't cooperate with the Nazis were also imprisoned and killed. Millions of Soviet soldiers captured by the Nazis were starved to death in prison camps. The Roma people, Gypsies, were also imprisoned, starved, and murdered. The Nazis wanted to wipe out all of the Gypsies too, and they killed hundreds of thousands of them.

The Nazis murdered two out of three European Jews, almost half of the Jews in the world. They also destroyed the thousand-year old homeland of Jewish life. The *shtetls* of Eastern Europe were wiped off the map. Towns that were the homes of great Hasidic dynasties were left without a single *Hasid*. Jewish Vilna, the "Jerusalem of Lithuania," home of great yeshivas and of the Vilna Gaon, birthplace of the Bund, was no more. Warsaw, which had hundreds of thousands of Jews before the war and was the center of Yiddish literature, was now a city without Jews. The Yiddish language itself, and all of the culture that went with it, never recovered from the Nazi persecution. After the war, no babies would ever again be born into a Yiddish-speaking town.

The trials for these crimes were held in the German city of Nuremberg. At the Nuremberg trials some Nazis were convicted and punished. The Commandant of Auschwitz, Rudolph Hess was executed. But most Nazi criminals escaped justice. Some top Nazis, such as Hitler, Goebbels and Himmler, killed themselves before or after they were caught. Other Nazi criminals, with the help of fascist or anti-Semitic friends, escaped. Many of these escaped Nazi criminals, like Adolf Eichmann, lived in South America, protected by right-wing military dictatorships. Some criminals were never put on trial because the United States or the Soviet Union found them useful. After World War Two, there was a "Cold War" between the United States and the Soviet Union. It was not a real fighting war, but each considered the other an enemy and thought that a real war would probably start soon. Any German that could help in this Cold War, as a spy or as a rocket scientist, for example, even if he was a Nazi criminal, was protected by whoever captured him. Both the United States and the Soviet Union protected these "useful Nazis." For the next fifty years people searched for war criminals, but only a small percentage of them were ever found and put on trial.

FIGURE 36 – Defendants at Nuremberg Trials of Nazi officials after World War II.

Some people thought the Nuremberg trials were unfair. They said that the Soviet Union was also a dictatorship that imprisoned and starved millions of innocent people. They said that the United States and Britain also killed innocent men, women, and children during the war. In Dresden and Hiroshima alone, hundreds of thousands of Germans and Japanese were killed by allied bombings. Some even said the Nazi activities weren't real crimes because the Nazis were the official government and Germans were just following the government policies and laws. But most people, even if they agreed with most of these points, thought that what the Nazis did deserved punishment, even if not everyone else who deserved punishment was punished. The Nuremberg trials also taught that certain laws themselves are criminal, and that it is a crime to follow those criminal laws.

Survivors

When the war ended, the Jews still alive in Europe had nothing. They came out of their hiding places in the forests, out of their hidden rooms, and out of the liberated concentration camps to find everything of their old world destroyed. All of those in the camps, and most of those who had been in hiding, had been starved for years, their health ruined. Some could not recognize themselves in mirrors. Only a few had any relatives left. Mothers, fathers, brothers, sisters, sons, and daughters—all were murdered. All their neighbors and friends from home had been killed. Their homes, businesses, and possessions had been taken over by others and stolen.

There was nothing at their old homes to return to. Those survivors who tried to return home often found they weren't welcome or even safe. In Kielce, Poland, there was an anti-Semitic pogrom one year after the war. Over forty Jewish survivors of the Nazi persecution who had returned home to Kielce were killed in the pogrom. Jews realized that there was no place for them in Poland. Most survivors did not want to stay in Europe. For them, Europe was now only an old slaughterhouse and a graveyard.

But even after the war few countries were willing to take in Jews. There were refugees admitted to the United States, Australia, South Africa, Britain, and France, but not nearly all who needed a new home. "Displaced Person" (DP) camps were set up in Europe for the survivors who couldn't find a new home. There were hundreds of thousands of survivors who lived in these camps for years. Of course they had food, medicine, and shelter in the DP camps. They were not tortured or murdered there. In fact, Jews organized schools, political groups, and social events in the DP camps. But years after the Nazi defeat, Jews still found themselves living in camps. They wanted to get out of the camps and get out of Europe.

Palestine, where Zionists were trying to establish a Jewish homeland and state, was where most displaced persons wanted to live. For three years after the war, while Britain controlled Palestine, Jews could not legally settle there. Some Jews sneaked in past the British. In 1948, the State of Israel was established in part of Palestine. The new state's first law was to allow any Jew to come and live in Israel. Many of the displaced European Jews became Israelis because they finally found the home they truly wanted. Other displaced Jews emigrated there because it was the only place that would accept them.

FIGURE 37 – Members of Kibbutz Ein Harod, 1941.

FIGURE 38 – Israeli leaders in a military review, 1949.

Chapter 18

The Creation of Israel

In Chapter 14 we described the beginning of Zionist ideas and the Zionist movement in Europe. Now we turn to the story of how the state of Israel was established and grew. It is a story not only of Jews, but also of Palestinian Arabs.

Palestine Before Zionism

Most of the Jews of Palestine were expelled after the Romans put down the Bar Kokhba rebellion in 134 AD. A majority of the people still living in Palestine after the expulsion eventually became Christian. When the Muslim Arabs conquered it in 640, Palestine became a mostly Muslim land and the people living there became an Arab people. Some of these people remained Christian, and there always remained some Jews in the land, but by the nineteenth century, Palestine had been a land inhabited mostly by Muslim Arabs for over a thousand years. At times during these thousand years, Palestine was part of large Arabic empires, called Caliphates. Caliphates were ruled from Damascus or Baghdad, but in 1516, the Ottomans, a Turkish Muslim people, started ruling Palestine.

At the end of the nineteenth century, Palestine was still part of the Ottoman Empire and had about 450,000 people. Around 400,000 were Muslims, 50,000 were Christian, and 17,000 were Jews. The Jews were very religious and were concentrated in the Jewish holy cities of Hebron, Safed, Tiberias, and Jerusalem (where Jews had come to be the largest group). The Zionists called this Jewish Palestinian population the Old Yishuv, the old settlement. Some Arab towns, such as Bethlehem and Nazareth, were heavily Christian, some, such as Jaffa, Haifa, Nablus, and Jenin, were Christian and Muslim mixed. Most of the people of Palestine were poor peasants living in Muslim villages. There were also Arab nomads, Bedouins, moving throughout the land. Jerusalem, a city holy to Muslims, Christians and Jews, had large populations from each group living within its city walls.

So when the first Zionists came, they came to an Arab land with a few old religious Jews living in a few towns. The Turkish rulers were in faraway Istanbul. The Arab peasants, called *fellahin*, were poor and uneducated. Locally, the *fellahin* were ruled by wealthy notable families called *ayan*. The *ayan* consisted of large, extended families and their friends. *Ayan* such as the Husseinis, and the Nashashibis were very powerful locally, but still had to obey the Ottoman government officials (sometimes the *ayan* were the local Ottoman officials). Local *ayan*, and some *ayan* that lived outside of Palestine, in Damascus or Cairo, owned most of the land. The *fellahin* were usually tenants of these great landlords. Some village peasants, however, did own their own land.

There was hardly any industry in Palestine. It was an agricultural land of fruit trees and shepherds, although of course there were merchants and commerce in the towns. Parts of Palestine didn't have many people. As in ancient times, and as is the case today, much of it was desert. Parts were swampy and parts were hilly. Although there was vibrant town culture in the towns mentioned, Palestine mostly was a land of poor farmers visited by religious pilgrims.

The Early Immigrants

At the very beginning of the Zionist movement, before it was even a political movement, a few wealthy European Jews, like Baron Edmund de Rothschild, gave money to settle Jews in Palestine. These settlements were near the Mediterranean coast. They were poor and were just barely kept going by the money given by the wealthy benefactors. A few other Jews also came, settling in cities such as Jaffa and Jerusalem. Jerusalem began to expand outside of its old walls. The Jews that came at this time are known as the

First *Aliyah. Aliyah* means "going up" and in Jewish tradition, going to Palestine was thought of as going to a higher place.

After 1905, right up until World War I, another wave of Jews came to Palestine. That wave is known as the Second *Aliyah.* These were mostly socialist Jews. They wanted to establish cooperative Jewish agricultural settlements all over Palestine. Eventually they established farming communities, *moshavim,* that cooperated in selling their crops. They also created farming communes in which the people cooperated in everything and shared equally all their responsibilities and all their wealth. Those are called *kibbutzim.* In *kibbutzim* the people ate together in big dining rooms, shared clothing and even brought up their children together in children's houses. Bosses were elected by the *kibbutz* members and were changed frequently. *Kibbutzniks* really tried to live as socialists.

The Jews that came to Palestine in the Second *Aliyah*, such as David Ben Gurion, became leaders of the Yishuv. (The Jews of Palestine, old and new together, were called the Yishuv.) Eventually they also became the first leaders of the State of Israel. The immigrants of the Second *Aliyah* started many of the Palestinian Jewish organizations that built up the Yishuv, such as Jewish workers' unions, Jewish health clinics, and Jewish militias to defend and expand the Yishuv.

Rebirth of Hebrew and Development of the Yishuv

The First *Aliyah*, which began after the anti-Semitic pogroms in Russia, did not bring many Jews to Palestine. But these pioneers, whom the Zionists called *chalutzim*, laid a few of the most important building blocks of a Jewish homeland. They started the first Jewish settlements, such as Petah Tikvah and Rishon Lezion near Jaffa, and Rosh Pina in the Galilee. In the time of the First *Aliyah*, the Jewish National Fund was begun. The JNF collected money from Jews around the world for the purpose of buying land in Palestine. The land was then used to build new Jewish settlements. The JNF's blue and white tin collection boxes eventually became familiar sights in many Jewish homes around the world. But perhaps the greatest contribution the First *Aliyah* made to the creation of a modern Jewish homeland was the revival, the bringing back to daily life, of the Hebrew language.

Before the *Haskalah*, for thousands of years, Hebrew had only been used as a religious language by Jews. With the *Haskalah*, some educated Jews began to use Hebrew to write modern literature. But when Zionism began, Hebrew was still not used as an everyday language by anybody. One reason for Zionism was to create a center for Jewish culture. That is what some Zionists, like Achad Ha'am, cared most about. But among the early Zionists there was no agreement about which language should be spoken by Jews in the new homeland. Some, like Herzl, didn't seem to care much. Other thought that Yiddish was the right language, because it was the language that most of the world's Jews spoke and the mother tongue of almost all of the Jewish immigrants coming to Palestine. Some suggested German, which was the language of the country many Jews considered the most scientifically and culturally advanced. German also had the advantage for Jews of being very similar to Yiddish. But for the rebuilding of the ancient Jewish homeland most Zionists wanted Hebrew, the ancient Jewish language. The problem was that no one had used Hebrew as a modern language, and no "dead" language had ever before been brought back to life.

Eliezer Ben Yehuda, who immigrated to Palestine in 1881, decided to change that. He brought up his child speaking only Hebrew. His son was the first person in over two thousand years to have Hebrew as his native language. Ben Yehuda began to write a modern Hebrew dictionary, making up new words for all of the modern things Biblical Hebrew had no words for. He spent all of his time encouraging people in the Yishuv to speak, read, and write Hebrew. Ben Yehuda did more than any other person to establish Hebrew as the language of the Yishuv and the State of Israel. Only a few generations after he lived, there are Hebrew-language theaters, films, newspapers, television, fire departments, nurseries, universities, and government, and millions of people whose mother tongue is Hebrew.

With the Second *Aliyah*, from 1905-1914, the Yishuv grew even more. These immigrants were mostly East European Labor Zionists. They started the first *kibbutz*, Degania, by the Sea of

Galilee, in 1909, and the first *moshav*, Nahalal, in the Jezreel Valley, in 1921. In fact, throughout the Jezreel Valley and all to the north and southwest of the Sea of Galilee small Jewish settlements began to be established. There were also Jewish settlements along the Mediterranean coast. In 1909, a Jewish suburb of Jaffa was started. It was called Tel Aviv and it soon became the biggest Jewish city in Palestine.

The next large Jewish immigration to Palestine came after World War I, when there was yet another wave of pogroms in Eastern Europe. This immigration is known as the third *aliyah*. It was at that time that the Yishuv formed almost all of the institutions it would need to be an organized, independent society. Besides the *Haganah* as a militia, the Jewish Agency was created as an unofficial government, with the *Va'ad Leumi* as a sort of Jewish legislature. The Jewish workers unions joined together into single big organization, the *Histadrut*. The *Histadrut*, in turn organized Jewish insurance programs, health clinics, and worker's cooperative businesses. More *kibbutzim* and *moshavim* were established. By 1933, a Jewish community of about 200,000 people had arisen in Palestine.

Zionism and the Palestinian Arabs

Life for the immigrants of the First and Second *Aliyahs* was difficult. They came as poor people to a poor land, but they did not come to an empty land. Palestine had a long-established Arab population. In some ways this made it easier for the Jewish immigrants but in other ways it made it harder. It made it easier because there were already inhabited towns to live in. There were Arab merchants that the Jews could buy things from and Arab people that the Jewish immigrants could sell things to. The many poor Arab people would also work cheaply in Jewish businesses and on Jewish farms. Some Jewish businesses wouldn't hire Arabs because they wanted to save jobs for new Jewish immigrants, and some workplaces, such as the *kibbutzim*, didn't like the idea of taking advantage of any cheap labor; that was against their socialist beliefs. But much of the Yishuv economy grew because it hired Arab workers. In all these ways, the fact that the Zionists were coming to a land that already had people living in it helped Zionism.

But it also created problems. The biggest problem was that after a while the Arab people realized that the Jews were trying to take over. Naturally, the Arabs didn't want that to happen and did things to try and prevent it. They feared becoming second-class citizens in their own homeland. It's true that the Arabs didn't like being ruled by the Turks, but at least the Turks were fellow Muslims, like the majority of Arabs living in Palestine, and had been in charge a long time. In addition, unlike the Jews, the Turks were not pushing the Arab Palestinians off of any land.

Some of the land the Jews bought and settled on was uncultivated land that no one was using, but lots of it was land that the Jews bought from rich landlords, land that *fellahin* had rented and used for centuries. The new Jewish owners, who bought the land to settle it with fellow Jews, would make the Arabs living on the land leave. Being kicked off of their land, more than anything else, made the Arab Palestinians enemies of Zionism. They saw Zionism as a movement to take their land away from them. So even though having people already settled in Palestine made it easier for Jews to settle there, it also made it harder to take the land over and turn it into a Jewish-ruled homeland, simply because that's not what the vast majority of Palestinians living there wanted.

Another problem for the Zionists was that many of them felt bad about displacing the Palestinians. As Jews, liberals, and socialists they were mostly against driving people from their homes. But it was hard to see how a Jewish homeland could be established without doing that to at least some of the Arab Palestinians. Some Zionists pretended to themselves that Palestine was empty. Others thought that since most Palestinians were Arabs, it would not really be so bad if the Palestinians had to leave their homes and relocate in the Arab lands surrounding Palestine. Many Zionists ignored the problem and just believed that somehow making Palestine into a Jewish homeland would not force Palestinian Arabs to leave and would even benefit them by modernizing the country. A few Zionists just said it was tough luck for the Palestinian Arabs, but that Jews needed their ancient homeland more than Palestinian Arabs needed their current homeland.

A few Zionists, such as Martin Buber, Henrietta Szold, and Judah Magnes, thought the only good solution was to make all of Palestine the homeland of both the Jewish people and the Palestinian Arab people. They were strong Zionists who believed that Jews deserved a homeland, desperately needed a safe place to live, and had a right to settle in their ancient homeland Palestine, the Land of Israel, but they also believed that the Arabs of Palestine had a right to stay in Palestine as equal citizens in their own homeland.

These people were called bi-nationalists. The bi-nationalists thought there was plenty of room for Palestine to be the homeland of the two peoples. So they wanted a "bi-national" state, one country with two equal peoples—the homeland of two cultures.

FIGURE 39 – Henrietta Szold, U.S. Jewish Zionist leader and founder of Hadassah, who advocated for a bi-national state.

But only a small minority of Zionists wanted a bi-national state, and almost no Palestinians did. For most Zionists, it was important that Jews have one country where they could be the majority and control the government. They were afraid that a bi-national state wouldn't be Jewish enough for Jewish culture to flourish in. They also worried that it wouldn't be a completely safe home for Jews.

The Palestinians were against a bi-national state because they saw no reason to share their homeland with newcomers. They felt as if these newcomers were robbing their country from them, and they didn't want to share it with the robbers. In addition, because there were so many more Arabs than Jews in the country, the Palestinian Arabs felt that democracy meant that Palestine should be the country of the Palestinian Arabs. Because Arabs and Jews, and especially the leaders on both sides, did not accept bi-nationalism, there was bound to be a struggle between the Zionists and the Palestinian Arabs for control of Palestine.

Beginnings of Palestinian Resistance to Zionism

It took a while after the Zionist movement began to settle Palestine for the Palestinian Arabs to fight against Zionism. At first, when Jews were so few in number, the Arabs were more concerned with getting rid of their Turkish rulers. In fact, before Zionism began, many Palestinians didn't think of themselves as Palestinians. They thought of themselves as belonging to a local clan, like the Husseinis, or as part of the entire Arab nation, or perhaps as part of the Muslim world. It was in large part the Zionist threat to the Arabs in Palestine that made them come to think of themselves as Palestinians. And until they thought of themselves as Palestinians, it was difficult to have a strong, united fight against the Zionist movement.

There were also many divisions in Palestinian society. There were divisions between the *ayan* and the *fellahin*, between one part of the country and another, between settled folks and Bedouin nomads, and between Christian Arabs and Muslim Arabs. The Zionist movement was able to take advantage of these divisions. As a matter of fact, up until 1948 almost all of the land the Jews settled on in Palestine was sold to them by Arabs.

The British Mandate and the Balfour Declaration

The Ottoman government was a Muslim government, and it was not in favor of helping Jews make a homeland in Palestine. It tried to limit and even stop Jewish immigration to Palestine. But the Ottoman government did not work very well. Its officials were often corrupt, that is, they could be bribed to break rules. The Ottoman government slowed down the Zionist movement but was not able to stop it.

In World War I, Britain conquered Palestine and ended four hundred years of Ottoman rule. After World War I, the League of Nations, an organization of mostly European countries, said that Britain should continue to govern Palestine until Palestine was ready to be an independent nation. This permission to govern Palestine was called a "mandate," and the period of British rule of Palestine is called the Mandate Government. Probably the British government was hoping to rule Palestine forever and make it part of the British Empire. Britain even had a secret agreement with the French to divide up the Middle East. But officially the British Mandate was supposed to be temporary.

The Zionists were very pleased that Britain took control of Palestine. During World War I, in 1917, Zionists convinced the British to say publicly that Britain was in favor of a Jewish homeland in Palestine. This was known as the Balfour Declaration. With the announcement of the Balfour Declaration, the world's then most powerful country, and the one that was in control of Palestine, had said to the whole world that Jews should have a homeland in Palestine. It looked as if the British were going help the Jews establish a homeland in Palestine.

But the Balfour Declaration also said that the Jewish homeland in Palestine should be created without hurting or discriminating against the Arabs in Palestine. In addition, during the World War I the British had promised some Arab leaders, Arab leaders who helped the British fight the Ottomans, that the Arabs would have independence in their own country. Nobody, including the British, knew how the British were going to keep their promises to both the Arabs and the Jews.

In the 30 years of British rule of Palestine, they sometimes favored the Jews and sometimes the Arabs. The overall effect of British rule was to help the Zionist movement, even when the British weren't trying to do so. The British kept order and tried to stop fighting between Jews and Arabs. In the first years of the Zionist movement, when there were few Jews in Palestine, the Jewish settlement in Palestine, the Yishuv, needed a peacekeeper. It gave the Yishuv time to grow. When the Yishuv became stronger, able to defend itself from Arab attacks and able to fight for Palestine, the British Mandate became an enemy to the Zionists.

The Armed Conflict between Jews and Arabs Begins

Starting after World War I, Arabs began to attack Jewish settlements in Palestine. The Jews organized defense units, and some Jewish groups launched revenge attacks on Arabs. Then the Arabs took revenge for the revenge attacks. This pattern continued for most of the twentieth century. During these attacks, many Jews were murdered by Arabs and many Arabs were murdered by Jews. Sometimes there were pauses between attacks and counter attacks, and, as we will see, there were times of all-out war.

The first major Arab attacks on Jewish settlements took place in 1929. There were massacres of Jews in Hebron and Safed and attacks throughout the country. The Jews defended themselves, but the main leadership of the Yishuv decided not to counter-attack against the Arabs; they preferred to have the British punish the Arabs for starting the fighting. But the 1929 Arab attacks made it clear to the Yishuv that the Palestinian Arabs were not going to allow a Jewish state to be set up in Palestine without a fight. The *Haganah*, the Yishuv's main military organization, had been formed right after the First World War. The attacks of 1929 convinced Zionist leaders to do everything they could to strengthen the *Haganah*. Some Zionists thought that the *Haganah* wasn't doing enough to punish the Arabs for attacking Jews, so they started their own Jewish military organization, called the *Irgun*. The *Irgun* shot Arabs in revenge whenever Jews were shot by Arabs. They sometimes planted bombs in Arab marketplaces to avenge attacks on Jews.

The Peel Plan and the Arab Revolt

Hitler came to power in 1933. Soon all Jews, even those who had not been supporters of Zionism, believed that Jews needed a safe place to live. Most German Jews were denied permission to go to other European countries or to America. Tens of thousands of German Jews, who had never planned on leaving Germany, came to Palestine, and even more wanted to come. But Britain was not letting them.

From early in the Mandate, Britain tried to limit Jewish immigration to Palestine. Even though Britain had said in the Balfour Declaration that it was in favor of a Jewish homeland in Palestine, the British still wanted to stay friendly with the Palestinian Arabs, who were the large majority in Palestine. Britain also wanted to stay friendly with all the Arabs in the Middle East. In 1921 Britain gave all of the Mandate territory east of the Jordan River to a traditional Arab ruler from the Arabian Peninsula, who became King Abdullah of the new country Transjordan (which today is known as Jordan). But most of this land was empty desert and only a little of it was part of the area considered to be Palestine. The creation of Transjordan did not in the least satisfy the Palestinian Arabs.

Sometimes Britain was strict about limiting Jewish immigration to Palestine and sometimes it was less strict. It usually depended on whether Britain was more worried about the opinions of the Jews in the world or of the Arabs in the world. But when Hitler came to power, when Jews were most desperate to leave Europe and come to Palestine, Britain became very strict. Britain understood that it might soon have to fight a war against Germany. Britain thought that no matter what it did in Palestine, the Jews around the world would have to support Britain in a war against Nazi Germany. But the Arabs wouldn't. And the Arabs were the majority in an important part of the world, the Middle East. Oil comes from the Middle East. The Suez Canal, Britain's main water route to its Indian Empire, is in the Middle East

(Egypt), and ports on the Mediterranean and Persian Gulf are in the Middle East. Britain didn't want to turn Arabs into enemies in the 1930s, so Britain turned against Zionism.

But Britain didn't completely stop Jewish immigration. It continued to allow some Jews to come into Palestine, and even more Jews were sneaked into Palestine illegally by the Yishuv. The Arabs became nervous and angry as more and more Jews came in and more Jewish settlements were created. Finally, in 1936, the Palestinian Arabs revolted. They attacked Jewish settlements all over the country. The Arabs wanted to throw the British out so they could have their own Palestinian Arab country and stop the Zionists from making Palestine into a Jewish country. When Britain tried to restore order, the Arabs fought against the British too. The *Irgun* started attacking Arab villages, but the *Haganah* mostly just tried to defend Jewish settlements. The main Jewish leadership thought it would be better to let the British fight the Arab revolt.

The Arab Revolt lasted from 1936 till 1939. It was a courageous but not very successful revolt. While it was the first time the Arabs tried to fight the Yishuv in an organized way, it really wasn't very well organized. There were still deep divisions among Palestinian Arabs. They did not always cooperate with each other. Some of the *ayan* didn't strongly support the revolt. The defeat of the revolt greatly weakened Palestinian society. Wealthy Arabs left the country, militants were killed or exiled, and weapons were taken away. Many more Arabs were killed in the revolt than British or Jews. As a result of the revolt, the Yishuv was stronger and the Palestinian Arab community was weaker.

In 1937, one year after the Arab Revolt began, Britain decide to try to find a solution to its problem in Palestine. It sent Sir Robert Peel to study the situation there and suggest a solution. Peel said that Palestine should be partitioned, that is, divided into two parts; one part would be Jewish and one would be Arab. Jerusalem would stay British.

One group of Zionists hated this idea. They were the Revisionist Zionists. They wanted all of Palestine for the Jews. The Labor Zionists, who were the leaders of the Yishuv, didn't like the plan either. They thought the partition didn't give enough land to the Jews. But the Labor Zionists didn't want to turn the plan down. They believed that Jews should accept whatever was being offered, and then worry later how they could make the Jewish state bigger. They wanted a big state because they believed there had to be space enough to settle the millions of the Jews of Europe, who the Zionists were certain would soon need to come to Palestine.

The Arabs hated the Peel partition plan as much as the Revisionist Zionists did. They didn't want to give any land to the Jews. In addition, even if they had thought the Jews should get some land in Palestine (which they didn't) they believed the Peel Plan gave the Jews too much land. There were about as many Arabs as there were Jews living in the parts of Palestine that the Peel Plan offered the Jews. The Arabs said the plan was terrible and turned it down completely. They continued their revolt for two years after the Peel Plan.

WWII and the Yishuv

In 1939, the year World War II broke out, Britain announced a new policy toward Palestine in a document called "the White Paper." Now more than ever it was important for Britain to make friends in the Arab world. The White Paper said that Britain planned to let Palestine become an independent state in ten years. Until then, Jews would not be allowed to buy any more land in Palestine. In addition, Britain was going to permit very few Jews to immigrate to Palestine. The White Paper basically told the Jews that Britain would not let the Yishuv grow any larger.

The Jews were very angry. Jews were trapped in Hitler's Germany with no place to go. Although no one could have known how great the threat was, Zionists realized that millions of Jews throughout Europe were in danger. And at just that moment Britain was closing Palestine to the Jews. Jewish forces, especially the *Irgun*, rebelled against the British, attacking government buildings and forces. But when World War II started in September, the *Haganah* and even the *Irgun* called a truce with the British. They did not want to weaken Britain in its fight against the worst enemy the Jewish people had ever had, Nazi

Germany. David Ben Gurion, the leader of the Yishuv, said, "we will fight the war as if there were no White Paper, and fight the White Paper as if there were no war." The Yishuv fought the White Paper by trying even harder to sneak Jews into Palestine. But Jewish fighters would not attack the British. In fact many Jews joined the British Army so they could fight the Nazis. Hannah Senesh, a young Palestinian Jew who was mentioned in the last chapter, was one of those volunteers. She was sent by the British into Nazi Germany during the war to help organize the resistance to the Nazis. She was caught and executed by the Gestapo. The military training that Jews received in the British Army would be of great help to the Yishuv after the war.

One group of Jewish fighters would not stop fighting the British even during the war. They quit the *Irgun* and formed a tiny group called *Lehi* (sometimes known as the Stern Gang, because they were led by a man named Avraham Stern). *Lehi* was small, but their assassinations of British officials and their terror operations against Arabs had a large influence on world opinion.

Some Palestinian Arabs were satisfied with the White Paper, but others were not. The dissatisfied ones didn't like it that any Jewish immigration, even a small amount, was allowed. The Arabs also didn't want to wait ten years for independence. The leader of this group was Haj Amin Muhammed al-Husseini. Years before the British had made him Mufti of Jerusalem, a leader in the Arab community. The British hoped to win his cooperation, but it didn't work. The Mufti became a leader of the Arab Revolt and during the war he helped the Germans. Many Arabs thought and hoped that the Nazis would win the war. The Nazis seemed very strong at first, and everyone knew how much Nazis hated Jews. The Mufti, and some other Palestinian leaders, thought a Nazi victory would help them win their fight against the Zionists and against the British.

Rebirth and Catastrophe

When World War II ended in 1945, hundreds of thousands of Jews were in displaced persons camps in Europe. They had survived the death camps. Most of their families had been murdered by the Nazis, and most wanted to go to Palestine. But even after the war the British refused to let them emigrate to Palestine.

The Jewish revolt against British rule increased. British soldiers were killed and British buidings were bombed. In 1946, the King David Hotel in Jerusalem was blown up by a bomb planted by the *Irgun*. The hotel was used by the British for government offices. Over 90 British, Jewish, and Arab persons were killed. *Irgun* and *Lehi* terror attacks against the British continued and the British fought back by executing some of *Lehi* members. There was increased fighting between all of the Jewish forces and Palestinian Arab forces. British soldiers got into fights trying to protect Jews from Arabs and Arabs from Jews. Finally, Britain gave up trying to control Palestine and gave up trying to find a solution to the conflict between the Yishuv and the Palestinian Arabs. Britain announced that it was leaving Palestine in 1948. It asked the United Nations to decide what to do with Palestine.

The countries of the world felt sorry for the Jews after the Holocaust. Perhaps they also felt guilty for doing so little to stop the murder of millions of Jews. In 1947 the United Nations voted to partition Palestine into one Jewish and one Arab state. The Jews were offered more land than they got in the Peel Plan. The Zionist Revisionists still hated the idea of partition and wanted to fight to conquer all of Palestine. The Labor Zionist would have preferred to have all of Palestine too, but they were happy to accept a part of Palestine so they could establish an independent Jewish state, a state that could then take in all of the European Jewish refugees. The disagreement between the Labor Zionists, who were the leaders of the Yishuv, and the Revisionist Zionists was very bitter. It even caused some armed fighting. There could have been a Jewish civil war in the Yishuv, but the *Irgun*, which was the main Revisionist fighting force, decided to give up, so that the Jews would be united in the war that was coming between the Yishuv and the Palestinian Arabs.

All of the Arab peoples, including the Palestinians, thought that the United Nations had no right to give any of Palestine to Jews. The Arabs were convinced that when the British were out of the way, they would easily be able to defeat the Jews, but they were mistaken.

On May 15, 1948, at midnight, the moment the British rule in Palestine ended, David Ben Gurion proclaimed the new State of Israel as an independent country that was to be a homeland for the Jews. Its first new law, called the Law of Return, said that any Jew in the world could come to Israel and automatically become a citizen. There was dancing in the streets of Tel Aviv. Ben Gurion said he wanted to live at peace with the Palestinians and with the surrounding Arab countries. But he knew that that was not going to happen. Even before the British left, the Jews and Palestinian Arabs had been battling for advantage. Now the Arab countries of Egypt, Jordan, Lebanon, Syria, and Iraq sent troops into Palestine to fight and destroy the Yishuv, and to conquer chunks of Palestine for themselves.

Most of the world thought the Jews of Palestine would be slaughtered, but even though many Arab armies participated in the war and the Arab Palestinian population was larger than the Jewish population of Israel, Israel was actually better prepared to win the war than were the Arabs. The Jewish population was more united than the Arabs. The Jewish fighters were now all part of the same army, the Israeli Defense Forces. The Arabs were split up into different armies that did not always cooperate with each other. Even the Palestinian fighters themselves were divided into different groups that did not always cooperate. The Jews had a well-organized government that could coordinate its civilians during the war, and almost all of its citizens were literate. The Palestinians lost many of their leaders and best educated people during the Arab Revolt. Even though the Jewish population of Israel in 1948 was only about 600,000 people, and they were supposed to be fighting the whole Arab world of over 30 million people, the Jews actually had more soldiers than all of the Arab armies fighting in Palestine combined. Every Jew that could possibly fight became a soldier. After the first few months of the war, with the help of Jews in the Diaspora, the Israelis were able to get enough weapons from France and Czechoslovakia to be better armed than the Arabs. The Jews also believed that they were fighting for their lives, that if they lost they would all be massacred. Some of the Arab war talk made this a reasonable thing for the Jews to believe. The Arabs said things like "we will drive the Jews into the sea." No army could have been better motivated to fight a war than a Jewish army, three years after the Holocaust, fighting for their lives and their new country in their ancient homeland. So even though the war was a bloody, desperate, and difficult fight for the Yishuv, the community's unity and determination led to victory.

For Jews the world over, the birth of the State of Israel was a miracle. After the thousands of years of suffering in the Diaspora, after the most murderous persecution ever, at the lowest point in Jewish history, Jews had created a center for Jewish life and a place to live under the rule and protection of their own Jewish government and their own Jewish army.

But the 1948 Israeli War for Independence was a disaster for Palestinians. It is known in Palestinian history as the *Nakba*, the catastrophe. That is because hundreds of thousands of Palestinians were driven from their homes and became refugees during the war. Although Israel had accepted the United Nations partition plan, once the war started the Israeli government wanted to conquer as much of Palestine as possible for its new country. It also wanted as few Palestinians in the country as possible. It knew that a large Palestinian population would be a problem for a country that the Israeli government wanted to be Jewish. So during the war the Israeli Army sometimes kicked the Palestinians out of villages that Israel conquered.

Other Palestinians fled their villages to avoid the fighting. They thought they would return to their homes when the battle was over, or at least when the war was ended. But Israel never let them return to their homes. Sometimes the Israelis destroyed the village houses to make sure the Palestinians had no homes to return to. In Lydda, a city of over 30,000 Palestinians, Israeli troops killed many civilians. The rest were terrorized and expelled and later their homes were destroyed. There were also some massacres of Palestinians to frighten them into leaving their land. One terrible massacre took place at the Palestinian village of Deir Yassin, where *Irgun* fighters murdered many Palestinian civilians. The Palestinians were very frightened by reports of these events and fled their homes before the Israeli army arrived.

FIGURE 40 – Palestinian refugees in the Galilee.

The Israeli government did not have a written, publicly-announced, official policy of driving out the Palestinians; plenty of Palestinians, especially those in villages that did not fight the Jews during the war, were left alone. But many of Israel's leaders believed that a Jewish homeland needed to have as few Arabs in it as possible. By war's end, over half a million Palestinian refugees had lost their homes. The Palestinian *Nakba* of 1948 created a Palestinian diaspora and the strong sense that Palestinians, although a part of the Arab people, were a separate nation.

There were also Arab massacres of Jews, and Jews driven from their homes in the war. The Jewish settlements of Gush Etzion, south of Jerusalem, were wiped out by Arab forces during the war. Most painful for the Jews, the ancient Jewish quarter of the old city of Jerusalem was conquered by Arabs. All of the Jews had to leave and were not allowed to return. But because the

Israeli Army was triumphant in most places, far fewer Jews of Palestine lost their homes during the war than did Palestinians.

When the war was over, Israel had won lands throughout Palestine that had been assigned to the Palestinians by the UN Partition plan. The parts that it had not won were not left for the Palestinians; Jordan had taken over the West Bank and East Jerusalem, including the holy Old City of Jerusalem. Egypt had taken over the land around Gaza. Some Palestinians were living as a minority in the new Jewish State and some became citizens of Jordan; most became refugees, many living in poor, crowded refugee camps. No Palestinian lived in an independent Palestinian country. The war was truly a catastrophe for them.

FIGURE 41 – Tel Aviv in 2012.

FIGURE 42 – Jerusalem in 2013.

Chapter 19

Israel Develops

Israel's First Decades

The Zionist movement had created a Jewish state, but now it had to build the country. There were lots of problems. Israel was poor. It was surrounded by countries that hated it and might attack it at any time. It had a large minority Arab population that the Jewish government didn't trust. But the biggest problem was how to take in and care for the millions of Jewish immigrants the Zionists hoped would come to live in Israel.

The first Jews to come to the State of Israel were the refugees in the Displaced Persons (DP) camps of Europe. They joined their fellow Russian, Polish, and German Jews who had come to Palestine before the war. It was hard to settle these Jews who had been through the horrors of the Nazi camps, but at least they were familiar with many of the customs of the Israeli Jews, who had come from the same European countries and followed the same Ashkenazi Jewish traditions.

Sephardim

Over the next eighteen years, from 1949 to 1967, most of the Jews who immigrated to Israel were not Ashkenazim. Instead they came from Muslim lands around the Mediterranean and the Middle East—Yemen, Iraq, Egypt, Morocco, Algeria, and Iran. These Jews came from Jewish communities that had existed for hundreds or thousands of years. Sometimes they had suffered terrible persecution, including large massacres. They had almost always been discriminated against as *dhimmis*, non-Muslims, who did not have equal rights with the Muslim majority. In some countries they had had to live in separate neighborhoods, for instance the *mellahs* of Morocco. Still, these communities often prospered and produced great cultural riches. They may have been kept down as non-Muslims, but there was no special hatred for them as Jews. The Jews in Muslim lands did not suffer the constant, murderous hatred that the Jews of Christian Europe did.

When Israel was established, these Jews began to be looked on with suspicion by their Muslim neighbors. The governments and the people of these lands wondered whether their Jews were loyal to them or to their enemy, Israel. In addition, many of these countries had just become independent themselves. They had finally thrown off European rule. They were nationalist and not friendly to foreigners. Even though the Jews had been living there for a very long time, because Jews were different they were sometimes looked upon as foreigners. This was especially true because often Jews had held official positions in the European colonial governments. It soon became very uncomfortable for Jews to live in these countries. They were accused of being Zionist spies and some were executed. Jewish property was sometimes taken by the government and there were anti-Semitic riots in which Jews were killed and Jewish property stolen or destroyed.

The Jews of these lands were usually religious. Returning to the Land of Israel had always been part of their religious faith. So when the State of Israel was established, their traditional faith and their troubles at home led in time to emigration to Israel. The governments didn't let them take their money or valuable property with them. So they arrived in Israel very poor. But by the middle of the 1960s over a half a million Jews had emigrated from Muslim lands to Israel, leaving only a very few Jews behind.

Although the Jews of these countries did not all have the exact same customs, as Jews in Muslim lands they had developed many common traditions. Their religious rituals were mostly Sephardic. Many Jews who had been exiled from Spain had settled in these Muslim lands. In fact, although most families spoke Arabic or Persian and most had no ancestors who came from Spain, there were some families who still spoke Ladino. The Israeli

Ashkenazim called all these non-European Jews Sephardim or Mizrachim, (Oriental) Jews.

The Ashkenazim came from the modern, industrial nations of Europe. The Sephardim came from countries that were not industrialized or modern. The Ashkenazim had created Israel and controlled all of the powerful organizations in Israel, such as the government, schools, army, unions and kibbutzim. The newcomers controlled none of these things. The European Jews were mostly secular, the Sephardim were mostly religious. The European Jews had some racist European attitudes that made them look down upon all non-European, darker skinned people.

All of these things led the Israeli Ashkenazim to discriminate against the Sephardim, even as the Ashkenazim were also trying to help their fellow Jews adjust to life in Israel. Ashkenazim sent the Sephardim to live in new towns away from the Ashkenazi settlements. Sephardim were kept out of good jobs and schools. Along with the Israeli Arabs, Sephardim did most of the hard, dirty jobs. The Sephardim felt that the Ashkenazim looked down upon them. The Sephardim stayed poor, even as the Ashkenazim began to climb out of poverty. A divide grew in Israeli society between the Jews from Europe and the Jews from the Middle East.

Still, the work of building a life for all the immigrants in Israel was fairly successful. The immigrants learned Hebrew. They moved out of the tents they first lived in, into permanent houses. They found work, started businesses and joined the army. Israel did not attract the Jews of the United States or Western Europe as much as Zionists had hoped. And, of course, the millions of Jews of Eastern Europe murdered by Hitler would never make it to Israel. But by the 1960s, the Yishuv Jews, the Holocaust survivors, and the Jews from Muslim lands had combined to make Israel into a Jewish homeland that would last.

Continued Conflict with the Arabs

The Arab world would still not accept Israel. They felt Israel had stolen an Arab land and they were embarrassed that Israel had won the war. Arabs were also angry that Israel would not allow

Palestinian refugees to return to their homes in Israel. The Arab countries believed that the Palestinian refugees were Israel's fault and responsibility. Except for Jordan, none of the Arab countries would let the Palestinians become citizens. Most Palestinians became people without a country. Many stayed in poor crowded camps.

Israel had small border fights with Jordan, Syria, and Egypt during all of these years. Arab countries sent in fighters to raid Israel. These raiders were called *fedayeen* and they sometimes killed Israelis. Israel revenged these attacks by raiding Arab villages and killing Arabs, usually as innocent as the Israelis whom the *fedayeen* had killed.

In 1956, Egypt took control of the Suez Canal and wouldn't let any ships with products for Israel through. The British and French wanted to get control of the Canal away from the Egyptians. The Israelis were angered that Israel couldn't use the Canal and were also looking for an excuse to fight the Egyptian Army so it would become weak and not threaten Israel. Britain, France and Israel made a secret plan to go to war against Egypt. At first the plan worked, and Israel, with British and French help, conquered the Sinai desert in Egypt. But America was angry and made Israel, Britain and France return the Canal and all of its territory back to Egypt.

But the 1956 war showed the Arabs how strong the Israeli Army had become. Some Palestinians decided that they could not depend on the Arab countries to win Palestine back from the Jews. They decided that they would have to fight to return to their homes and to liberate their country on their own. Following the example of other liberation movements, they decided to use guerilla war tactics. They formed an organization called the Palestine Liberation Organization, the PLO. The PLO was made up of a number of smaller groups. The main group was *Al Fatah,* and it was led by a man named Yasser Arafat. Its official goal was to win all of Palestine back for the Palestinians and send most of the Jews in Israel back to Europe, North Africa and other Middle East countries.

June 1967: the Six Day War

Between 1956 and 1967, United Nations soldiers patrolled the Egyptian-Israeli border. The soldiers were supposed to prevent the countries from attacking each other. In 1967, the leader of Egypt, Gamal Abdel Nasser, ordered the United Nations troops out. Nasser also closed the opening to the Gulf of Aqaba and wouldn't let any ships go to the Israeli port of Eilat. Most historians don't think that Egypt planned to go to war in 1967, but at the time, Israel could not be sure. Israel felt that Egypt's blockade of Eilat was an act of war. Some Israeli generals wanted to fight Egypt before Egypt's Army became very strong from the weapons it was starting to get from the Soviet Union. In June 1967, Israel attacked Egypt. Syria and Jordan then attacked Israel. In six days the war was over and Israel had won a very big victory. It had conquered all of the Sinai up to the Suez Canal from Egypt. From Syria, Israel won the Golan Heights. From Jordan, Israel won the West Bank, including East Jerusalem.

In the days right before the 1967 war, Jews around the world and Israeli civilians were worried that Israel was about to be destroyed. Israeli political and military leaders were more confident, but even they were surprised at how big and fast the Israeli victory was. There was a feeling in Israel that the victory was a miracle and that Israel could accomplish anything.

Of all the land the Israelis conquered, the Israelis cared most about the West Bank and Jerusalem. The Sinai was important because it gave Israel space between itself and the Egyptian Army and made Israel easier to defend. The Golan was important because Syria had been using it to bomb the Israeli settlements in the Galilee in the border clashes that took place between Israel and Syria since 1948. But the West Bank was a part of historic Palestine, the traditional Land of Israel. The Old City of Jerusalem was the holiest place in all of Judaism, and no Jews had been allowed to live there since Jordan took control in 1948. This was the territory Israelis cared most about.

Yom Kippur War and Rise of Likud to Power

In 1973, on Yom Kippur, Egypt and Syria launched a surprise attack against Israel. At first the attacks were successful. Israel had been so confident from the 1967 victory that it did not take the Arab armies seriously and was unprepared for the Arab attack. The war lasted 18 days. By the time it was over, Israel had fought back and won a military victory. But the victory cost more Israeli lives than the people of Israel expected, and at times during the war there was a danger that Israeli towns would be conquered by Syria. The 1973 war made Israelis realize that it was possible for Israel to lose wars.

Labor Zionists were the leaders of the Yishuv and the heads of all of the first Israeli governments. But the Yom Kippur War shook the Israeli people's confidence in the Labor leadership because it had been so unprepared for the war. Sephardim were also growing unhappy with the Labor Zionist leadership. The Labor Zionists were mostly Ashkenazim and the Sephardim held them responsible for the discrimination the Sephardim suffered in Israel. In the 1977 elections, the Labor Party lost to Likud. Likud was a Revisionist Zionist party. Likud believed that all of the West Bank should become a permanent part of Israel. The Revisionists, such as Menahem Begin and Yitzhak Shamir, had always been against sharing Palestine with the Palestinians. They had fought with the *Irgun* and *Lehi*. In 1977 they came to power in Israel.

After 1967, the Labor government said it would return some of the West Bank to Jordan if Jordan made peace with Israel. It would not return it all, it said, because it needed some West Bank land to defend Israel and because it wanted Jerusalem to stay the united capital of Israel. The Labor government settled Israelis on the parts of the West Bank it said should remain Israeli forever. But when Likud was elected, it tried to settle Israelis all over the West Bank. The Likud believed all of the West Bank should remain a part of Israel, and its government encouraged Israelis to settle there by giving settlers favors of many kinds.

Some Israelis chose to settle on the West Bank because the government would give them nice houses for very little money.

Other Israelis went for religious reasons. Even though most of the first Zionists were secular, after 1967 there was a small but very strong group of religious Zionists who wanted Jews to own all of the Land of Israel because they believed that God had given it all to the Jews. These religious Zionists were the main part of the Israeli movement to take over the West Bank. They thought that settling the West Bank and being in charge there was part of fulfilling the requirements of Judaism. These religious settlers had the support of the Likud government. As we will see, in time these settlers' activities caused a Palestinian uprising.

Israeli Occupation and Palestinian Resistance

As in the 1948 war, Palestinians were made refugees by the 1967 war. But the majority of Palestinians of the West Bank did not get driven out or flee from Palestine in 1967. As a result, Israel took control of a million more Palestinians after the 1967 war. The West Bank and Gaza became Israeli-occupied territory, with West Bank and Gaza Palestinians under the direct rule of the Israeli Army.

The PLO was not having great success using regular guerilla tactics against Israeli soldiers. After 1967, groups in the PLO began to bomb and assassinate Israeli civilians to win publicity for the Palestinian cause. Some groups began to attack Jewish civilians in other countries. This did win attention for the Palestinian cause, but it also made many people and governments in America and Europe angry at the Palestinians. They began to think of all Palestinians as terrorists, who hijacked airplanes, killed Olympic athletes, took Israeli children hostage, and bombed synagogues. All of these things were done by groups that were part of the PLO. Because of the bad public opinion these activities caused, the main PLO group, *Al Fatah*, decided to stop using terror tactics. But some PLO groups continued to murder innocent Israelis, Jews, and people they thought helped Israelis.

Israel fought back by assassinating PLO members or bombing Palestinian refugee camps, where Israel said PLO terrorists were trained. In the attacks on refugee camps, Israelis killed many innocent Palestinians, including children. This gave Israel the reputation of being a brutal country. But the strongest and bloodiest Israeli attack on the PLO came in 1982, when the Likud government attacked deep inside Lebanon.

Peace with Egypt

Five years before the Israeli invasion of Lebanon, Israel made peace for the first time with an Arab country. In 1977, Anwar Sadat, the President of Egypt, visited Israel and offered to make peace. Sadat said Egypt would accept Israel and in live in peace with it if Israel would give Egypt back the Sinai and let the Palestinians on the West Bank have some self-rule. After long negotiations, with the help of the President of the United States, Jimmy Carter, Egypt and Israel made peace and promised to be friends. The peace held. Israel did give back all of the Sinai. But Israel didn't give the Palestinians real self-rule and the Palestinians were not interested in phony self-rule. The Egyptians kept the peace, but didn't make it a friendly peace. Egypt was angry because Israel did not live up to the Palestinian part of the agreement.

The other Arab countries, the Palestinians, and some Egyptians were angry at Sadat for making peace with Israel. They wanted all Arabs to stay united enemies of Israel. In 1981 Sadat was assassinated by religious Egyptian Muslims who were against peace with Israel. But the new Egyptian leaders stayed at peace with Israel, even when Israel invaded Lebanon and fought the Palestinians.

The First Lebanon War

The PLO main headquarters and fighters had been in Lebanon for ten years. From southern Lebanon the PLO attacked northern Israel with rockets. There had been a civil war between the Lebanese Christian Arabs and the Lebanese Muslim Arabs, and in the disorder the PLO had grown strong. In 1982, to destroy the PLO, Israel invaded Lebanon. The invasion caused the deaths of many Lebanese. At one point in the war, Israel surrounded Beirut, Lebanon's main city, and allowed Lebanese Christian fascists to enter the Palestinian refugee camps of Sabra and Shatilla. The Israelis knew that the Christians hated the Palestinians, and asked the Christians to fight and kill the PLO fighters. But the Christians didn't find many PLO fighters in the refugee camps. Instead, for three days they massacred hundreds of Palestinian civilians in the camps. Israeli Army officers said they didn't know that the massacre was taking place. But the Israeli Army was in control of the camps, and even many Israelis said that Israel had some responsibility for the massacre. In Tel Aviv half a million Israelis protested the massacre and the whole invasion of Lebanon. Finally, Israel made a deal to let the PLO fighters leave Beirut and the Israeli Army withdrew to southern Lebanon, the part of Lebanon near Israel. In time the Shi'ite Muslims in southern Lebanon started fighting the Israelis. For decades, the Israelis remained in south Lebanon fighting the Shi'ites.

Repression and The First *Intifada*

At first the Palestinians actually living in the West Bank and Gaza did not strongly resist the Israeli occupation. But in time that changed. Gradually, West Bank and Gaza Palestinians lost hope that the Arab countries or the PLO would be able to free them from Israeli rule. As Israeli settlers took more and more Palestinian land, West Bank and Gaza Palestinians became concerned that they would be pushed from their homes and become refugees. They also became angrier and angrier at the way the Israelis treated them. They had no secure rights in their own country. They couldn't move around without Israeli permission. They were always being stopped and searched by soldiers. Israel imposed curfews, that is, Israel wouldn't allow Palestinians to come out at night. Palestinians were put in jail without any trial. In jail they were usually mistreated and sometimes tortured.

In 1987, the Palestinians rose up against the Israeli occupation. They refused to pay taxes to Israel. They closed their shops every afternoon to protest the occupation. Young people threw rocks at Israeli soldiers in Palestinian towns and villages and at Israeli settlers in the West Bank and Gaza. This uprising of the whole Palestinian people on the West Bank and Gaza was called the *Intifada*. It included the *ayan* and *fellahin*, the educated and uneducated, Christian and Muslim Palestinian people. Although they had no advanced weapons, for the first time Palestinians as a united people fought Israelis. The *Intifada* lasted for five years.

The Israelis tried to fight the *Intifada* by being even tougher with the Palestinians. Israeli soldiers received orders to beat up Palestinian rock throwers and break their bones. Soldiers fired into crowds of protestors with rubber bullets. These bullets killed some Palestinians and injured many. Thousands of Palestinians were put in jail without trial, and torture of Palestinians increased. Palestinian homes were torn down. Leaders of the *Intifada* were exiled from the country. Palestinians suffered greatly, but the *Intifada* continued.

The *Intifada* made many Israelis realize that Israel could not go on ruling the West Bank and Gaza. Some of course, had always felt it was wrong to permanently occupy the West Bank and Gaza. Other Israelis didn't like the way the occupation turned some Israelis into torturers, jailers, home destroyers, and people who shot into crowds of children. Many Israelis simply wanted peace and realized there would be no peace as long as the occupation continued. Israelis were sick of the *Intifada*. More than at any time since 1967, many Israelis were willing to make compromises for peace. The Arabs and the rest of the world were also now ready for peace in the Middle East.

The Oslo Accords

During the 1980s, many Arabs, including many Palestinians, decided that they would not be able to get rid of Israel. They started to say that they would make peace with Israel if Israel gave back all of the land it had conquered in 1967. In the late 1980s and early 1990s, the Soviet bloc of nations, including the Soviet Union, collapsed. These East European Communist countries had been the Arabs' main supporters. Without Soviet help, it seemed impossible that the Arabs could defeat Israel in war, for Israel had the strong support of the United States. In addition, it was an open secret that Israel had developed an atomic bomb. No Arab country could destroy Israel without being destroyed itself. Then, in 1991, the United States totally and easily defeated Iraq in the First Gulf War. That war began when Iraq, an Arab country, conquered another Arab country, Kuwait. Then Iraq was thrown out of Kuwait by a group of countries led by the United States. Some Arab countries fought with the United States against Iraq, but some, including the Palestinians, supported Iraq. The United States told Israel to stay out of the war, even though Israel was attacked by missiles from Iraq.

The First Gulf War made everyone more ready for peace. Israel, which was still fighting the *Intifada,* now saw that faraway Arab countries could attack Israeli cities with missiles that would fly right over the Golan and West Bank. Israelis saw that the extra land did not protect them. The Palestinians saw how the strong Arab country of Iraq was no match for the United States, Israel's close ally. The United States saw how hard it was to keep all the Arab countries friendly and cooperative with the United States, as long as Israel occupied the West Bank and Gaza.

Pushed by the United States, a peace conference was organized at Madrid. Israel had a Likud government, headed by Yitzhak Shamir, who was a Revisionist Zionist and had been a member of *Lehi.* Shamir was against any compromise for peace. The American government and Israeli public opinion forced him to go to the Madrid Peace Conference, but Shamir was not planning on making peace.

When a new Israeli Labor government came to power in 1992, secret talks between Israelis and Palestinians began in Oslo, Norway. At Oslo, the Palestinians were represented by the PLO. Soon these talks led to a Declaration of Principles for peace, that is, an outline of how the Israelis and Palestinians could share the Land of Israel/Palestine. Once this outline agreement was reached with the Palestinians, Israel and Jordan made peace. Jordan no longer wanted the West Bank, and had been waiting for a chance to make peace with Israel without getting its own Palestinian population angry. The Oslo agreement gave Jordan that chance.

FIGURE 43 – Israeli Prime Minister Yitzhak Rabin and Chairman of the Palestinian Liberation Organization Yasser Arafat shaking hands on the White House lawn on the signing of a Declaration of Principles for peace between Arabs and Israelis, 1993.

The Oslo outline left out many details. It basically said that Israeli troops would start to leave the West Bank and Gaza, and the PLO could be the government in the parts that Israel left. The agreement said that in five years there would be a new permanent agreement. The new agreement would spell out how much land the Palestinians would get, what would happen to the Jewish settlers on the West Bank and Gaza, what would become of Palestinian refugees around the world, what would become of Arab East Jerusalem, and whether the PLO-ruled areas could become a real independent state. In other words, the outline didn't solve any of the hard disagreements. But it did say that Israelis and Palestinians recognized that each had a right to live in their own state, and that they should solve their conflict through negotiations, not violence. The agreement was made between two leaders who had been hated enemies of each other: Yasser Arafat who had ordered terror attacks against Israeli civilians, and Yitzhak Rabin, who had ordered brutal violence against Palestinian civilians.

There were both Palestinians and Israelis who were very much against the Oslo peace agreements. Each side had people who said it was surrender. Each side had people who said the whole land belonged only to its own people. These Jewish and Palestinian opponents of Oslo did what they could to stop the peace negotiations. Baruch Goldstein, a Jewish settler on the West Bank, massacred Palestinian Muslims while they were at prayer in a mosque. Hamas, a Muslim Palestinian group, set off bombs among Israeli civilians, murdering dozens of Israelis. During the negotiations the Israeli government punished all Palestinians for the bombs by not letting them work in Israel. This angered Palestinians and led to more violence. Still, through all the terror attacks against Israeli civilians and all of the brutal suppression and punishment of innocent Palestinians, the negotiations continued.

In 1995, a Jew who was against compromising for peace assassinated Yitzhak Rabin, the Prime Minister of Israel. Rabin had been a soldier for Israel most of his life and he was no friend of Palestinians, but it seemed that he had become willing to make a deal with the Palestinians for the sake of peace. The Israelis who disagreed with Rabin, such as the Likud and the West Bank settler Jews, said that Rabin was a traitor and a danger to Israel. They called him an anti-Semite. Finally, a Jew who strongly supported the settlers murdered him.

Israelis were shocked by the assassination of Rabin. New elections were called. But before the elections could be held, *Hamas* planted many bombs throughout Israel, on buses, in malls, on the streets. The bombs made Israelis feel that perhaps peace was impossible, and it certainly made them angry with all Palestinians. Benjamin Netanyahu, a Likud Revisionist Zionist who was against compromising for peace, won the elections. He tried to stop the peace process. There was more violence against Israelis and against Palestinians. Finally, Israelis and Palestinians decided to try once again to have real peace negotiations. Netanyahu was thrown out of office and Ehud Barak, a Labor Party Israeli soldier, very much like Rabin, became Prime Minster. Peace negotiations started again.

Those negotiations, held at Camp David near Washington, DC, did not succeed. Israelis and Palestinians tried to make peace still again a few months later at Taba, Egypt, and again seven years later when Ehud Olmert led Israel and Mahmoud Abbas led the Palestinians, but all those talks failed. Each time Israelis and Palestinians seemed to come very close to agreeing to live in peace. Most Israelis, most Palestinians, and most people around the world, thought there could be a fair peace if the land was shared. The West Bank and Gaza would be a homeland for Palestinians; Israel, in the borders it had before the 1967 War, would remain the Jewish homeland.

But the leaders of the Palestinians and the leaders of Israel could not agree on how to share Jerusalem or how to treat the Palestinians who lost their homes and fled from Palestine in the war of 1948. It was also hard to make peace because those Israelis and Palestinians who wanted to keep all of the land for themselves more than they wanted peace made their leaders afraid that, if they made peace, they would lose political power. So instead of moving toward peace, over the next 15 years there was more terror, more oppression, more war, more distrust and more death.

The Second *Intifada*

Ariel Sharon was an Israeli politician who did not want the Palestinians to have a country in the West Bank. An Israeli investigation had held Sharon responsible for making possible the Christian Lebanese massacre of Palestinians in the war in Lebanon in 1982. Palestinians hated him. In the year 2000, Sharon decided to visit the Temple Mount in Jerusalem. Muslims call that place the Haram al Sharif. It is a very holy place to Muslims and Jews and everyone knew that having this Israeli politician visit the Temple Mount with all his body guards would anger Palestinians. Some people thought that the Palestinian leaders, because they were frustrated that the Oslo negotiations had not given them their own country yet, were looking for an excuse to become violent. The violence probably would have happened anyway, but Sharon's visit gave Palestinians an excuse to become violent if they were looking for one.

The Palestinians once again started actively resisting the occupation. This resistance was called "the Second *Intifada.*" With the exception of some stone throwing, the First *Intifada* was mostly non-violent. But this Second *Intifada* was very violent. Restaurants, cafes, and buses were bombed. Many Israelis were murdered in these terrorist attacks. The Israeli government reacted with violence. Palestinians were shot during protests. They were kept prisoners in their homes. Israeli soldiers set up "checkpoints" throughout the West Bank and Gaza. Palestinians had great trouble getting to work, school, or their farmlands because of the checkpoints. West Bank cities, the town of Jenin for example, were invaded by the Israeli army, and many Palestinians died or were arrested and kept in jail for years without receiving a trial.

FIGURE 44 – The Separation Wall, near Bethlehem.

To stop terror attacks and keep Palestinians out of Israel, Israel built a barrier made of a concrete wall and a barbed wire fence. This fence and wall separated Palestinians from land they expected would be part of Palestine, if peace ever were to come.

Palestinians thought the wall was not made to stop attacks. They believed it was built to take more Palestinian land for Israel.

The violence of the Second *Intifada* made Israelis angry and frightened. They elected Ariel Sharon Prime Minister because they knew he would be very tough on the Palestinians. When he became responsible for Israel's future, Sharon decided that keeping the occupation without any changes would be bad for Israel. Without negotiating with the Palestinians, Sharon arranged for the withdrawal of all Israelis living in Gaza and all Israeli soldiers occupying Gaza. The Palestinians were happy the Israelis left Gaza, but they wanted Israel to leave the West Bank too, because Gaza was only a small part of the land they needed to build their own country.

After the Second *Intifada* there were elections in Palestine. *Hamas,* a Palestinian Muslim political party that wanted Palestinians to follow a strict religious life, gained government power in those elections, even though it did not get a majority of Palestinian votes. *Hamas* was against peace with Israel. Their Palestinian political opponent was *Al Fatah*, Yasser Arafat's party, now led by Mahmoud Abbas. *Al Fatah* wanted to make a peace agreement and was not a religious party. The election results soon led to a short Palestinian civil war between *Hamas* and *Al Fatah*. In this bitter fight, *Hamas* got complete control of Gaza, which Israel had already left, and *Al Fatah* got some control of the West Bank, which remained under Israeli occupation.

Hamas, probably in part because it was against peace with Israel altogether, allowed some people in Gaza to attack Israel with missiles. These missiles killed a few Israelis and made many Israelis frightened every day of their lives. In return Israel bombed Gaza and invaded it. In these invasions and bombings many hundreds of Gazans were killed by Israel, and thousands had their homes destroyed. Israel also did not let products into Gaza, except for basic food and medicine, and didn't let out of Gaza the products the Gazans needed to sell. The people of Gaza felt trapped in their crowded, small area and became very poor.

Different Palestinians tried different things to end the occupation and become an independent country. In the West Bank *Al Fatah* tried to cooperate with Israelis to stop all terrorism. They also tried to make the Palestine economically stronger and ready to rule itself independently. Other Palestinian activists started a worldwide non-violent movement to pressure Israel to end the occupation. This movement, called Boycott, Divestment and Sanction (BDS) asked everyone in the world to stop having anything to do with Israel; no buying or selling; no visiting Israel or inviting Israelis to your country; no contact at all. Most Israelis felt that BDS was aimed not at ending the occupation, but at ending Israel as a Jewish homeland. Palestinians mostly felt BDS was the only non-violent way they had to stop the Israeli occupation of their land and violation of their human rights.

Israeli Economic Changes

After 1967, Israel changed. To begin with, it became richer. The 1967 victory made Israelis confident and offered them new business opportunities. After 1973 Israel began to get lots of money from the United States government. Contributions to Israel from the Jewish diaspora also increased. So did tourism to Israel. Israel became more connected to the outside world.

Israel also became less socialist. As time passed, the Labor Zionists did not remain very loyal to the socialist values of Israel's founders. The Likud, which came to power in 1977, was against socialist values. In addition, Israel became close to the United States and depended on the United States for money and weapons. The United States wanted all of its allies to be friendly to business and not to workers. When the Soviet Union collapsed, the United States was the only very powerful country left in the world. American opinions and ways of doing things had a great deal of influence everywhere, but especially in Israel. Americans in general were against socialism, and that helped weaken Israeli socialism.

In Israel, all of this meant that the worker's unions and their federation, the *Histadrut*, became weaker. The government also gave less help to workers cooperatives, such as *kibbutzim*. The *kibbutzim* themselves became less socialist. In some *kibbutzim*, members began to have private bank accounts, and on all *kibbutzim* children stopped being raised collectively. Strict equality stopped being the *kibbutz* rule. In fact, all of Israel went from being a society that had a lot of equality, to one where there began to be more and more of the very rich and the very poor.

Israel developed into a very modern country, full of modern appliances, communications, buildings, and roads. An advanced computer industry became a central part of the Israeli economy. By 2000, Israel had more cell phones per person than any other country in the world. By 2013 Israel had a very prosperous high-tech industry, but also growing inequality between rich and poor people. Israel itself was richer than it had ever been. But there was much less equality than in Israel's first years and many Israelis were still poor. A large protest movement in 2011 demanded that the government be fairer to poor and middle income people. But even though the government did not do much to make it fairer in Israel, the movement fell apart because the never-ending conflict with the Palestinians kept Israelis from paying continued attention to any other political problem.

FIGURE 45 – Housing protest in Beersheva, Israel, 2011.

The makeup of the Israeli population also continued to change. In 1948, Israeli Arabs were less than 10% of the population, but by 2013 they were over 15%. Israeli Arabs were still the poorest Israelis and were still discriminated against, but they were starting to demand full equal rights and full inclusion in Israeli society.

The Sephardim also began to improve their position in Israel. There were Sephardim in top jobs in government and the Army, even though by 2013 Sephardim had still not caught up with the Ashkenazim.

Secular-Religious Conflict

Another group that grew in size and power were the ultraorthodox religious Jews in Israel. These Israelis kept themselves apart from other Israelis, dressed in traditional Hasidic clothing, and rejected modern, liberal values. They were small groups, mostly anti-Zionist, when Israel was founded in 1948, and had been especially hard hit by the Nazi murders. Ben Gurion thought they were bound to disappear in the modern world. But instead, they grew.

In the late 1970s the ultraorthodox in Israel started to make political deals with the Zionist Revisionists: the ultraorthodox would support Israel taking over the West Bank if the Zionist Revisionists—the Likud—supported making Israel a society run by religious Jewish laws. This deal gave the ultraorthodox lots of power in Israel.

By the 1990s, one of the main conflicts in Israel was between the ultraorthodox and the non-religious Israeli Jews. The ultraorthodox wanted only orthodox rabbis to have the power to decide who was Jewish, who could marry, who could divorce, who would serve in the Army, and what was allowed on Shabbat. The non-religious, the secularists, who were by far the majority, wanted to give other rabbis, such as Reform and Conservative rabbis, equal rights in Israel. More importantly, the secularists didn't want any rabbis, Reform, Conservative, or Orthodox, to make these decisions for all Israelis. They wanted these public policies decided democratically by the majority of Israelis, and they thought personal decisions should be left up to individuals to decide for themselves.

The disputes between the ultraorthodox and the secularists sometimes became very angry. For instance, the ultraorthodox often protested secularists driving on Shabbat by throwing stones at cars riding through religious neighborhoods. The ultraorthodox also tried to force other Israelis to follow their customs of denying women equality in public places such as on buses and at holy sites. Israelis who wanted equality for women and did not want to be forced to obey religious rules fought back, and this disagreement caused tension in Israeli society. The tension between the ultraorthodox citizens and the secular citizens grew in the first decade of the 21st century as the ultraorthodox minority wanted religious laws to rule more and more parts of Israeli society.

Soviet Immigrants

In the 90s, Israel was greatly affected by immigrants from the former Soviet Union. Starting in the 1970s, some Soviet Jews became Zionist. The Soviet Union didn't allow much religious or cultural freedom for anyone, but in addition, the Soviet government was anti-Semitic, and so there was even less religious and cultural freedom allowed Jews. A few Jews decided that they wanted to go to Israel. Most were refused permission to leave by the Soviet government. They were called *refuseniks*. Sometimes they were put in jail and almost always they lost their jobs. A few did get permission to leave the Soviet Union.

In 1985, Mikhail Gorbachev became the leader of the Soviet Union. He tried to bring more freedom to the Soviet Union and he let many more Jews leave. When the Soviet Union collapsed in 1991, a flood of Russian-speaking Jews left Russia, Ukraine, Belarus, the Baltics countries, and the Caucasus—all parts of the former Soviet Union. Many went to the United States or Europe, but almost a million went to Israel.

These Russian immigrants were a challenge for Israel. They had almost no Jewish culture, and the orthodox rabbis would not even treat many of them as Jews. They needed places to live, but they didn't want to go to the development towns where the Sephardim had been sent decades earlier. Russian Jews needed jobs, but most were well educated and didn't like doing the unskilled jobs that were available. For instance, many Russian Jews who came to Israel were professional musicians, but there aren't that many paying jobs for violinists in a small country like Israel. Some Israelis, especially Sephardim, resented the Russians. The Sephardim thought the Russians were favored by the government and were taking away opportunities from Sephardim.

By 2013 these problems remained but were lessening. The Russians added a lot of skill and talent to Israel and helped the Israeli economy. They started to find the jobs they wanted. They built Russian neighborhoods throughout Israel, with their own restaurants, newspapers, and political parties. The Russians were succeeding as Israelis.

Ethiopians

A smaller but still important new group to Israel came from Ethiopia. In ancient times a group of Jews had made their way to Ethiopia and settled there. They did not have the Talmud because they separated from other Jews before the Talmud was written, but through the centuries these Ethiopian Jews had kept the ancient Jewish customs and remained a separate group. In the 1980s, terrible civil wars came to Ethiopia. All Ethiopians suffered from the violence and starvation. The Ethiopian Jews were also hard hit. World Jewry, and then the Israeli government, worked to bring Ethiopian Jews to Israel. In two operations, Operation Moses and Operation Solomon, Israel flew almost all of the Ethiopian Jews to Israel.

There were far fewer Ethiopian immigrants than Russian ones, but the Ethiopians presented special problems. They came from a poor, traditional society to a wealthy modern one. They did not have the habits or education to do well quickly in their new country. Also, as dark skinned Africans, they were easily singled out and sometimes discriminated against. Many Israelis still had some of their European anti-African prejudice. Along with the Arab Israelis, Ethiopians became the poorest people in Israeli society. But because they were Jewish, the Ethiopians were basically welcomed and did begin to make progress in Israel.

In 2013, although there remained tension between various Israeli ethnic groups—Ashkenazim, Sephardim, Russians, and

Ethiopians—each group added to the culture of Israel, and many in Israel seemed determined to learn to live together and respect each other. Moreover, the groups were beginning to intermarry and merge into one national Israeli identity.

However, one group of Israelis was still kept mostly separate from the mainstream of Israeli society; Palestinian Arab citizens of Israel. By 2013, the Arab-Israelis were growing frustrated by the discrimination they continued to suffer. They were demanding to be included as full and equal citizens of Israel.

The Middle East Region and the Chances for Peace

At the beginning of the twenty first century it looked as if the majority of Palestinians in Gaza and the West Bank for the first time ever, and the majority Israelis for the first time since 1967, were ready to share Palestine. Arab countries also seemed serious about accepting Israel. We must say "seemed," because some Palestinians groups still spoke of getting rid of Israel completely, and Israel still took over land on the West Bank and expanded its settlements. All sides were doing things that made peace difficult. Still, in 2000, peace appeared to have a real chance. However, as we have seen, the Second *Intifada* and the failure of the talks at Camp David and Taba badly hurt the hopes for peace. The re-election of Benjamin Netanyahu in 2009, a man who opposed Oslo and Palestinian independence his whole life, did not help. After he was elected he said that he supported an independent Palestine, but he still encouraged taking more land away from Palestinians and increasing Jewish settlements, so few thought he really wanted a fair peace agreement with the Palestinians.

The situation in the Middle East also hurt the chances for peace. On September 11, 2001, religious Islamic terrorists, mostly from Saudi Arabia, and based in Afghanistan, attacked the United States and killed thousands of people. The United States started hunting for radical Islamic terrorists throughout the world, jailing and torturing people it suspected of terrorism wherever it found them. It went to war in Afghanistan to overthrow the government which supported the September 11th attackers.

A few years later the United States started a war in Iraq, the Second Gulf War, for stated reasons which didn't make sense or were based on falsehoods. Many innocent people were killed in these wars which lasted for years, and Muslims throughout the world lost trust in the United States and were angry with it. For many years the United States was busy fighting wars, and was less able to help make peace between Israel and the Palestinians. For ten years it did not even try very hard.

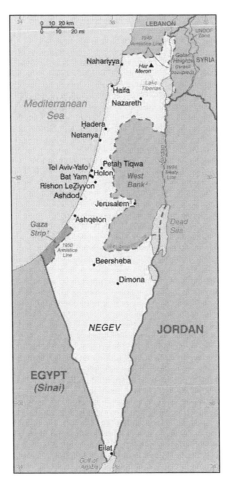

FIGURE 46 – Map of Israel and the occupied Palestinian Territories today.

Israeli Democracy and Peace

The biggest problem facing Israel in 2013 remained how to make peace with the Palestinians. The occupation that started in 1967 threatened to destroy Israeli democracy. It is impossible to oppress millions of people without hurting your own democracy. The Palestinians in the West Bank had almost no democratic rights that were respected by Israel. After nearly 50 years of occupation, many Israelis in the police, army, and the government got used to ignoring people's rights, and began to act within Israel as if democratic rights were not so important. By 2013 many people believed that if there was no peace deal soon, Israeli democracy would not last long, and that Israel itself, as the homeland of the Jewish people, would not survive.

Israel had many of the problems common to most countries in the modern world, such as preserving the environment and finding good jobs for its people. But Israel also faced a special problem: how to be a free, democratic country, a country that treats all its citizens equally, and yet could remain a Jewish homeland. The challenge to Israel of being a Jewish homeland and full democracy with a large minority of non-Jewish citizens would be hard even if there was no occupation of the West Bank, but Israel's continuing occupation of the West Bank makes Israeli democracy truly impossible, for it is impossible to be a democracy and control generations of Palestinians who are not allowed either their own country or citizenship in Israel.

In 2011 the Arab world started to change. It was called the "Arab Spring." Arab nations had been military dictatorships or non-democratic kingdoms since they won independence from European colonial powers. In 2011 street protests began in almost all Arab nations. In Tunisia, Egypt, Yemen, and Libya, new governments came to power. In other countries protests were put down by the dictators. In Israel's neighbor Syria, there was a horrible civil war. It is unclear if these changes in the Arab world will lead to freedom and democracy, or to religious or new military dictatorships. But because no one could be sure what was going to result from all these changes, many Israelis were afraid to make peace. They thought any change was too dangerous when things along their borders were so uncertain.

However, in late 2013, encouraged and helped by President Obama's government, the Israelis and Palestinians began negotiations again. As I write there is hope for peace.

FIGURE 47 – Hasidic children in Jerusalem prepare for Shabbat.

FIGURE 48 – Workmen's Circle Boston protests racism against immigrants.

Chapter 20

Jewish Identity Today

Today there are many different types of Jews—perhaps more types than there have ever been before. There are Jews who are fanatically religious, and there are Jews who make a point of not being religious at all. In between these two extremes, almost every attitude toward religion and religious tradition is represented among today's Jewish groups. Ultraorthodox, Modern Orthodox, Conservative, Reform, Reconstructionist, Humanistic, and Secular—these are only some of the large religious and non-religious categories of Jews. Within these groups there are smaller groups, such as Hasidic Ultraorthodox and Misnagdim Ultraorthodox.

It is not only in religious ideas and behavior that you can find a great variety of Jews today. You also find many different political ideas. As in the beginning of the 20th century, Jews are mostly liberal. But you can find many politically conservative Jews throughout the world. In Israel, as we saw in the last chapter, and throughout the Diaspora too, there are Jews in favor of compromising with the Palestinians for the sake of peace and Jews against any compromises. Although most of the world's Jews have some sympathy for Zionism, there are groups that are strongly anti-Zionist and many groups, even in Israel, that believe that Zionism as a political philosophy is no longer relevant. They think that now that Israel is a strong, established country there is no need for a movement to return to Zion.

There is also great cultural variety among the world's Jews. There are Jews who grow up speaking, as their first language, almost every language of Europe, plus most languages of the Middle East and some of Asia and Africa too. Along with the languages, the Jews are part of the culture of the people around them. Dutch Jews are culturally Dutch, Italian Jews culturally Italian, Persian Jews culturally Persian, Mexican Jews culturally Mexican, and so forth.

Even in the way Jews look we find great variety. There are Jews of every human skin color, eye shape, and nose length. While most Jews still look European or Middle Eastern, there are African American Jews who look African American, Chinese-American- Jews who look Chinese-American, and Jews of almost all nations who look like the non-Jews of those nations. So what makes a Jew a Jew?

Who's a Jew Today?

Jews are represented by a wide array of customs and skin colors, yet Ethiopian Jews from Addis Ababa, Moroccan Jews from Fez, Indian Jews from Bombay, Russian Jews from Moscow, Iranian Jews from Teheran, Irish Jews from Dublin, American Jews from Atlanta, Israeli Jews from Tel Aviv, New York Jews from Brooklyn, Los Angeles Jews from New York, and so on and so on, with all their different skin colors and customs, have a great deal in common. (See Appendix I for an account of some little known Jewish communities.)

We do not know how many of today's Jews are biological descendants of the ancient Israelite Jews. Of course, over the centuries some people have converted into Judaism, but until our own times, conversions were probably mostly rare. But all Jews, including those who have converted and have no direct biological link to ancient Israelites, are the *historical and spiritual* descendants of ancient Israelites, and that historical and spiritual descent is what really makes them Jewish. It is interesting that there seems to be evidence that many of today's Jews have a biological connection to the ancient Israelites, for it tells us something about Jewish history, namely that the Jews were kept separate and kept themselves separate. But throughout history the Jewish people incorporated some people who were not biologically descended from the ancient Israelites.

Nowadays many people who have no biological connection to the ancient Israelites are becoming Jewish. Some convert when they marry Jews, some are adopted by Jews, some become Jews because they want to live with equal rights in Israel, and some are drawn to the Jewish religion. But whatever the reason, it is choosing to remain part of the Jewish people, to call yourself a Jew and become part of Jewish history, choosing to have non-Jews consider you Jewish and treat you as a Jew—all that is what makes someone Jewish. Today, more than ever before, for people born to Jewish parents as well as people not born to Jewish parents, being a Jew is a choice someone makes. That means that not being Jewish is a choice people are also free to make.

If being a Jew today is a choice people make, we should ask why people make that choice. Different people of course, probably have different reasons for making that choice. Often that choice is made on the basis of how the person views Jewish history. Below are two examples.

Different Ways of Looking at History:
Anti-Semitism

When some people learn about Jewish history, they are most impressed by the terrible persecutions Jews have endured and the Jew-hatred that has lasted for centuries. Historians still debate why anti-Semitism has such a long and terrible history, and whether it will ever go away. Some people think it won't, and a few of those people stay Jews just because they don't want the Jew-haters to win. Jew haters, such as Hitler, want Jews to disappear, so some people stay Jews just to make sure Hitler's dream never becomes true. Others consider themselves Jews because they think that Jew-haters will always treat them badly no matter what, so, they reason, since the anti-Semites are going to make them suffer the bad parts of being a Jew, they may as well accept being Jews and enjoy the good parts of Jewish life too.

But there are people who believe it is a mistake to overemphasize the role of anti-Semitism in Jewish history. They admit that anti-Semitism has been an important part of Jewish history. But they do not think Jew-hatred is what kept Jews together as a people. There are also people who do *not* believe that just because anti-Semitism has been around almost two thousand years it will be around forever. They think there were particular causes for Jew-hatred, and when those causes go away Jew-hatred too will go away. Not all the people who think this agree on what the causes of anti-Semitism were or are—they only agree that whatever the causes, they are not permanent and not impossible to change.

So there are different ways of looking at the past and future of anti-Semitism, different ways of understanding what it was and is. These different perspectives can affect whether a person might choose to stay or become Jewish

Different Ways of Looking at History: Zion and the Diaspora

The anti-Semitism example shows that there are different ways to look at history. At the beginning of this book, I told you what my biases were so that you could better judge how my way of looking at history might be influenced by my values and experience. The different possible ways of looking at things affect all the great debates in Jewish history. For instance, some Zionists think that the main story of Jewish history takes place in the Land of Israel. They think that Jews began there, grew up there, and created their lasting books, legends, and ideas there. The important thing about the exile to them was that it was a break from the main story. To them, the return to the Land of Israel restarts the next important section of Jewish history, the future of the Jews in their own land.

Other people think that living dispersed among other nations of the world, the Diaspora, is the most important fact about Jewish history. What makes Jews the particular people they are is that they had to figure out how to remain a people without having their own land. For those who think like that, the Diaspora is the natural and best condition for Jews. It is what fed Jewish creativity. It is what taught Jews to be critical of society, because it gave them a stranger's perspective. And the Diaspora helped develop Jewish values because it showed Jews what it was like to be a minority. Without the Diaspora, some believe, the heart of Jewish culture would not have developed and could not stay alive.

Between Zionism and what we can call "Diasporism" there may be other ways at looking at this issue in Jewish history, ways that agree with some parts of each of these extreme views. Clearly, your perspective on the Zionism/Diasporism debate might affect whether and how you are Jewish. Some people might think the only folks who will remain Jewish are Israelis and others think that Israelis are the Jews most likely to stop being Jewish!

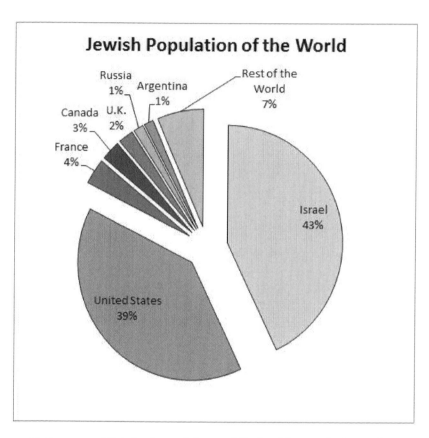

FIGURE 49 – Distribution of the world's Jewish population today.

Appendix I

World Jewish Populations Today

The main story of today's Jews is taking place in two countries: Israel and the United States. There are about 13 million Jews in the world today—over 5 million of them live in Israel and over 5 million of them in America. The development of Israeli society and of Jewish life in America have been talked about in detail in the preceding chapters. However, there continues to be Jewish life throughout the world.

Europe and Latin America

There are large Jewish communities in many Western European countries, particularly France and England, but they are still less than one tenth of the world's Jewish population. In many ways the communities there are still feeling the long effects of the Holocaust and the Second World War.

Not very directly affected by the Second World War, Latin America Jewry is a significant part of today's world Jewish community. It was not until the countries of Latin America won their independence in the early 1800s that Jews were allowed to live there. At first very few Jews came—tiny groups of mostly Sephardic and a few Ashkenazi Jews. But by at end of the 1800s and the first part of the 1900s a fair number of Jews did come to Latin America. In the 20th century, Argentina became the largest Jewish community in Latin America, with hundreds of thousands of Jews living there, mostly in the main city, Buenos Aires. Although Argentinian Jews became a generally accepted and established part of the country, a strong attitude of Jew-hatred existed among parts of the Argentinian people. Argentina was notorious for letting Nazi war criminals live there in safety after

World War II. When brutal dictators took power in Argentina in 1979, they killed and tortured their political opponents and were especially cruel to any Jews who they thought were against them. Still, for the most part, the Jewish community of Argentina flourished, and remains today a strong community. Substantial Jewish communities were also formed in Brazil, Uruguay, and Mexico. Synagogues, social centers, and religious schools were created by the Jewish communities in all of these countries. In Buenos Aires, Montevideo, and Mexico City, communities of Jews devoted to Yiddish culture thrived for decades.

Western European and Latin American Jews are fairly well-off and well-organized, with pretty strong Jewish institutions. There is no official anti-Semitism, and popular anti-Semitism is weaker than it has ever been. In Eastern Europe, even though lots of Russian Jews have left for Israel and America, Jewish life is reviving again. With the help of American Jews, Jewish schools are being opened, Hebrew and Yiddish are being studied, and rabbis are being trained. The East European Jewish homeland was destroyed by the Nazis and oppressed by the Stalinists. It cannot be recreated. But the tiny Jewish communities of Poland, the Czech Republic, Slovakia, and Hungary are trying to preserve and restore its sites. Russian Jews, because there are more of them left, are trying to build a strong, living Jewish community.

Though there are great differences among Jews from different countries, there are important ways in which Jews are coming closer together than ever before. Jews know more about each other and affect each other more than they have for long time. First, of course, as with everyone else, modern technology has connected Jews. Telephones, television, cars, airplanes and the internet all allow Jews to communicate with, travel to, and learn about other Jews. In addition, the end of the Cold War has brought the remaining Jews in Eastern Europe closer to Jews in Western Europe, Israel, and the Americas. There are now worldwide Jewish organizations that operate in practically every Jewish community on earth.

One result of these increased connections between Jews is that small communities of Jews who had been isolated for centuries have been reconnected to the main body of the Jewish people. We have already discussed (Chapter 19) the Jews of Ethiopia, most of who emigrated to Israel in the 1980s and 1990's. Here are some other examples.

Kaifeng Jews

There is evidence of Jewish merchants in China from earliest medieval times. By the Ming Dynasty in the 1300s, there was a well-established Jewish community in the Chinese city of Kaifeng.

FIGURE 50 – Rubbings from two of three stone tablets dated 1489-1663 describe historical events of the Kaifeng Jewish community of China.

The Kaifeng community had rabbis, a synagogue, and Jewish schools located on Teaching the Torah Street. Kaifeng Jews appear to have lived in peace but separately from their Chinese neighbors. The Kaifeng community lasted for hundreds of years. When Christian missionaries came to China, the Kaifeng Jews thought that the missionaries must be Jews. They had never heard of Christians and thought that anyone preaching the Bible had to be Jewish. The missionaries at first thought the Jews must be Christians because they couldn't imagine that they would find any Jews in China. Once the confusion was straightened out, the missionaries tried to convert the Jews, but the Kaifeng Jews remained loyal to their Jewish traditions.

Eventually the Jewish community in Kaifeng blended into the larger Chinese population. In the middle of the 1800s, the last Kaifeng rabbi died, but there are still people in the city of Kaifeng today who know of their Jewish ancestry and consider themselves Jewish.

The Jews of India

The Book of Esther mentions India, so we know that Jews knew about India from ancient times. Indian Jewish legends say that the first Jews came to India during the time of King Solomon. But the earliest Jewish settlements in India that we have real evidence for is from the tenth century C.E. In the Middle Ages, there were a number of Jewish settlements on the southwestern coast of India. We have the plaque given by the local Indian ruler, the Maharaja, to the Jews of Cranganore about the year 1000. The plaque says that the Jews are given the right to live in Cranganore under the Maharaja's protection. The most important Jewish settlement in India was Cochin, where the Jews built a community that lasted into our own times. You can still visit the beautiful synagogue in Cochin located on Jew Street. Cochinese Jews became great merchants, and Cochin was a strong community for centuries. Recently it has become very small, as most of its younger members have left to settle in Israel.

More Jews came to India with the Portuguese, Dutch, and British from the 1500s to the 1800s. All these European nations came and conquered different parts of India. Jews came with the Portuguese in part to escape the Inquisition. They came with all three nations to trade and set up businesses. At one point there were 29 synagogues in India. There was a Jewish community in Calcutta and a large one, called the Bene Israel, in Bombay. Both Bombay and Calcutta still have synagogues and Jews. But like Cochin, the communities have gotten smaller and weaker because so many Indian Jews have left India to go to Israel.

India is a large country containing different languages, religions, customs, and physical types of peoples. Indian Jews shared the culture of the other Indians around them. Calcutta Jews developed Bengali-style kosher cooking (Calcutta is in the

Indian region of Bengal). Jews in Bombay (now Mumbai) translated the Torah into Marathi, the local language in that part of India. Cochinese Jews became part of the traditional local caste system. Although a small stream, Indian Jewish culture has now flowed into the mainstream of Jewish culture and become part of the whole.

African Jews

The major African Jewish communities were in the North, in Morocco, Algeria, Tunisia, and Egypt. We have discussed those important communities in previous chapters and told of how they had emigrated to Israel. We have also already described the Ethiopian Jews of East Africa.

European Jews came to South Africa at first to escape East European pogroms and poverty. Later they came fleeing the Nazis. They became a wealthy community, in part because they were classified as "white" in the racial discrimination system called "apartheid." Although most Jews profited from the oppression of the Black Africans, along with the other "whites" in South Africa, more Jews were active in the anti-apartheid struggle than any other South African European group. The many of Nelson Mandela's white colleagues in the African National Congress liberation movement, people such as Joe Slovo, were Jewish.

The Lemba, a Black African people living in South Africa, considered themselves Israelites who had come from the north to southern Africa centuries ago. Scientists are now able to test peoples' genes to help trace their family ancestry. They have found that the Lemba are genetically related to other Jewish groups. Apparently, as the Lemba legends say, the Lemba came from the Yemen city of Sana, which had an ancient Jewish population. Although they had never had the Talmud and lost many ancient Jewish traditions, they maintained many Jewish customs. Long cut off from the rest of the Jewish world, the Lemba have rejoined the Jewish people and world Jewish history.

FIGURE 51 – Passover seder at the White House, 2013.

Appendix II

American Jewry Today

In many ways, no Jews have ever had it better than the American Jews of today. There are still some poor American Jews—elderly people living in old neighborhoods in the city—but most American Jews are comfortably middle class and many are wealthy. In fact, Jews are among the wealthiest Americans. Jews are also in all leading areas of American society. There are many Jews that publish, edit, and write books, magazines, and newspapers. Jews produce, direct, write and act in movies, television, and plays. Jews are also prominent musicians and artists. Many of the most important American novelists and poets are Jews. The professions have many Jewish representatives: doctors, dentists, lawyers, architects, scientists, and teachers. Universities have many Jewish professors and students. Jews are found throughout American government. There are Jewish Senators, Congressional representatives, cabinet officers, and Supreme Court justices.

Jews play such an outstanding part in American life that it is surprising that fewer than 3 out of 100 Americans are Jewish. You might think that Jews were a very large minority in the country given how often Jews and Jewish customs are publicly discussed in America, but they are not. Small in numbers, Jews still play a large role in America.

It is interesting that there is so little anti-Semitism in America. Every other time in Diaspora history when Jews were successful and had some power, non-Jews resented the Jews. This happened in Spain before the Inquisition and in Germany before the Nazis. Yet in America, where Jews are more successful than they have ever been, there is no government anti-Semitism at all.

Jews are part of government and American politicians try to be friendly with the strong Jewish community. There is some anti-Semitism in America, but very little for a traditionally Christian country. Most Americans consider outright anti-Semitic groups, such as American Nazis, the White Aryan Nation, the Ku Klux Klan and some wings of the Black Muslims to be nuts. Of course some anti-Semitic attitudes are widespread in America, but they are not considered proper or polite and they usually don't result in violence or discrimination. For the most part, American Jews are accepted by other Americans as being just as American as everybody else. Never before has this happened in the Diaspora.

American Jews have many organizations, but no one organization contains them all. A few different groups specialize in fighting anti-Semitism, some in remembering and teaching about the Holocaust. There are many charitable organizations that try to fight world hunger, or support hospitals, or house the homeless. There are political organizations that try to get American government help for Israel or to get American policy to agree with Israeli policy.

These organizations can be very effective. They have gotten Holocaust museums and memorials built throughout the country and Holocaust lessons taught in the public schools. America has been a very strong ally of Israel since 1967, giving it money and weapons. American Jewish organizations have helped make sure that America keeps religion and government separate (this is called "the separation of church and state"). Jewish supported hospitals are important health and medical research centers throughout the United States. When Soviet Jews, the refuseniks we spoke of earlier in the book, were being persecuted in the 1970s and 1980s, American Jews got America to stand-up for the refuseniks. Many Russian Jews came to America, the first large group of immigrant Jews to America in decades. They were able to come because of the strength of Jewish organizations.

The most numerous American Jewish organizations are the synagogue congregations. Each congregation is self-ruling, but most are connected to a national Jewish religious movement organization, Reform, Conservative, Reconstructionist, Humanist, and a number of different Orthodox and Ultraorthodox organizations. The national organizations train rabbis and help organize religious schools. There are also non-religious cultural and educational organizations, such as the Workmen's Circle and the YMHA's and YWHA's.

In many cities, most of these different organizations belong to an "umbrella organization," that is, an organization that has other organizations as its members. There is often a Combined Jewish Philanthropies that collects money for Jewish causes and a Jewish Community Relations Council that tries to coordinate some of the policies and events of the city's Jewish organizations. These umbrella organizations often maintain a Jewish Community Center that is used as a community pre-school, senior center, gymnasium, adult education center, and Jewish community auditorium.

There are also umbrella organizations on a national level. The Conference of Presidents of Major Jewish Organizations has leaders from many of the big Jewish organizations. The "Conference" tries to represent organized Jewish opinion both to Jews and to other Americans.

Not all Jewish organizations belong to these umbrella groups. Some, such as some Hasidic groups, want to have nothing to do with them; they don't consider the umbrella groups Jewish enough. Other organizations don't belong to the umbrella groups because they are not invited to join. American Jewish organizations which think Zionism was a bad idea, or criticize the Israeli government's treatment of Palestinians, like the Jewish Voice for Peace, are kept out of the umbrella organizations. Even organizations, such as J Street and Americans for Peace Now, are not fully accepted by the traditional Jewish organizations. J Street and Americans for Peace Now strongly support Israel, but they think Israel is hurting itself by not doing enough to end the occupation of the West Bank. They also believe Israel does not do enough to respect the rights of Palestinians, and so J Street and Americans for Peace Now will sometimes publicly disagree with the Israeli government. The umbrella organizations don't want any public criticism of Israel's treatment of Palestinians, so they dislike these groups.

With so many organizations of so many types, you would think that every Jew would belong to at least three of them. Many Jews do belong to more than one, but the majority of American Jews are actually "unaffiliated," that is, they don't belong to any Jewish organization at all. Some Jewish leaders and thinkers are worried about these unaffiliated Jews. Many unaffiliated Jews do only a couple of "Jewish things" a year (perhaps they go to a Passover Seder, or light Chanukah candles, or go to synagogue on Rosh Hashanah) and some do nothing Jewish at all. In addition, affiliated and unaffiliated Jews are living, working, playing and marrying with non-Jews as never before. Some Jewish leaders fear that most American Jews will eventually assimilate—blend in with the majority of non-Jewish Americans and stop being Jewish. In America, being completely free to be Jewish has also meant being free not to bother being Jewish. American Jews who want there to be as many Jews as possible are trying to figure out ways to keep Jews Jewish.

Other American Jews say: don't bother with those Jews who don't care about staying Jewish. They say it is more important that there be "good" Jews than that there be lots of Jews. They say that even though most American Jews don't do much of anything Jewish, there are still plenty of Jews leading full Jewish lives in traditional and new ways. Jewish day school enrollments are getting larger. There are congregations of gay Jews. College students are studying Yiddish. Hasidic groups are building new dynastic centers. Feminist Jews are writing new, non-sexist prayers. Pointing to all this activity, some Jewish leaders are not concerned about the majority of American Jews who seem headed for assimilation. This question of how to respond to assimilation is a very controversial issue facing American Jewish organizations today.

However, it is not the only issue. Starting in the 1960s and continuing to the present, some Jews have been unhappy that most Jewish Americans remain progressive in their politics—that is, most Jews care about being fair to the poor, care strongly about the rights of women and minorities, are against most wars, and, in general, are what is called in America, very "liberal."

FIGURE 52 – Jews in a gay pride parade.

Those Jews who do not want other Jews to be so liberal are sometimes called "neo-conservatives." They were unhappy that Jews mostly voted for Barack Obama, and unhappy that Jews do not automatically vote against any politician that the right wing governments of Israel do not like. The neo-conservatives find it confusing that most Jews stay liberal, because most Jews in America are no longer poor and no longer powerless. Usually, when a group becomes wealthy and powerful it stops being progressive and becomes conservative, because it does not want to share its wealth and power with people who do not have it. This may eventually happen to American Jews, but it had not happened much by the first years of the 21st century, and this surprised and upset conservative Jews. Perhaps after reading this book you will not find it so surprising.

Questions to Consider

Chapter 1

Is there any value in a people telling themselves stories of how they became a people, even if those stories are false? Known to be false by the people? Is there a downside to repeating such stories?

Chapter 2

The prophets said God wanted the Israelites to be "righteous": what was the prophets' idea of righteousness? How does it compare to today's ideas? The prophets thought God would punish wickedness. Does the world appear to reward good actions and punish bad ones?

Chapter 3

The rebellion against the Greeks, which Jews remember with the Hanukah festival, in part started because some Jews did not like the way Greek culture was influencing traditional Jewish culture. Under what circumstances, if any, is foreign influence on a culture bad?

Chapter 4

The Jews rebelled against Roman oppression, with little chance of ultimately defeating Rome. Is it wrong to wage an armed struggle for freedom if there is a good chance you will not win that war?

Chapter 5

Some historians believe that it was strict adherence to the Talmud's rules for living that kept Jews being Jews and a separate people throughout the long diaspora? Does that seem correct? Might generations of Jews remain Jewish without following a Talmudic way of life?

Chapter 6

Christianity, in large part, grew out of Judaism, and Islam in large part, grew out of both Judaism and Christianity. What makes something a separate, new religion, rather than just a variation of the same old religion?

Chapter 7

The Jews were severely persecuted through much of medieval times in Christian Europe. What do you think Christian society got out of treating the Jews so badly? Did it serve any purposes, bad or good, or was it just cruelty?

Chapter 8

Many Spanish Jews converted to Christianity so they could get ahead in Christian Spain, or, when expelled, so they could remain in their homeland. For what motives is formally converting to another religion or belief system justifiable?

Chapter 9

The Jews in Eastern Europe spoke Yiddish, an exclusively Jewish language, and for over a thousand years lived separately from the people around them. To what extent does the language you speak affect how you live, what you think, and how you feel? Did Yiddish have any such effects?

Chapter 10

What is called "mysticism" is found in many religions and cultures. Mysticism, wherever it arises, usually has some or all of these beliefs: there is secret knowledge about the universe, special techniques can put a person in contact with God, there is a real world very different than the world we see, some special people can serve as bridges or guides to God, intense feeling are the most valuable experience in life, or the opposite, no feelings at all are the best experience a person can have. Do you think that difficult times—times of war, persecution and extreme poverty— make such beliefs especially attractive to people?

Chapter 11

The oppression of Jews in Europe began to end around when the first modern economies started to develop. Instead of most people making most of what they need for themselves, more people started to do one job, earned money, and bought most of what they needed. Small shops grew to big businesses that had lots of workers and sold goods for large profits. Trade increased greatly, and wealth which had mostly been in the hands of only the nobility, who were also the political rulers, and a few rich merchants, spread to other groups who started private businesses. A large middle class arose for the first time. Do you think there is a connection between these economic developments and respect for human rights? What might it be?

Chapter 12

Moses Mendelssohn believed a person could be an orthodox Jew and also be a full German citizen living and working in the modern world. Can one be an orthodox Jew and full American citizen living in the modern world? Can a person believe in the Torah and fully accept modern science?

Chapter 13

Is there something about the origins of America that made, and will continue to make, Jewish experience in America very different than Jewish experience in Europe?

Chapter 14

How do the roles in *shtetl* society compare to the roles in modern American society, especially in terms of sources of prestige and power?

Chapter 15

What about socialism made it so attractive to so many Jews in the 19th and 20th centuries?

Chapter 16

How much do American Jews today appear to be shaped by the experiences and actions of East European Jews and their children who came to America between 1881 and 1924? Jewish Americans are far more politically liberal than any other prosperous American ethnic group: why might that be?

Chapter 17

Hitler wanted to annihilate all Jews, and did manage, with the help of his followers and other Jew haters, to murder about 6 million Jews. Besides killing many Jews, what effects did the holocaust have on the Jewish people?

Chapter 18

Was Zionism a good idea?

Chapter 19

Why has it been so difficult for Palestinians and Israelis to resolve their conflict and make peace?

Chapter 20

What makes someone a Jew in your eyes?

Selected Bibliography

Here is a list of some of the books I found most useful while I was writing. The list is only a small portion of all the books and articles that I drew upon, and that longer list would only be a tiny fraction of all of the writings on Jewish history.

Avishai, Bernard. *The Tragedy of Zionism*. New York: Farrar, Strauss, Giroux, 1985.

Cantor, Norman. *The Sacred Chain: A History of the Jews*. New York: Harper Personal, 1994.

Dawidowicz, Lucy. *The Golden Tradition*. New York: Schocken, 1984.

Encyclopedia Judaica. Jerusalem: Keter Publishing, 1972.

Fast, Howard. *The Jews*. New York: Doubleday, 1968.

Friedman, Philip. *Their Brother's Keeper*. New York: Crown Publishers, 1957.

Grayzel, Solomon. *A History of the Jews*. New York: Jewish Publishing Society, 1947.

Howe, Irving. *World of Our Fathers*. New York: Simon and Shuster, 1976.

Johnson, Paul. *A History of the Jews*. New York: Harper and Rowe, 1987.

Khalidi, Rashid. *The Iron Cage*. Boston: Beacon, 2006.

Laqueur, Walter. *A History of Zionism*. New York: Schocken, 1972.

Morris, Benny. *The Birth of the Palestinian Refugee Problem, 1947-1949*. Cambridge: Cambridge University Press, 1987.

Morris, Benny. *Righteous Victims: A History of the Zionist-Arab Conflict*. New York: Knopf, 1999.

Netanyahu, Benzion. *The Origins of the Inquisition*. New York: Random House, 1991.

O'Brien, Connor Cruse. *The Siege*. New York: Simon and Shuster, 1986.

Potok, Chaim. *Wanderings*. New York: Knopf, 1978.

Rudavsky, David. *Modern Jewish Religious Movements*. New York: Behrman, 1967.

Sacher, Howard. *The Course of Modern Jewish History.* New York: Dell Publishing, 1958.

Sacher, Howard. *A History of Israel.* New York: Knopf, 1979.

Sarna, Jonathan. *American Judaism.* New Haven: Yale University Press, 2004.

Scholem, Gershon. *Sabbatai Sevi.* Princeton: Princeton University Press, 1973.

Shulvass, Moses. *The History of the Jewish People, Volumes I-III.* Washington, DC: Regnery, 1982.

Yahil, Leni. *The Holocaust.* Oxford: Oxford University Press, 1990.

Zborowski, Mark and Elizabeth Herzog. *Life is with People.* New York: Schocken, 1952.

List of Illustrations

FIGURE 1 – The territories of the 12 Tribes of Israel according to the Bible.
Source: Wikimedia Commons, user:Richardprins / CC-BY-SA-3.0.

FIGURE 2 – Engraving by Rembrandt showing the Bible story of Joseph telling his dreams, one of the many works of art inspired by the Bible.
Source: Wikimedia Commons / Public Domain.

FIGURE 3 – Map of the Kingdoms of Israel and Judah.
Source: Wikimedia Commons, user:Richardprins / CC-BY-SA-3.0.

FIGURE 4 – Print of Mattathias, leader of Macabbean rebellion against the Greeks.
Source: Wikimedia Commons, engraving by Gustave Doré / Public Domain.

FIGURE 5 – Bust of Antiochus IV.
Source: Wikimedia Commons /© user:Jniemenmaa / CC-BY-SA-3.0 / GFDL.

FIGURE 6 – Detail of the stone carving on the Roman Arch of Titus commemorating the conquest of Jerusalem in the year 70.
Source: Wikimedia Commons, user: Steerpike / CC-BY-SA-3.0.

FIGURE 7 – The fortress of Masada.
Source: Courtesy of Dorothée Rozenberg, photographer.

FIGURE 8 – A page of the Talmud.
Source: Wikimedia Commons, from The Jewish Encyclopedia */ Public Domain.*

FIGURE 9 – Engraving of Moshe ben Maimon (Maimonides).
Source: Wikimedia Commons / Public Domain.

FIGURE 10 – Page of a manuscript written by Maimonides, in Arabic written in Hebrew script.
Source: Wikimedia Commons, from The Jewish Encyclopedia */ Public Domain.*

FIGURE 11 – Modern statue of medieval Jewish poet Judah HaLevi.
Source: Wikimedia Commons / he:user:Raananms / Public Domain.

FIGURE 12 – Medieval manuscript painting showing a Jewish man (at right).
Source: Wikimedia Commons, from the Codex Manesse, *in the collection of the Universitätsbibliothek Heidelberg / Public Domain.*

FIGURE 13 – Print of Jews being burned to death in medieval Europe during the Black Death.
Source: Wikimedia Commons, from the Nuremberg Chronicle */ Public Domain.*

FIGURE 14 – Medieval synagogue in Sopron, Hungary.
Source: Wikimedia Commons, photograph by Daniel Kovacs / CC-BY-SA-3.0.

FIGURE 15 – Sephardic couple from the city of Sarajevo, around 1900.
Source: Wikimedia Commons / Public Domain.

FIGURE 16 – Print of Jews burned at the stake in an auto-da-fé during the Inquisition.
Source: Wikimedia Commons / Public Domain.

FIGURE 17 – Drawing of an 18th Polish Jewish boy.
Source: Wikimedia Commons, drawing by Johann Christoph Brotze / Public Domain.

FIGURE 18 – Print of Sabbatai Zevi.
Source: Wikimedia Commons / Public Domain.

FIGURE 19 – Painting of the Vilna Gaon.
Source: Wikimedia Commons / Public Domain.

FIGURE 20 – A street in the Jewish ghetto, Frankfurt, Germany.
Source: Wikimedia Commons, photograph by Th. Creifelds / Public Domain.

FIGURE 21 – Painting of the interior of Portuguese Synagogue in Amsterdam.
Source: Wikimedia Commons, painting by Emanuel de Witte / Public Domain.

FIGURE 22 – Poolstrasse Reform Temple in Hamburg, around 1850.
Source: Wikimedia Commons / Public Domain.

FIGURE 23 – The first Jewish publication in the Americas.
Source: Library of Congress website / Public Domain.

FIGURE 24 – 19th century American Jewish anti-slavery and women's rights activist Ernestine Rose.
Source: Wikimedia Commons / Public Domain.

FIGURE 25 – Jewish family, Eastern Europe, 1909.
Source: Wikimedia Commons, user: Хомелка/ CC-BY-SA-3.0.

FIGURE 26 – Map of the Pale of Settlement, the area of the Russian Empire where Jews were required to live.
Source: Wikimedia Commons, from The Jewish Encyclopedia */ Public Domain.*

FIGURE 27 – Ceremony discharging Alfred Dreyfus from the French army, a cover illustration of a French newspaper, 1895.
Source: Le Petit Journal *(illustrated supplement), 13 January 1895, cover / Public Domain.*

FIGURE 28 – Karl Marx.
Source: Wikimedia Commons / Public Domain.

FIGURE 29 – Theodor Herzl at the First Zionist Congress in Basel, Switzerland, 1897.
Source: Wikimedia Commons / Public Domain.

FIGURE 30 – "Welcome to the Land of Freedom," a newspaper illustration from 1887 showing immigrants, including Jews, on the steerage deck of a ship looking at the Statue of Liberty.
Source: Wikimedia Commons, from Frank Leslie's Illustrated Newspaper, *2 July 1887 / Public Domain.*

FIGURE 31 – Sweatshop on Ludlow Street.
Source: Wikimedia Commons, from the collection of the Library of Congress' Photographs and Prints Division / Public Domain.

FIGURE 32 – Women surrounded by posters in English and Yiddish supporting Franklin D. Roosevelt, teach other women how to vote, 1935.
Source: Flickr Creative Commons, posted by Kheel Center for Labor-Management Documentation and Archives, Cornell University / CC-BY-2.0.

FIGURE 33 – Front page illustration from a 1936 issue of *Der Stürmer*, an anti-Semitic German newspaper. The bottom headline says "Jews are our misfortune."
Source: Image courtesy of Randall Bytwerk.

FIGURE 34 – A synagogue burning during Kristallnacht, 1938.
Source: Wikimedia Commons / Public Domain.

FIGURE 35 – Jews driven by Germans from the Warsaw ghetto.
Source: Wikimedia Commons, photo from Jürgen Stroop Report to Heinrich Himmler, 1943 / Public Domain.

FIGURE 36 – Defendants at Nuremberg Trials of Nazi officials.
Source: Flickr Creative Commons; photograph from collections of United States National Archives and Records Administration / Public Domain.

FIGURE 37 – Members of Kibbutz Ein Harod, 1941.
Source: Wikimedia Commons, from the Government Press Office, Israel / CC-BY-SA-3.0.

FIGURE 38 – Israeli leaders in a military review, 1949.
Source: Wikimedia Commons, from the Government Press Office, Israel / CC-BY-SA-3.0.

FIGURE 39 – Henrietta Szold, U.S. Jewish Zionist leader and founder of Hadassah, who advocated for a bi-national state.
Source: Wikimedia Commons, photograph by Alexander Ganan, from the collection of the National Library of Israel / CC-BY-SA-3.0.

FIGURE 40 – Palestinian refugees in the Galilee.
Wikimedia Commons, photograph by Fred Csasznik / CC-BY-SA-2.5.

FIGURE 41 – Tel Aviv in 2012.
Source: Wikimedia Commons, photograph by Ksenia Smirnova / CC-BY-2.0.

FIGURE 42 – Jerusalem in 2013.
Source: Courtesy of Dorothée Rozenberg, photographer.

FIGURE 43 – Israeli Prime Minister Yitzhak Rabin and Chairman of the Palestinian Liberation Organization Yasser Arafat shaking hands on the White House lawn on the signing of a Declaration of Principles for peace between Arabs and Israelis, 1993.
Source: National Archives and Records Administration, deposited by White House Photograph Office / Public Domain.

FIGURE 44 – The Separation Wall, near Bethlehem.
Source: Flickr Creative Commons, photograph by Paolo Cuttitta / CC-BY-2.5.

FIGURE 45 – Housing protest in Beersheva, Israel, 2011.
Source: Wikimedia Commons, user:Eman / Public Domain.

FIGURE 46 – Map of Israel and the occupied Palestinian Territories today.
Source: Adapted from Israel map in CIA World Factbook / Public Domain.

FIGURE 47 – Hasidic children in Jerusalem prepare for Shabbat.
Source: Wikimedia Commons, "Breslov kids prepare for Shabbat, Mea Shearim, Jerusalem," photograph by Yoav Elad / CC-BY-2.5.

FIGURE 48 – Workmen's Circle Boston protests racism against immigrants.
Source: Courtesy of Edward Elbers, photographer.

FIGURE 49 – Distribution of the world's Jewish population today.
Source: Based on data from: Sergio DellaPergola. "World Jewish Population, 2012." American Jewish Year Book (2012) (Dordrecht: Springer) p. 212-283.

FIGURE 50 – Rubbings from two of three stone tablets dated 1489-1663 describe historical events of the Kaifeng Jewish community of China.
Source: Wikimedia Commons / Public Domain.

FIGURE 51 – Passover seder at the White House, 2013.
Source: Wikimedia Commons, photograph by White House photographer Pete Souza / Public Domain.

FIGURE 52 – Jews in a gay pride parade.
Source: Wikimedia Commons, photograph by Quinn Dombrowski / CC-BY-SA-2.0.

COVER UPPER LEFT – Painting by Polish artist Maurycy Gottlieb, Jews Praying in the Synagogue on Yom Kippur, 1878.
Source: Wikimedia Commons / Public Domain.

COVER UPPER MIDDLE – Protest against child labor in a labor parade, probably 1909.
Source: Wikimedia Commons, photograph from the Bain News Service, from the collection of the Library of Congress / Public Domain.

COVER UPPER RIGHT – Illuminated painting from the Sarajevo Haggadah, depicting the maror (bitter herb) as an artichoke.
Source: Wikimedia Commons / Public Domain.

COVER LOWER LEFT – Albert Einstein.
Source: Wikimedia Commons, photograph by Oren Jack Turner, cleaned/leveled and cropped by user:Jaakobou / Public Domain.

COVER LOWER MIDDLE – Painting of Jerusalem by Hungarian artist Tivadar Kosztka Csontváry, 1905.
Source: Wikimedia Commons / Public Domain.

COVER LOWER RIGHT – Klezmer musicians at a wedding, Ukraine, about 1925.
Source: Wikimedia Commons / Public Domain.

AUTHOR PHOTO – Mitchell Silver
Source: Courtesy of University of Massachusetts-Boston / Photo credit: Harry Brett.

Timeline

Three Thousand Years of Jewish History

1300 BCE - 2013 CE

1300 BCE	30 CE	500 CE	622 CE	1492	1789	2013
Israelites Leave Egypt According to Traditional Jewish Legend	Beginnings of Christianity	Talmud Completed	Beginnings of Islam	Expulsion from Spain	French Revolution, Modern Era Begins for	

The Modern Era
1789 - 2013

1789	1818	1882	1897	1933	1948	2013
French Revolution	Reform Judaism Begins in Germany	Anti-Jewish May Laws in Czarist Empire, Pogroms	Jewish Labor Bund Formed	Hitler Comes to Power	Founding of Israel	

The Last Century-and-a-Third
1882 - 2013

1882	1907	1917	1938-1945	1948	1967	1987	1993	2013
Anti-Jewish May Laws in Czarist Empire, Pogroms	Peak Year of Eastern European Emigration to America	Russian Revolution, Third Aliyah to Palestine	Murder of European Jews	Israel's War of Independence, Palestinian Nakba	Six Day War, Occupation of West Bank and Gaza	First Intifada	Oslo Peace Accords	

About the Author

Mitchell Silver was educational director of the I.L. Peretz School of the Boston Workmen's Circle from 1992-2009 and cultural director of Camp Kinderland from 1989-2006. He received his Ph.D. from the University of Connecticut and has taught philosophy at the University of Massachusetts/Boston since 1982.

Silver is the author of *A Plausible God* (2006) and *Respecting the Wicked Child: A Philosophy of Secular Jewish Identity and Education* (1998). Mitchell writes and speaks regularly on issues relating to health care ethics, Jewish secularism, and Middle East politics. He was born in New York City, and lives with his wife in Newton, Massachusetts, where he raised his family.

27697120R00202

Made in the USA
Charleston, SC
19 March 2014